THE CAMBRIDGE BIBLE COMMENTARY

NEW ENGLISH BIBLE

GENERAL EDITORS

P. R. ACKROYD, A. R. C. LEANEY

J. W. PACKER

2 KINGS

THE SECOND BOOK OF
KINGS

COMMENTARY BY
J. ROBINSON
Canon of Canterbury

CAMBRIDGE UNIVERSITY PRESS
CAMBRIDGE
LONDON · NEW YORK · MELBOURNE

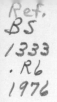
Published by the Syndics of the Cambridge University Press
The Pitt Building, Trumpington Street, Cambridge CB2 IRP
Bentley House, 200 Euston Road, London NW1 2DB
32 East 57th Street, New York, NY 10022, USA
296 Beaconsfield Parade, Middle Park, Melbourne 3206, Australia

© Cambridge University Press 1976

First published 1976

Printed in Great Britain
at the
University Printing House, Cambridge
(Euan Phillips, University Printer)

Library of Congress cataloguing in publication data

Bible. O.T. 2 Kings. English. New English. 1976.
The second book of Kings.

(The Cambridge Bible commentary, New English Bible)
Bibliography: p.
Includes index.
1. Bible. O.T. 2 Kings – Commentaries.
I. Robinson, Joseph, 1927– II. Title. III. Series.
BS1333.R6 1976   222′.54′077   76–6863
ISBN 0 521 08646 9 hard covers
ISBN 0 521 09774 6 paperback

GENERAL EDITORS' PREFACE

The aim of this series is to provide the text of the New English Bible closely linked to a commentary in which the results of modern scholarship are made available to the general reader. Teachers and young people have been especially kept in mind. The commentators have been asked to assume no specialized theological knowledge, and no knowledge of Greek and Hebrew. Bare references to other literature and multiple references to other parts of the Bible have been avoided. Actual quotations have been given as often as possible.

The completion of the New Testament part of the series in 1967 provides a basis upon which the production of the much larger Old Testament and Apocrypha series can be undertaken. The welcome accorded to the series has been an encouragement to the editors to follow the same general pattern, and an attempt has been made to take account of criticisms which have been offered. One necessary change is the inclusion of the translators' footnotes since in the Old Testament these are more extensive, and essential for the understanding of the text.

Within the severe limits imposed by the size and scope of the series, each commentator will attempt to set out the main findings of recent biblical scholarship and to describe the historical background to the text. The main theological issues will also be critically discussed.

Much attention has been given to the form of the volumes. The aim is to produce books each of which will be read consecutively from first to last page. The introductory material leads naturally into the text, which itself leads into the alternating sections of the commentary.

The series is accompanied by three volumes of a more general character. *Understanding the Old Testament* sets out to provide the larger historical and archaeological background, to say something about the life and thought of the people of the Old Testament, and to answer the question 'Why should we study the Old Testament?'. *The Making of the Old Testament* is concerned with the formation of the books of the Old Testament and Apocrypha in the context of the ancient near eastern world, and with the ways in which these books have come down to us in the life of the Jewish and Christian communities. *Old Testament Illustrations* contains maps, diagrams and photographs with an explanatory text. These three volumes are designed to provide material helpful to the understanding of the individual books and their commentaries, but they are also prepared so as to be of use quite independently.

P. R. A.

A. R. C. L.

J. W. P.

CONTENTS

List of maps and time chart   *page* ix

The footnotes to the N.E.B. text   x

*   *   *   *   *   *   *   *   *   *   *   *   *

What the book is about   1

The earlier history of the Israelites   1

Samaria and Israel   2

The story told in 1 Kings   3

Ahab and Elijah   4

The influence of the prophets on the compiler of
     Kings   5

The deuteronomists   6

The point of view of the deuteronomists   7

The end of the two kingdoms   8

The motive for the writing of the book   9

The Deuteronomic History   10

How the book was compiled   11

The story of King Hezekiah   12

The chronology of Kings   12

The faith of the writers   13

*   *   *   *   *   *   *   *   *   *   *   *   *

Elisha and the end of the house of Ahab   14

Kings of Israel and Judah   106

Downfall of the northern kingdom   143

CONTENTS

The last kings of Judah   page 200

Downfall of the southern kingdom   234

✻   ✻   ✻   ✻   ✻   ✻   ✻   ✻   ✻   ✻   ✻   ✻   ✻

The message of the book   246

✻   ✻   ✻   ✻   ✻   ✻   ✻   ✻   ✻   ✻   ✻   ✻   ✻

A NOTE ON FURTHER READING   250

APPENDIX:

MEASURES OF LENGTH AND EXTENT;

MEASURES OF CAPACITY; WEIGHTS AND COINS   252

INDEX   255

LIST OF MAPS AND TIME CHART

MAPS

1. The Near East in the time covered by 2 Kings *page* xii
2. Palestine during the time of the divided kingdom 30
3. The kingdom of Israel 80
4. The kingdoms of Aram and Phoenicia 126
5. Plan of Jerusalem in the time of Hezekiah 191

A TIME CHART OF THE PERIOD 251

THE FOOTNOTES TO THE N.E.B. TEXT

The footnotes to the N.E.B. text are designed to help the reader either to understand particular points of detail – the meaning of a name, the presence of a play upon words – or to give information about the actual text. Where the Hebrew text appears to be erroneous, or there is doubt about its precise meaning, it may be necessary to turn to manuscripts which offer a different wording, or to ancient translations of the text which may suggest a better reading, or to offer a new explanation based upon conjecture. In such cases, the footnotes supply very briefly an indication of the evidence, and whether the solution proposed is one that is regarded as possible or as probable. Various abbreviations are used in the footnotes.

(1) Some abbreviations are simply of terms used in explaining a point: *ch(s).*, chapter(s); *cp.*, compare; *lit.*, literally; *mng.*, meaning; *MS(S).*, manuscript(s), i.e. Hebrew manuscript(s), unless otherwise stated; *om.*, omit(s); *or*, indicating an alternative interpretation; *poss.*, possible; *prob.*, probable; *rdg.*, reading; *Vs(s).*, version(s).

(2) Other abbreviations indicate sources of information from which better interpretations or readings may be obtained.

Aq. Aquila, a Greek translator of the Old Testament (perhaps about A.D. 130) characterized by great literalness.

Aram. Aramaic – may refer to the text in this language (used in parts of Ezra and Daniel), or to the meaning of an Aramaic word. Aramaic belongs to the same language family as Hebrew, and is known from about 1000 B.C. over a wide area of the Middle East, including Palestine.

Heb. Hebrew – may refer to the Hebrew text or may indicate the literal meaning of the Hebrew word.

Josephus Flavius Josephus (A.D. 37/8–about 100), author of the *Jewish Antiquities*, a survey of the whole history of his people, directed partly at least to a non-Jewish audience, and of various other works, notably one on the *Jewish War* (that of A.D. 66–73) and a defence of Judaism (*Against Apion*).

Luc. Sept. Lucian's recension of the Septuagint, an important edition made in Antioch in Syria about the end of the third century A.D.

Pesh. Peshitta or Peshitto, the Syriac version of the Old Testament. Syriac is the name given chiefly to a form of Eastern Aramaic used by the Christian community. The translation varies in quality, and is at many points influenced by the Septuagint or the Targums.

Sam. Samaritan Pentateuch – the form of the first five books of the Old Testament as used by the Samaritan community. It is written in Hebrew in a special form of the Old Hebrew script, and preserves an important form of the text, somewhat influenced by Samaritan ideas.

Scroll(s) Scroll(s), commonly called the Dead Sea Scrolls, found at or near Qumran from 1947 onwards. These important manuscripts shed light on the state of the Hebrew text as it was developing in the last centuries B.C. and the first century A.D.

Sept. Septuagint (meaning 'seventy'); often abbreviated as the Roman numeral (LXX), the name given to the main Greek version of the Old Testament. According to tradition, the Pentateuch was translated in Egypt in the third century B.C. by 70 (or 72) translators, six from each tribe, but the precise nature of its origin and development is not fully known. It was intended to provide Greek-speaking Jews with a convenient translation. Subsequently it came to be much revered by the Christian community.

Symm. Symmachus, another Greek translator of the Old Testament (beginning of the third century A.D.), who tried to combine literalness with good style. Both Lucian and Jerome viewed his version with favour.

Targ. Targum, a name given to various Aramaic versions of the Old Testament, produced over a long period and eventually standardized, for the use of Aramaic-speaking Jews.

Theod. Theodotion, the author of a revision of the Septuagint (probably second century A.D.), very dependent on the Hebrew text.

Vulg. Vulgate, the most important Latin version of the Old Testament, produced by Jerome about A.D. 400, and the text most used throughout the Middle Ages in western Christianity.

[...] In the text itself square brackets are used to indicate probably late additions to the Hebrew text.

(Fuller discussion of a number of these points may be found in *The Making of the Old Testament* in this series)

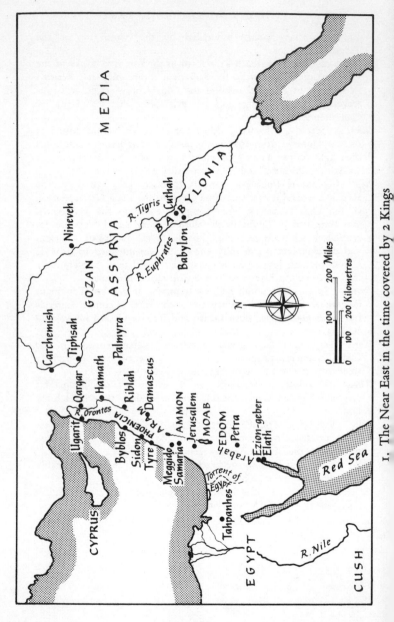

I. The Near East in the time covered by 2 Kings

xii

THE SECOND BOOK OF

KINGS

✳ ✳ ✳ ✳ ✳ ✳ ✳ ✳ ✳ ✳ ✳ ✳ ✳

WHAT THE BOOK IS ABOUT

The Second Book of Kings tells the story of the decline and
fall of the two Hebrew kingdoms of Israel and Judah. Each in
turn was defeated by a stronger enemy and its territory
annexed. In the end both Israel and Judah had ceased to exist
as independent states. Thus, this book completes the story of
the two Israelite kingdoms. The earlier part of that story has
already been told in the books that precede 2 Kings in the
Old Testament. Indeed, 2 Kings was not intended to be a
separate book. It is the second part of the book of Kings
which, in the original Hebrew, is one book, and the whole of
Kings was itself the concluding part of the story of the
Israelites which had already been told in Joshua, Judges and
the two books of Samuel. Kings like Samuel was divided into
two by the men who translated it into Greek for the very
practical reason that the Greek took up more space than the
Hebrew and the Greek version of Kings was too long for one
scroll.

THE EARLIER HISTORY OF THE ISRAELITES

The story of the settlement of the Hebrew tribes in Palestine
is told in the book of Joshua. Then in the book of Judges there
follows a description of the life of the people as a group of
tribes led by tribal leaders from the time of the settlement until
they became a kingdom. The account of the creation of that
kingdom under Saul and David is told in the two books of
Samuel. 1 Kings follows with the story of the united kingdom

I

under David's son Solomon and also tells of the break which followed after his death when the kingdom was split in two. Of the twelve tribes which had made up the united kingdom, only two, Judah and Benjamin, remained loyal to the successors of David and Solomon. They formed the kingdom of Judah with Jerusalem as its capital. The other ten tribes refused to accept the rule of Solomon's son and formed their own kingdom, called the kingdom of Israel with its capital at first situated at Shechem. By the time of the events which are narrated in 2 Kings the capital of Israel had been transferred to another city, Samaria. One of the stronger kings of Israel, Omri, had built a new city on the hill of Samaria and transferred the capital there. Samaria remained the capital of the kingdom for the rest of its history and even after the destruction of the kingdom remained the chief city of the area so that the region around it was known even in New Testament times as Samaria.

SAMARIA AND ISRAEL

The use of names can cause confusion. Samaria is first the name of a city. Then it is sometimes used as an alternative name for the kingdom, and later it was used as the name of a geographical area. Similarly, the name Israel can be used in more than one sense. It can refer to the united kingdom of the twelve tribes created by David and ruled, after his death, by Solomon. It is also the name of the northern kingdom of the ten tribes who rebelled against Solomon's son. To add to the difficulty, it can be used in a rather different sense, to refer to the Hebrews as the particular people with whom God had entered into covenant and who therefore ought to live in obedience to his will and seek to fulfil his purposes. In this last use, the name is being used with a religious rather than a political significance.

THE STORY TOLD IN I KINGS

The reader of 2 Kings is thus thrust into the middle of a story that has already been more than half told. It is as though he or she opened a book and began to read only the last half of it, or went into a cinema when the film was already half over. A summary of the story of 1 Kings may, therefore, help the reader to understand 2 Kings better. 1 Kings tells of Solomon's accession to the throne and his reign, giving great prominence to his building of the temple at Jerusalem. After Solomon's death his kingdom was torn apart. His son Rehoboam followed him as king in Jerusalem but he had authority only over the much reduced kingdom of Judah. The northern ten tribes formed their own kingdom, Israel, and appointed the man who had led their revolt, Jeroboam, as their king. This division opened up again long-standing differences between northern and southern Israelites which had been a feature of Israelite life ever since the original settlement. David had for a time united the two groups and Solomon had managed to avert division in his own lifetime, but neither had been able to create any lasting bond of unity between the northern and southern parts of the kingdom. 1 Kings tells the story of this division and then gives an account of the reign of each successive king of both Israel and Judah. The story of each king is told in chronological order and so the narrative continually moves to and fro from Judah to Israel and back again. At first the two kingdoms were hostile to each other but by the time 1 Kings has come to an end with the reigns of Ahab in Israel and Jehoshaphat in Judah, the original hostility had turned to alliance. In part this alliance was a recognition of the fact that Israel was much stronger than Judah. It contained more fertile land and the international trade routes between Mesopotamia and Egypt passed through its territory. Judah had come to accept the fact of Israel's dominance. There was also the fact that both kingdoms were thrust together by a mutual threat from another power which menaced their very existence.

3

That power was Assyria, an empire with its homeland in northern Mesopotamia. By the ninth century B.C. Assyria had made herself the dominant power in Mesopotamia and begun to send her armies westwards along the valley of the upper Euphrates to attack the kingdoms of Syria. Her aim was to control all the land along the river systems of Mesopotamia and Syria in order to contain the power and influence of Egypt, the great rival empire, and eventually to attack Egypt itself. Ahab and Jehoshaphat had both been members of a coalition of the armies of the various Syrian states which had fought the Assyrian army at Qarqar on the river Orontes in 853 B.C. and forced it to retreat.

AHAB AND ELIJAH

Ahab was a strong king and has a prominence in 1 Kings second only to Solomon, though his strength was not the reason for that prominence. Just as Solomon was portrayed in 1 Kings before all else as the builder of the temple, so Ahab is shown as the king who refused to listen to a true prophet of God. Ahab was the son of Omri who had built the new capital of Samaria. Omri was also the founder of a new dynasty of kings and the originator of a new foreign policy. He made alliances of friendship with his neighbours which may have helped to pave the way for the alliance of forces against Assyria in 853 B.C. The marriage of his son Ahab to Jezebel, a Phoenician princess, was a part of that policy. Yet by pursuing such a policy he aroused the opposition of the prophet Elijah and much prominence is given in the latter part of the narrative of 1 Kings to the controversy between these two men.

Elijah saw the people of his day as being corrupted from their true allegiance to Yahweh their God by the influence of the religion of their Canaanite neighbours. Israel had originally taken the land from Canaanites and many Canaanites still lived among the Israelites. Canaanite religion was thus already well known to the Israelites and alliances with Canaanite

4

states could only add to that influence. Elijah, and those who shared his point of view, feared that the religion of Israel which had been the most creative and active force among the people since the time of the settlement, and even before, would be destroyed by Omri's policy. In 1 Kings Omri is only briefly mentioned but Ahab his son is shown as one of the main characters in the book because of his struggle with the prophet Elijah. The narratives in 2 Kings which give great prominence to Elisha, the disciple and successor of Elijah, are to be understood as further illustrations of the conflicts between loyal prophets and disloyal kings.

THE INFLUENCE OF THE PROPHETS ON THE COMPILER OF KINGS

The compiler of Kings was convinced that prophets such as Elijah or Elisha were right, and that kings such as Ahab were wrong. In fact the point of view from which Kings is written is very similar to that of the prophets whose teaching is given in the Old Testament. (It may be noted that in the Hebrew Bible the books Joshua–2 Kings are not described as history books but as 'The Former Prophets', and as such are linked with the books of the prophets, Isaiah–Malachi, which are called 'The Latter Prophets'.) Now the story of the two kingdoms is a story of failure and disaster, and with a very few notable exceptions kings are presented as the villains who, by their bad policies, brought about the disaster, while prophets, notably Elijah and Elisha, are portrayed as God's spokesmen who stood for what was right and true but were ignored by the kings. The one great difference between the point of view expressed in Kings and that expressed in the writings of the prophets is that in Kings the temple at Jerusalem and all that went on in it is looked upon as the chief glory of the people of Israel, while some at least of the prophets were strongly critical of the place that the temple had come to fill in the life of the people, and all were critical of the significance attached by the people to the sacrifices that took place in the temple. In Kings the only kings who are unreservedly praised are Solomon who built the temple, and Hezekiah and Josiah, the two kings who tried to reform and purify the religious practices carried out there.

THE DEUTERONOMISTS

This attitude towards the temple and the kings which is found consistently throughout the two books of Kings points to the conclusion that the writer or writers were members of a school of theologians who are generally known as the deuteronomists. Kings was not written by any one man. It was created by an editor collecting together material written by other men in such a way as to use that material to express his own point of view. And even when this had been done, a second editor might have altered the work of the first. We do not know who these men were individually, but they have been given the name deuteronomists from a reform of the temple which was undertaken by King Josiah in 621 B.C. A good deal of space in 2 Kings is devoted to the details of that reform. 2 Kings 22: 3–13 relates how Hilkiah, one of the temple priests, discovered an old book of law in the temple. It set out regulations for temple worship, particularly for the offering of sacrifice, which were not being followed in Judah at that time. It laid down, for example, that the Jerusalem temple was the only place where Israelites could legitimately offer sacrifice. Josiah instituted his reform to bring practice into conformity with the regulations set out in that book. Although the account of the reform does not specifically state it, it is usually accepted that the law book which Hilkiah discovered was the whole or part of the book Deuteronomy. Hence the reform is commonly referred to as the deuteronomic reform. Such a reform would have interpreted and modified Israelite law in the direction suggested by the prophets, and a writer of the deuteronomic school would have looked upon the temple as the most important institution in the kingdom, and the prophets as the true religious teachers of the people. This is very clearly the point of view of the editor of Kings.

The deuteronomists also taught that Yahweh, the God of Israel, had freely chosen Israel to be his people. This he had done because he loved them and he had demonstrated his love not only by his original choice but also by saving Israel from slavery in Egypt and giving them the land of Palestine to be their home. The defeat of the Egyptians at the Red Sea, and the victories which had gained for Israel her place in Palestine alongside the Canaanites, were all seen as being due to God's support for his people. Yahweh had also shown his love by giving to Israel a law so that they would know how to live in a manner pleasing to him. In response to this love, he looked in return for love from the people to whom he had given so much. That response of love, he made clear, should take the form of loyal obedience to his law.

THE POINT OF VIEW OF THE DEUTERONOMISTS

The deuteronomists were not interested in political and economic issues, in conquests and foreign alliances, in building and trade, except in so far as these things were related to and illustrated their own theological interests. Consequently their evaluation of kings and events must seem strange to us. A king who repaired or reformed the temple merited more attention in their eyes than one who gained new territory. For them Israel was first and foremost the covenant people of God to whom God had given the privilege and responsibility of living by his law. That was Israel's purpose and vocation in life. All other interests were secondary, and to the degree in which they could deflect Israel from her primary obligation to her God, they were dangerous and even sinful. So kings who were primarily concerned with political issues were suspect, and when their concerns and policies led to close alliances with neighbouring states and thus opened up the people to the influence of the culture and religion of those states, then the kings were looked upon as sinners and enemies both of God and his people. All the kings of Israel, the northern kingdom, from Jeroboam, who led the rebellion against Solomon's son, onwards were condemned. Each one 'did what was wrong in the eyes of the LORD' in that they encouraged their subjects to worship and offer sacrifice at temples other than the temple at Jerusalem. Ahab received particular attention and extra condemnation because his policy of alliance with foreign states was pursued vigorously and successfully, and because it attracted the opposition of the prophet Elijah.

The prophets are portrayed as men of affairs who entered the political arena of their time. They criticized the actions of the kings and always from one simple point of view: that any involvement with neighbouring states must inevitably lead to a blurring of the distinctive community life of Israel and therefore, to a lessening of the response of obedience to God's law which was the true measure of Israel's love for her God. To the comment that it is the business of kings to ensure the stability of their kingdoms by diplomatic and other means, the prophets offered one simple answer of which the classic statement is to be found in the exchanges described between King Hezekiah and the prophet Isaiah: 'I will shield this city to deliver it, for my own sake and for the sake of my servant David' (19: 34; see the whole of 19: 20–34). Israel was God's own people, and so long as she responded with loyal obedience to the law she could look to God to maintain the life of the nation and deliver it from all perils, as he had already done in earlier times.

THE END OF THE TWO KINGDOMS

Such an answer may seem particularly pointless in view of the story which 2 Kings tells. Samaria was destroyed by the armies of the Assyrian emperor, Sargon II, in 722 B.C. and with its destruction Israel ceased to exist. Its territory became one of the provinces of the Assyrian Empire. Judah was left from that time as the sole Hebrew kingdom, the one remaining witness to the old traditions. For a time all seemed to be well with her. The Judaeans could confidently assert that God had destroyed the northern kingdom because of its rebellion against the house of David and its refusal to close down its sanctuaries and acknowledge in religious matters the undisputed authority of the temple at Jerusalem. When the Assyrian Empire began to decline and her hold upon Syria and Palestine was relaxed, it seemed as though God was defending his people as in former times. Josiah, who was king of Judah at that time, was able to expand his territory and act more freely than his predecessors had been able to do for a very long time. He may well have thought of himself as a second David, and his reform of the temple was in part at least dictated by nationalist motives. But the empire of Assyria was in a short space of time replaced by the empire of Babylon which simply continued where Assyria had left off. Josiah interfered in the wars between the empires and was defeated and killed in the battle of Megiddo, 609 B.C. After that Judah became an unwilling vassal of the Babylonian Empire. Egypt was continually trying to stir such vassal states into revolt and she had some success with Judah. In 597 B.C. the Babylonians attacked Judah as both a warning and a punishment but the lesson was not learned. The consequence was that in 587 B.C. Jerusalem was destroyed and the kingdom of Judah brought to an end by the Emperor Nebuchadnezzar. Such a story seems to refute absolutely the deuteronomic faith that God can be relied upon to protect his own people.

THE MOTIVE FOR THE WRITING OF THE BOOK

Yet one of the reasons for the writing of Kings was the concern of the deuteronomists to defend their faith and, as they believed, vindicate their God. They did it by the use of another basic tenet of their theology. This was that God punished the wicked and rewarded the righteous, and that his rewards and punishments were visible and unambiguous. The rewards were wealth and national prosperity, the punishments defeat, poverty and, ultimately, the destruction of the nation. They applied this doctrine to the history of their people and drew the conclusion that what had happened to the Hebrew kingdoms did not indicate God's inability or unwillingness to protect his people so much as his punishment for their sinfulness. Far from the Assyrians or Babylonians being beyond the power of God, they were in fact the very instrument which he had chosen to enforce his will and teach his lessons (cp. Isa. 10: 5). Their purpose in writing the history of their people in this way was to teach their contemporaries, and generations yet to come, that they should learn lessons from the past; that they should live in loving obedience to God's law, and thus ensure that out of defeat and destruction would come eventually restoration and renewal. For the deuteronomists were convinced that when the people did turn to their God in loving obedience he would forgive them and restore their fortunes.

THE DEUTERONOMIC HISTORY

Kings was written then not out of despair, but in confidence and hope. It forms the last part of the story of the rise and fall of the kingdoms, a story which is begun in the book of Joshua and continued in Judges, Samuel and Kings. This group of books has been called the Deuteronomic History. It was compiled probably towards the end of the exile to set before the people the lesson they should learn from their present plight and the sins of their forefathers. It was a call for repentance and for faith in God. For faith that a restoration would come: for repentance so that when it did come, the pattern of the earlier history would not be repeated. We do not know the exact date at which Kings was written. The last event which it records is the release of the former King Jehoiachin from his Babylonian prison: 25: 27–30. This probably took place in

560 B.C. and so some time shortly after this is the earliest date that Kings could have been put together in the form that we now have it, and the whole Deuteronomic History compiled.

HOW THE BOOK WAS COMPILED

Probably the book that was compiled then was a second and enlarged edition of an earlier book. That earlier book would have been a history of the two kingdoms written after the destruction of Samaria to show that God had destroyed that kingdom because of its defection from the house of David and the temple at Jerusalem. The hero of this first edition of Kings would have been King Josiah and it would have firmly supported the Davidic monarchy and the Jerusalem temple. It could have been written some time after 621 B.C. when the deuteronomic reform took place, and before 609 B.C. when Josiah was killed. Later, after the death of Josiah, the decline of Judah and the destruction of Jerusalem, this first book was enlarged and modified to take account of what had happened to Judah as well as Israel. In the writing of both these editions, written sources would have been used. Reference is made in both 1 and 2 Kings to 'the annals of the kings of Israel' (2 Kings 1: 18), and 'the annals of the kings of Judah' (2 Kings 8: 23), which seem to have been official records of the reigns of the monarchs of the two kingdoms. The Elijah–Elisha narratives may have existed as separate narratives since they contain a good deal of material, particularly about Elisha, which is not directly related to the main historical theme of Kings. These narratives have their place in Kings as illustrating the conflict between disobedient kings and faithful prophets, but they do not conform to the strict deuteronomic views about the Jerusalem temple. For example, Elijah is shown as offering sacrifice on Mount Carmel without any censure. For this reason it may be that they were only included in the book at the final revision when Judah and Jerusalem were seen to have been as sinful and worthy of punishment as Israel.

THE STORY OF KING HEZEKIAH

There is also a lengthy narrative of the reign of King Hezekiah in which the prophet Isaiah plays a prominent part (2 Kings 18: 13 – 20: 19). This also may originally have been a separate narrative. It is repeated as chapters 36–9 of the book of Isaiah, there forming an historical appendix to the collected teaching of the prophet. The original record of the reign of Hezekiah in Kings may have been 18: 9–12 and 20: 20–1 into which the fuller narrative which features Isaiah may have been inserted. In much the same way 2 Kings 24: 18 – 25: 21 has been added as an historical appendix to the book of Jeremiah. This may have originally provided the basis for the Jewish tradition that Jeremiah was the author of Kings. In fact, Kings was probably the work of several men, authors and editors, but in any case Jeremiah's fiercely critical attitude towards the Jerusalem temple makes it difficult to give any credence to the Jewish tradition. The authors and editors of Kings certainly had written records at their disposal. They may also have inserted parts, or even the whole, of written sources into their work, but in doing this they have welded the material together so well to serve their purposes that we can do no more than offer conjectures about these matters.

THE CHRONOLOGY OF KINGS

One particular feature of Kings has caused much conjecture in the past and will doubtless continue to do so in the future. It is the chronology which forms such a prominent feature of the book. For each king of both Israel and Judah, care is taken to give an accurate dating for the beginning and length of the reign. Thus, 'In the eighteenth year of Jehoshaphat king of Judah, Jehoram son of Ahab became king of Israel in Samaria, and he reigned for twelve years' (2 Kings 3: 1), and a similar introduction is given for all the other kings. The problem is that when all the dates are put together they are not consistent with each other, and the numbers as chronology seem quite meaningless, if not bogus. Some have seen this as evidence that the numbers were added to Kings to give a false historical authority to a work which was never more than theological propaganda. Such a judgement is difficult to accept in the light of all the evidence that needs to be taken into account. Numbers can be omitted or changed in copying manuscripts more easily than words, and inaccuracies may have crept into the text. But quite apart from scribal errors, we know that methods of reckoning in such matters in the ancient world were complex and varied. The editors of Kings may have taken dates over from various sources which used different methods of reckoning, with resultant confusion. There can be no certainty. The chronology used in Kings is a technical, and to some degree a controversial, matter. It is best, therefore, to place complete reliance only on such dates as can be confirmed by archaeological evidence from other sources.

THE FAITH OF THE WRITERS

In reading 2 Kings, then, we are reading the story of the Hebrews over a period of time when events of great importance happened to them which determined the course of their national life for centuries afterwards. The story is told to us by men who believed that all history was in the hand of God who used it to fulfil his purposes. They believed that God loved his people and that that love was to be discerned even in disasters and suffering. So the sufferings of their people and the disasters that befell them did not lead the authors to despair. On the contrary they offered firm hope to those who loved God and were willing to live in obedience to his will. In the circumstances out of which Kings was written, this was an act of faith which was as courageous as it was unexpected. For us the chief value in reading Kings is to come to understand better the faith and hope of the writers and thus to learn more of the nature of the God whom they worshipped.

✳   ✳   ✳   ✳   ✳   ✳   ✳   ✳   ✳   ✳   ✳   ✳   ✳   ✳

Elisha and the end of the house of Ahab

This title which is given to the first ten chapters – approximately two-fifths of the whole book – is some indication of the prominence which Elisha has been given in 2 Kings. This may seem surprising. Elisha was not a king, and to devote that amount of space to any one person in a narrative which is telling the story of two kingdoms over several generations, may seem to be out of proportion. Clearly such was not the view of the editors. They devoted such a large amount of space to Elisha because they believed that the events in which he was involved illustrated more clearly than others the religious issues which were at stake throughout the period of the Kings. In much the same way, and for the same reason, it has often been noted that great emphasis, and a seemingly disproportionate amount of space, is devoted in the gospels to the events of the last week of Jesus' life.

2 Kings tells the story of the decline and destruction of the kingdoms of Israel and Judah, but the editors were not simply concerned to record the facts. They wished also to point to the reasons why things had happened just as they did. They believed that the greatest single factor which had led to the disasters was the policy of the kings. They regarded them all, with the exceptions of Hezekiah and Josiah, as stupid and wicked. It was not just that the kings were ignorant or uncertain of what to do. God raised up particular men, prophets, whom he commissioned to declare clearly and openly his will for his people and the particular decisions to which the implementation of that will pointed. Unhappily the kings paid little attention to the true prophets and the result was hostility and tension between kings and prophets. This tension between

14

kings and prophets was a part of the situation for most of the period which 2 Kings covers, as anyone can easily discover by reading the books of Amos, or Hosea, or Isaiah 1–39. The editors of Kings chose to teach this point by concentrating on the conflict between one king and his successor, and one prophet and his disciple. The king in question was Ahab, and the prophet Elijah. Most of the latter part of 1 Kings is devoted to the conflict between these two persons and what they represent. When 2 Kings opens Ahab has been killed and succeeded by his son Ahaziah. Elijah does appear briefly in chapter 1 but then dies and is succeeded by his disciple Elisha, and the conflict is shown as continuing into another generation. One of the main points in the teaching of the deuteronomic editors was that God rewards with blessing the righteous, and punishes with misfortune the wicked, and that this moral process can be demonstrated in history. The story of Elisha is used to demonstrate this teaching. Elijah died before the cause for which he had fought was finally victorious. He did not live to see Canaanite religion and all its influence expelled from Israel and Judah, but it did happen. His disciple Elisha inspired a revolution which overthrew the dynasty of Omri, and abandoned its policy of friendship with the Phoenician states. By this revolt the teaching of Elijah was proved victorious, and the dynasty of Omri brought to an end. For the deuteronomists right had prevailed and the enemies of God been punished. The very great emphasis laid upon Elisha in the book thus occurs because to the editors he was such a clear example of the teaching they wished to present, and of the true meaning which they believed was present in all historical events.

The stories that are told of Elisha are very varied in character. Some show him dealing with kings in much the same manner as other prophets: others depict him as a wonder-worker who used supernatural power to enhance his own position and even buttress his own dignity. The latter stories are legendary. They may be exaggerated accounts of events with which the prophet was concerned, or stories made up about him by disciples who wished to magnify his power and authority. Some at least of the stories may have been popular folk-tales which can be told of any leader and in this instance have come to be associated with Elisha. Their purpose is to emphasize the power, resource and cleverness of their hero and to warn of the danger of opposing him, rather than to illustrate the moral and spiritual greatness of his person and teaching. To many modern readers they have proved a source of embarrassment and bewilderment since they describe a man who was said to be God's agent, acting in a morally repulsive fashion. Yet if we recognize their origin as folk-tales and seek to discover how and why they came to be associated with the figure of Elisha we shall begin to understand their purpose. The editors felt the need to depict Elisha as first and foremost a strong man with sources of supernatural power at his disposal because of the fierceness and importance of the struggle in which he was engaged. He was fighting for true religion against false religion. In their zeal to describe his victory the editors at times show him as being superior in strength rather than in moral and spiritual qualities. In so doing they have debased their portrait. To this judgement they might have replied that they merely sought to popularize it and thus bring its lesson home to a greater number of people. If so, the very features which gave the portrait greater impact in their day are in danger of lessening its impact in ours. Some modern readers may well feel that they can only recognize Elisha as an authentic prophet of God by abandoning altogether some of the stories with which his name has become associated.

AHAZIAH'S INJURY

AFTER AHAB'S DEATH Moab rebelled against Israel. **1** Ahaziah fell through a latticed window in his roof- **2** chamber in Samaria and injured himself; he sent messengers to inquire of Baal-zebub the god of Ekron whether he would recover from his illness. The angel of the LORD **3** ordered Elijah the Tishbite to go and meet the messengers of the king of Samaria and say to them, 'Is there no god in Israel, that you go to inquire of Baal-zebub the god of Ekron? This is the word of the LORD to your master: **4** "You shall not rise from the bed where you are lying; you will die."' Then Elijah departed. The messengers **5** went back to the king. When asked why they had returned, they answered that a man had come to meet them **6** and had ordered them to return and say to the king who had sent them, 'This is the word of the LORD: "Is there no god in Israel, that you send to inquire of Baal-zebub the god of Ekron? In consequence, you shall not rise from the bed where you are lying; you will die."' The king **7** asked them what kind of man it was who had met them and said this. 'A hairy man', they answered, 'with a **8** leather apron around his waist.' 'It is Elijah the Tishbite', said the king.

* I. *Moab* was a neighbour of Israel whose territory lay east of the Dead Sea and north of the brook Zared (see map on p. 30). Its northern boundary varied from time to time. It had been made a vassal of Israel by Omri, Ahab's father. More details of the revolt are given in chapter 3, where it is said to have taken place during the reign of Jehoram, Ahaziah's brother and successor. Probably the revolt began after Ahab's

death and continued for some years. A commemorative stone set up by Mesha, a king of Moab, was discovered in the nineteenth century. It is now kept in the Louvre in Paris. The inscription on it tells of the revolt of Mesha against Israel after a period of 'oppression' by Omri and Ahab, but its statements do not exactly fit with the information given in the biblical narrative (see comment on 3: 4).

2. The opening formula for the reign of Ahaziah has already been given in 1 Kings 22: 51-3. The *latticed window* was probably a first-floor balcony projecting out from the house. The window would have been covered with a fretted wooden screen which ensured privacy but allowed any cool breeze to enter. *Baal-zebub*: literally, Lord of flies. *Baal* means Lord or husband. Each city had its own baal, the god who was regarded as the husband of the land, and whose duty it was to ensure its continuing fertility. The *Baal* might be a god who was worshipped in that city alone, or the local form of the great Canaanite storm god who was also called Baal. *zebub* is probably a deliberate corruption of *zebul*, a word meaning 'prince'. This form of the name is also found in the New Testament, e.g. Matt. 10: 25. *inquire* means to consult the oracle and so seek a message from the god. Ekron was the most northern of the Philistine cities (see map on p. 30). It was about 10 miles (16 km) south-east of Jaffa, the old city (Joppa; cp. Jonah 1: 3), now closely linked with the modern Tel-Aviv.

3. *The angel of the LORD* was one who carried God's messages. The term can be used to indicate that a human agent was regarded for this purpose as God himself. The point of Elijah's question to the messengers was that no event was believed to happen by accident. Therefore Ahaziah's 'accident' would have been believed to have been caused by God as a punishment for sin, here the king's apostasy (cp. 1 Kings 22: 53). Ahaziah's action was an attempt to seek relief by asking help from another god. If his petition had proved successful, then Yahweh would have been even less regarded

18

in the eyes of the people. Elijah therefore, as Yahweh's spokesman, had to intervene and to put into plain words the judgement of God which the accident implied. This meant that Ahaziah was as good as dead since the words of a true prophet must be fulfilled (cp. Isa. 55: 11).

8. *A hairy man*: or alternatively, 'he wore a garment of haircloth' (Revised Standard Version). The Hebrew has been understood in both ways. With the latter translation the *leather apron* becomes 'a girdle of leather'. 'A robe of coarse hair' seems to have been the recognized uniform of a prophet (cp. Zech. 13: 4) which would account for the comment on the dress of John the Baptist in the gospels (cp. Matt. 3: 4). For this reason it seems more likely that Elijah was recognized by his dress than by his appearance.

This is the only story in 2 Kings in which Elijah appears, apart from the account of his death. It restates the issue which lay between the prophets and the kings which has been expounded most fully in the story of the conflict on Mount Carmel (1 Kings 18: 17–46). This was that Yahweh was the God of Israel and as such demanded total and exclusive allegiance from his people. He would not share his sovereignty with any other god, and those who sought to make him do so, acted at their own peril. *

FIRE FROM HEAVEN

Then the king sent a captain to him with his company 9 of fifty. He went up and found the prophet sitting on a hill-top and said to him, 'Man of God, the king orders you to come down.' Elijah answered the captain, 'If I am 10 a man of God, may fire fall from heaven and consume you and your company!' Fire fell from heaven and consumed the officer and his fifty men. The king sent another 11 captain of fifty with his company, and he went up[a] and

[a] *So Luc. Sept.; Heb.* answered.

said to the prophet, 'Man of God, this is the king's
12 command: Come down at once.' Elijah answered, 'If I
am a man of God, may fire fall from heaven and consume you and your company!' God's fire fell from heaven
13 and consumed the man and his company. The king sent
the captain of a third company with his fifty men, and
this third captain went up the hill to Elijah and knelt down
before him and pleaded with him: 'Man of God, consider me and these fifty servants of yours, and set some
14 value on our lives. Fire fell from heaven and consumed
the other two captains of fifty and their companies; but
15 let my life have some value in your eyes.' The angel of the
LORD said to Elijah, 'Go down with him. Do not be
afraid.' So he rose and went down with him to the king,
16 and he said, 'This is the word of the LORD: "You have
sent to inquire of Baal-zebub the god of Ekron,*a* and
therefore you shall not rise from the bed where you are
17 lying; you will die."' The word of the LORD which
Elijah had spoken was fulfilled, and Ahaziah died; and
because he had no son, his brother*b* Jehoram succeeded
him in the second year of Joram son of Jehoshaphat king
of Judah.
18   The other events of Ahaziah's reign are recorded in the
annals of the kings of Israel.

* The king recognized Elijah as an authentic prophet and his
words as God's judgement. His only hope, then, was to persuade Elijah to withdraw his prophecy. So a conflict follows
which Elijah wins. The story as it stands is probably a legen-

[a] So Sept.; Heb. adds is it because there is no god in Israel of whom you
may inquire?
[b] his brother: so Luc. Sept.; Heb. om.

dary expansion of the conflict. It has developed from a typically folklorish play on words. A man of God (Hebrew, *'ish 'elohim*) has been given the weapon of fire of God (Hebrew, *'esh 'elohim*) with which to defend himself. The original story may have been verses 2–8. To this verses 9–17 were probably added. These verses share the character of the Elisha legends which we shall meet in the following chapters. There is no story of Elijah in 1 Kings which is of this kind.

9. A *company of fifty* was a recognized unit in the armies of the time.

11. *went up* and 'answered' (N.E.B. footnote) only differ by the final letter of the words in Hebrew.

16. The N.E.B. follows the shorter text of the Septuagint. It regards the words which it has relegated to a footnote as being an addition to the text copied from verse 3. But the longer text may be original. The point is that the king already knows the will of the God of Israel but is unwilling to heed it.

17. *in the second year of Joram*: this dating disagrees with that given in 3: 1. This is an example of the chronological problems of Kings to which reference has been made on p. 12. *his brother*: these words are not found in the Hebrew, but are in most of the versions. They amplify the reference in 3: 1. *Joram* is a shortened form of Jehoram. The Hebrew here is Jehoram. The N.E.B. has changed this to *Joram* because this is the form of the name which is found in later chapters. ✳

THE COMMISSIONING OF ELISHA

The time came when the LORD would take Elijah up to **2** heaven in a whirlwind. Elijah and Elisha left Gilgal, and 2 Elijah said to Elisha, 'Stay here; for the LORD has sent me to Bethel.' But Elisha said, 'As the LORD lives, your life upon it, I will not leave you.' So they went down country to Bethel. There a company of prophets came out to 3 Elisha and said to him, 'Do you know that the LORD is

going to take your lord and master from you today?'
4 'I do know,' he replied; 'say no more.' Then Elijah said
to him, 'Stay here, Elisha; for the LORD has sent me to
Jericho.' But he replied, 'As the LORD lives, your life
upon it, I will not leave you.' So they went to Jericho.
5 There a company of prophets came up to Elisha and said
to him, 'Do you know that the LORD is going to take
your lord and master from you today?' 'I do know,' he
6 said; 'say no more.' Then Elijah said to him, 'Stay here;
for the LORD has sent me to the Jordan.' The other
replied, 'As the LORD lives, your life upon it, I will not
leave you.' So the two of them went on.

7   Fifty of the prophets followed them, and stood watching from a distance as the two of them stopped by the
8 Jordan. Elijah took his cloak, rolled it up and struck the
water with it. The water divided to right and left, and
9 they both crossed over on dry ground. While they were
crossing, Elijah said to Elisha, 'Tell me what I can do for
you before I am taken from you.' Elisha said, 'Let me
10 inherit a double share of your spirit.' 'You have asked a
hard thing', said Elijah. 'If you see me taken from you,
may your wish be granted; if you do not, it shall not be
11 granted.' They went on, talking as they went, and
suddenly there appeared chariots of fire and horses of
fire, which separated them one from the other, and Elijah
12 was carried up in the whirlwind to heaven. When Elisha
saw it, he cried, 'My father, my father, the chariots and
the horsemen of Israel!', and he saw him no more. Then
13 he took hold of his mantle and rent it in two, and he
picked up the cloak which had fallen from Elijah, and
14 came back and stood on the bank of the Jordan. There he

too struck the water with Elijah's cloak and said, 'Where is the LORD the God of Elijah?' When he struck the water, it was again divided to right and left, and he crossed over. The prophets from Jericho, who were watching, saw 15 him and said, 'The spirit of Elijah has settled on Elisha.' So they came to meet him, and fell on their faces before him and said, 'Your servants have fifty stalwart men. Let 16 them go and search for your master; perhaps the spirit of the LORD has lifted him up and cast him on some mountain or into some valley.' But he said, 'No, you must not send them.' They pressed him, however, until he had not 17 the heart to refuse. So they sent out the fifty men but, though they searched for three days, they did not find him. When they came back to Elisha, who had remained 18 at Jericho, he said to them, 'Did I not tell you not to go?'

* Attention has usually been concentrated in this passage on the ascension of Elijah since this is the aspect of the story which was given great prominence in later Jewish and Christian teaching. The story was interpreted as meaning that Elijah was so close to God in spirit that he was taken to heaven without passing through the experience of death. In this he was linked with the patriarch Enoch (cp. Gen. 5: 24) and both stories were seen in Christian thought as foreshadowing the ascension of Jesus. Yet the main point of the story for the editors of Kings is clearly the commissioning of Elisha. By it he is authenticated as the true successor of Elijah upon whom both the work and the authority of the master have descended. The details of the story are meant to indicate the source of the commission which Elijah held and here passed on to Elisha. Moses, under God, founded the covenant people. Both Elijah and Elisha were his successors in that their work was to ensure the continuance of that people in their own time. So both prophets divided the waters of Jordan as Moses had done at the Red Sea, and the purpose of Elijah's ascension may have been to link him with Moses rather than Enoch. Moses also had no known grave (cp. Deut. 34: 5–6). In the New Testament, at the transfiguration of Jesus, Moses and Elijah were also linked as the two authoritative figures of the Old Testament tradition (cp. Matt. 17: 1–5). Elisha has already appeared once in 1 Kings in a story which also told of his commissioning, but this story seems to know nothing of that one (cp. 1 Kings 19: 19–21).

1. *a whirlwind* would be a fairly frequent and therefore relatively well-known occurrence in the deserts of Transjordan. Wind and spirit were closely related in the minds of the Hebrews. The Hebrew *ruaḥ* means both. The link was probably the idea of energy, as in the New Testament where the double meaning of the word is used as a basis for teaching (cp. John 3: 8 and Acts 2: 1–4). *Gilgal*: this could not have been the Gilgal near the Jordan mentioned in Josh. 5: 9. The name means 'circle' and may have been used of several places particularly where there was a circle of stones as a sanctuary. One such place, called Jiljiliyeh by the Arabs, is about 8 miles (nearly 13 km) north of Bethel. This may have been the site of this Gilgal (see map on p. 30). Bethel was situated on the eastern side of the central hill-country. The city had probably grown up around an ancient shrine. The name means 'house of God', and its foundation was associated with Jacob's dream (cp. Gen. 28: 11–19).

2. *I will not leave you*: the disciple here and later uncharacteristically refuses to obey the command of his master. The command may possibly have been a test.

3. *a company of prophets*: many prophets seem to have lived together in schools or guilds near to the old sanctuaries. They were the groups upon whom the king called for advice and counsel (cp. 1 Kings 22: 6). Elijah had been a solitary figure seemingly deliberately dissociating himself from the other prophets and being highly critical of their willingness to support royal policies.

8. *struck the water with it*: a sign was needed to show the watching prophets that Elijah was still God's man. The divided water declared Elijah to be the inheritor of the Mosaic tradition.

9. *a double share of your spirit*: Elisha was asking that he might be treated as Elijah's firstborn son (cp. Deut. 21: 17).

10. *You have asked a hard thing*: because the prophetic spirit was a gift from God alone. The condition attached to the gift, *If you see me taken from you*, would indicate that God had approved of Elisha (cp. Gen. 32: 30 and Exod. 33: 18–23). It was believed that men could not see God and live. Even Moses who had ascended the mount of revelation was not allowed to see God face to face.

11. *chariots of fire and horses of fire* are mentioned here for the first time. We shall meet them again in later stories of Elisha. What the words precisely describe is not clear. Nor is their precise meaning. They present a pictorial symbol which had more than one association for Israel. Since the function of a symbol is to evoke a response rather than to communicate a precise meaning, and since that response may be made up of several elements which are not directly related to each other, it is difficult, if not impossible, to give a clear description of what the words were intended to convey.

Chariots had played a considerable part in the fortunes of the Israelite tribes in the early days of their settlement in Canaan. The Canaanites had then possessed chariots and this had given them weapon superiority over the Israelites. So the Israelites had been confined to the hill-country where chariots could not be used effectively. They could not settle at all on the plains where their foot-soldiers were no match for the enemy chariots. At that time the Israelites had neither the expertise for using chariots nor the economic resources to be able to maintain them. Thus chariots came to be for Israel the symbol of overwhelming military force, and when under David and Solomon, the kingdom grew strong and powerful, that power was displayed by the building of chariot cities which housed large forces of chariots. These were regarded as one of the greater bulwarks for the defence of the nation. The association of chariots with the prophets Elijah and Elisha may be pointing to them as fulfilling the same function, i.e. defending the nation against its enemies.

The imagery of chariots was also used in a quite different sphere, namely the worship and mythology of the Canaanites. The sun god was depicted as riding across the heavens each day in his heavenly chariot, and models of horses and chariots were kept in temples and used as a part of the cult of the sun god. Such ritual objects seem to have been destroyed in the temple at Jerusalem during the reform of King Josiah (2 Kings 23: 11). The chariot in this sense was the symbol of the sun god and conveyed the meaning of supernatural strength and power. Israel rejected the use of the chariots of the sun god in her worship as compromising the uniqueness of Yahweh, but took over literary images from the Canaanites. In Ps. 68 the power of Yahweh is visualized in terms of his chariots (Ps. 68: 17) and the same image is used by the prophet Habakkuk (Hab. 3: 8). Ezekiel also seems to picture God's presence in terms of a chariot (Ezek. 1: 15–21 and 10: 15–18).

Here the image of chariots seems to be used to evoke the idea of the power of Yahweh. The solar myth was probably in the mind of the writer as a means of visualizing Elijah's passage to heaven. In other passages where the image is used, it is impossible to say whether its source is human chariotry or divine chariots. Probably both were in the mind of the writer, though human chariots may have been dominant at 7: 6 and divine chariots at 6: 17 and 13: 14. It is a part of the artistry of the writer to link together the two aspects of the image in this way.

12. *rent it in two* as a sign of renunciation.

14. *with Elijah's cloak*: after these words many Greek manuscripts add 'and it was not divided'. These words may be original. They would explain Elisha's question. If they are accepted, then the words that follow, *When he struck the water*,

would be better translated, 'Then he struck the water', i.e. Elisha struck the water a second time after his question. The incident has made plain to him and the watching prophets that the power in him was the same in character and purpose as had been in Elijah.

16–18. The fifty prophets understood the whirlwind as God's instrument to bring about the death of Elijah. They did not understand it as an instrument to rescue him from the earth. To leave a corpse unburied was a shameful impiety, especially the corpse of a man as eminent as Elijah had been. Hence their concern to find it. Elisha's attitude seemed to them callous and lacking in filial respect, but the outcome indicated that Elisha had greater knowledge and insight than they had. He had, indeed, received the double share of Elijah's spirit. *

TWO EXAMPLES OF ELISHA'S POWER

The people of the city said to Elisha, 'You can see how 19 pleasantly our city is situated, but the water is polluted and the country is troubled with miscarriages.' He said, 20 'Fetch me a new bowl and put some salt in it.' When they had fetched it, he went out to the spring and, throwing 21 the salt into it, he said, 'This is the word of the LORD: "I purify this water. It shall cause no more death or miscarriage."' The water has remained pure till this day, in 22 fulfilment of Elisha's word.

He went up from there to Bethel and, as he was on his 23 way, some small boys came out of the city and jeered at him, saying, 'Get along with you, bald head, get along.' He turned round and looked at them and he cursed them 24 in the name of the LORD; and two she-bears came out of a wood and mauled forty-two of them. From there he 25 went on to Mount Carmel, and thence back to Samaria.

* Immediately following the commissioning the editors have added two stories to show that Elisha was endowed with God's power both to bless the good and to curse the wicked. The second story is morally repulsive to us, but it would not have been seen in that light by the deuteronomic editors. To them Elisha was the successor of Moses, who offered to the people a choice between good and evil, blessing and curse, as Moses had done (cp. Deut. 30: 15–20).

19. Jericho had been rebuilt in the time of Ahab (cp. 1 Kings 16: 34). The tradition was that it had been cursed by Joshua after its capture by him (cp. Josh. 6: 26) and the pollution of the spring was a part of that curse.

20. *a new bowl*: so that there could be no influence in the bowl left over from some previous use. Salt was essential to life. Therefore water with salt would bring life rather than death. A new-born child was rubbed with salt (cp. Ezek. 16: 4). The water was taking on a new function of giving life.

22. *The water* has been traditionally identified with Ain es-Sultan, the spring beside the mound of ancient Jericho.

23. *bald head*: a traveller would have had his head covered. The boys probably recognized Elisha as a prophet from his dress (cp. note on 1: 8) and mocked him as a prophet. The reference to baldness would be to the prophet's tonsure. The offence of the boys was therefore blasphemy in that mocking God's prophet was equivalent to mocking God himself (cp. Deut. 18: 19 and Lev. 24: 10–16).

24. *two she-bears*: the Hebrews believed that all things were caused; nothing happened by accident. Therefore what to us would be an accident was to them an act of God. Here punishment was being administered by God.

These stories may be based upon incidents in the life of Elisha but, as told here, they are legendary folk-tales, which indicate how Elisha was remembered as a popular hero. They have been included by the editors to illustrate a point they wished to make. All such stories make a single point with clarity and force at the expense of oversimplifying the issue and distorting the truth. Here the doctrine of retributive justice, a doctrine which was central to the teaching of the deuteronomists, has been set out in a crude way. The editors have made their point forcibly but at the cost of presenting a view of God's nature which is crude and insensitive. In the first story God is shown as working through magic; in the second he is a harsh tyrant rather than a compassionate father. These stories fall far below the sensitive spirituality of the best of the deuteronomic tradition (cp. Deut. 7: 7–10 and 6: 4–5) but the editors have included them as popular and effective teaching aids to instruct the people of the danger of turning away from their God, and to demonstrate that the only security lay in rigid obedience to the will of God as expressed in his law and spoken by his true prophets. *

THE INTRODUCTION TO THE REIGN OF JEHORAM, KING OF ISRAEL

In the eighteenth year of Jehoshaphat king of Judah, **3** Jehoram son of Ahab became king of Israel in Samaria, and he reigned for twelve years. He did what was wrong **2** in the eyes of the LORD, though not as his father and his mother had done; he did remove the sacred pillar of the Baal which his father had made. Yet he persisted in the **3** sins into which Jeroboam son of Nebat had led Israel, and did not give them up.

* Jehoram was the last of the house of Omri to reign over Israel. His death is recorded at 9: 24. This very large amount of space in the book has been devoted to his reign because it includes the stories of the prophet Elisha which the editors have collected.

   1. The dating given here does not agree with that given earlier (see p. 12; cp. note on 1: 17). This may indicate that the two stories came originally from different sources.

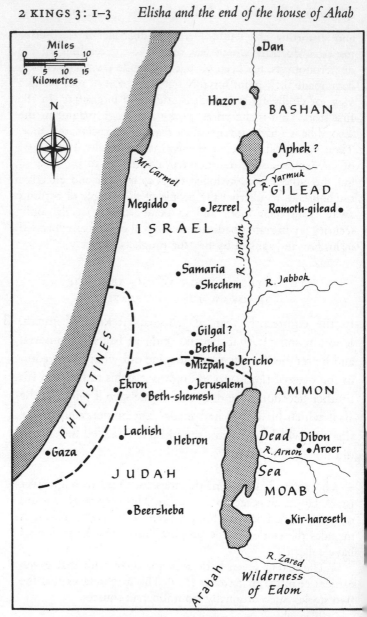

2. Palestine during the time of the divided kingdom

2. *the sacred pillar* was a standing stone pillar. An image of the god might have been carved on it. The name *Baal* is ambiguous. It means Lord or husband. Each city had its own *Baal* (see note on 1: 2) but the name was also used among the Canaanites for the storm god whom they regarded as the most prominent and active of all the gods. This is the Baal who was most probably being referred to here. ✳

THE REVOLT OF MESHA, KING OF MOAB

Mesha king of Moab was a sheep-breeder, and he used 4 to supply the king of Israel regularly with the wool of a hundred thousand lambs and a hundred thousand rams. When Ahab died, the king of Moab rebelled against the 5 king of Israel. Then King Jehoram came from Samaria 6 and mustered all Israel. He also sent this message to 7 Jehoshaphat king of Judah: 'The king of Moab has rebelled against me. Will you join me in attacking Moab?' 'I will,' he replied; 'what is mine is yours: myself, my people, and my horses.' 'From which direc- 8 tion shall we attack?' Jehoram asked. 'Through the wilderness of Edom', replied the other. So the king of 9 Israel set out with the king of Judah and the king of Edom. When they had been seven days on the march, they had no water left for the army or the pack-animals. Then the king of Israel said, 'Alas, the LORD has brought 10 together three kings, only to put us at the mercy of the Moabites.' But Jehoshaphat said, 'Is there not a prophet 11 of the LORD here through whom we may seek guidance of the LORD?' One of the officers of the king of Israel answered, 'Elisha son of Shaphat is here, the man who poured water on Elijah's hands.' 'The word of the LORD 12

is with him', said Jehoshaphat. So the king of Israel and
Jehoshaphat and the king of Edom went down to Elisha.
13 Elisha said to the king of Israel, 'Why do you come to
me? Go to the prophets of your father and your mother.'
But the king of Israel said to him, 'No; the LORD has
called us three kings out to put us at the mercy of the
14 Moabites.' 'As the LORD of Hosts lives, whom I serve,'
said Elisha, 'I would not spare a look or a glance for you,
if it were not for my regard for Jehoshaphat king of
15 Judah. But now, fetch me a minstrel.' They fetched a
minstrel,ᵃ and while he was playing, the power of the
16 LORD came upon Elisha and he said, 'This is the word of
17 the LORD: "Pools will form all over this ravine." The
LORD has decreed that you shall see neither wind nor rain,
yet this ravine shall be filled with water for you and your
18 armyᵇ and your pack-animals to drink. But that is a mere
trifle in the sight of the LORD; what he will also do, is to
19 put Moab at your mercy. You will raze to the ground
every fortified town and every noble city; you will cut
down all their fine trees; you will stop up all the springs
of water; and you will spoil every good piece of land by
20 littering it with stones.' In the morning at the hour of the
regular sacrifice they saw water flowing in from the
direction of Edom, and the land was flooded.
21   Meanwhile all Moab had heard that the kings had come
up to fight against them, and every man, young and old,
who could carry arms, was called out and stationed on the
22 frontier. When they got up next morning and the sun
had risen over the water, the Moabites saw the water in

[a] They fetched a minstrel: *so Luc. Sept.; Heb. om.*
[b] *So Luc. Sept.; Heb.* cattle.

front of them red like blood and cried out, 'It is blood. 23
The kings must have quarrelled and attacked one another.
Now to the plunder, Moab!' When they came to the 24
Israelite camp, the Israelites turned out and attacked them
and drove the Moabites headlong in flight, and themselves
entered[a] the land of Moab, destroying as they went. They 25
razed the cities to the ground; they littered every good
piece of land with stones, each man casting one stone on
to it; they stopped up every spring of water; they cut
down all their fine trees; and they harried Moab[b] until
only in Kir-hareseth were any buildings left standing, and
even this city the slingers surrounded and attacked.

When the king of Moab saw that the war had gone 26
against him, he took seven hundred men with him,
armed with swords, to cut a way through to the king of
Aram,[c] but they failed in the attempt. Then he took his 27
eldest son, who would have succeeded him, and offered
him as a whole-offering upon the city wall. The Israelites
were filled with such consternation at this sight,[d] that
they struck camp and returned to their own land.

* This story is similar in many respects to the story of the
attack made by the kings Ahab and Jehoshaphat against
Ramoth-gilead in 1 Kings 22. It owes its present position in
2 Kings, and maybe even its inclusion in the book at all, to the
fact that Elisha appears in it. Yet Elisha does not play a prominent part, and this is basically a story about the activities of the
kings rather than a folk-tale about the exploits of a prophet. It

[a] So Sept.; Heb. destroyed.
[b] and...Moab: so Luc. Sept.; Heb. om.
[c] So Old Latin; Heb. Edom.
[d] The Israelites...sight: or There was such great anger against the
Israelites...

may be that the incident upon which the story is based happened during the reign of Ahab who was a much stronger king than Jehoram. This would account for the mention of Jehoshaphat king of Judah which has caused difficulty for the editors (cp. the dating in 1 : 17 and 3 : 1), and fits in with the evidence of the Moabite Stone which dates Mesha's revolt during the reign of Ahab (see note on 1 : 1). Is the point of the story as used here simply to demonstrate the power of the word of Elisha?

4. *Mesha king of Moab* is also known from a non-biblical source. In 1868 a missionary, the Reverend F. A. Klein, discovered an inscribed stone at Dibon (see map on p. 30) which commemorated in the Moabite language the victories of Mesha against Israel. The stone was broken in pieces by local Arabs but the pieces have been reconstructed and are now exhibited as the Moabite Stone in the Louvre in Paris. A translation of the inscription will be found in *Documents from Old Testament Times*, pp. 196–7 (see also *The Making of the Old Testament* in this series, pp. 29–32). The inscription tells how Mesha in the name of Chemosh, the god of Moab, drove out the Israelites who had oppressed the Moabites in the time of Omri and his son.

5. *When Ahab died*: this does not agree with the Moabite Stone but it may be correct. The death of a king was frequently the signal for the revolt of his vassals, and Mesha may have exaggerated his success by describing it as a victory against the powerful Ahab.

6. *King Jehoram*: no mention is made of Ahaziah.

8. The most direct line of attack would have been across the Jordan at Jericho and then southwards into Moabite territory to the east of the Dead Sea, but Mesha had regained and fortified the strong points north of the Arnon. An attack through Judah and the Arabah to the south of the Dead Sea with a thrust north was made impossible by the precipitous north bank of the Zared (Wadi 'l-Ḥesa). So the allies chose to make a long detour eastward around the Zared entering Moab

from the east. This desert region was *the wilderness of Edom* (see map on p. 30).

9. The *king of Edom* was at this time a vassal of Judah. In fact the title *king* seems to be incorrect (cp. 1 Kings 22: 47 and 2 Kings 8: 20).

11. *who poured water on Elijah's hands*: the work of a servant.

12–13. It seems that Jehoram had consulted prophets before embarking on the expedition. Elisha repudiates them as no true prophets of Yahweh (cp. 1 Kings 22: 6–14). The king is now willing to listen to Elisha since events have shown that his own prophets have not truly interpreted the will of Yahweh.

14. *the LORD of Hosts*: this title was also used by Elijah (1 Kings 18: 15). The *Hosts* may be the sun, moon and stars over whom God was thought to rule, or the heavenly beings who were present at his court. LORD of Hosts, *Yahweh Sabaoth*, was the title by which Yahweh had especially been known in the days of the old tribal league. It was the rallying cry for the tribes in battle. The Hosts were then the tribes who made up the league. After the creation of the kingdom the title was particularly associated with Yahweh as the covenant God of Israel. Its use is particularly appropriate here in conditions of war, and it subtly makes the point that it is Elisha the prophet who is true to the traditions of Israel rather than the kings.

15f. *the power of the LORD came upon Elisha*: i.e. he became ecstatic. In this he was much nearer to the nationalistic prophets than his master Elijah had been. Music was frequently used by groups of prophets to induce ecstasy (cp. 1 Sam. 10: 5). "*Pools will form all over this ravine*": another possible translation is, 'Make this valley full of trenches', i.e. the soldiers are to dig trenches to collect water. This would have seemed pointless in a wilderness.

17. The source of the water was a freak storm over the mountains of Edom. The water ran down the valley and lay in pools in the ravine. Such storms are unpredictable but a

35

feature of the area. *army*: the Hebrew word differs in only one letter from the word for 'cattle'. The versions seem to have preserved the true reading which the Hebrew has lost by scribal error.

19. This verse describes a policy of systematic destruction of the land as a place of settlement. *you will cut down all their fine trees*: this is specifically forbidden in Deut. 20: 19-20. Either the law was thought only to operate in Canaan or this campaign was regarded as being outside the usual rules of warfare. The impression is given that the whole land is being put to the ban, i.e. offered as a sacrifice to God for victory in war.

20. *at the hour of the regular sacrifice*: the time of the daily sacrifice in the temple at Jerusalem. In the temple built after the exile this was dawn.

22. *the Moabites saw the water...red like blood*: the cause of this phenomenon was probably the red sand which is a notable feature of the Wadi 'l-Ḥesa. To this there may have been added a play on words. Edom means red (cp. Gen. 25: 30) and the Hebrew word for blood, *dam*, is almost identical.

24. The story emphasizes that the victory was won for Israel through God's help. The lesson the editors wished to teach was that God showed an active concern for his people, and that they in return should respond with obedient love by keeping his commandments and scrupulously avoiding all religious links with their pagan neighbours. This is the point which has been made again and again in most of the stories of Israel's battles told in the deuteronomic history from Joshua onwards. *entered*: the Hebrew word is very like that for 'destroyed' (N.E.B. footnote).

25. *and they harried Moab*: the text reads equally well without these words (see N.E.B. footnote). *Kir-hareseth*: the capital of Moab, now called Kerak. The importance and strength of the site is indicated by the fact that the crusaders built a castle there which was only captured after a year-long siege and famine.

26. *Aram*: the Hebrew reads 'Edom' (see N.E.B. footnote).

Since the king of Edom was fighting as an ally of Jehoram and Jehoshaphat this reads strangely. 'Edom' and 'Aram' are almost identical in Hebrew and it seems that Edom has replaced Aram in the Hebrew because of a scribal error. Aram was a kingdom to the north with its capital at Damascus which had become the chief rival of Israel (cp. 1 Kings 20). Aram would have been the obvious place for Mesha to seek refuge and assistance.

27. The sacrifice was offered to Chemosh the god of Moab. Their defeat would have been looked upon by the Moabites as a punishment from their god for some national sin. So this most costly offering was made to appease the anger of the god. It was made on the city wall in full view of the Israelites in order that the anger of Chemosh might be turned away from the Moabites and towards their enemies. Such sacrifices were rare but not unknown among the Israelites. Ahaz king of Judah sacrificed his son (2 Kings 16: 3) and Jephthah, one of the earlier judges, sacrificed his daughter (Judg. 11: 29–40). They seem to have been practised with greater frequency by the Phoenicians. The deuteronomists regarded such sacrifices with especial horror as a particularly wicked pagan practice. *whole-offering*: this is the name for the kind of sacrifice which was completely burned on the altar. In other sacrifices the priests and worshippers themselves ate a part of the offering. *The Israelites...at this sight*: the alternative translation given in the N.E.B. footnote is much nearer to the Hebrew. Its meaning is not wholly clear and the ambiguity had led to the translation which is given in the text. The difficulty is the 'great anger' of the footnote. Who was angry? The most natural answer to the question is 'Chemosh, god of Moab'. But would the deuteronomists have written as they have of a pagan god, or admitted that a sacrifice to Chemosh was so successful? Alternatively, the reference could be to the anger of Yahweh, but would Yahweh pay attention to a sacrifice offered to Chemosh?

The N.E.B. translation understands the Hebrew word to

mean 'consternation' rather than 'wrath', and then understands the Israelites as the subject rather than the object of the emotion. It also implies that the Israelites were so convinced of the efficacy of the sacrifice that they lost all confidence in their own cause. After the account given in the earlier verses of God's help and in view of the general attitude of the deuteronomists, this seems very unlikely. The translation given in the footnote is to be preferred even though its meaning is not clear. It can best be interpreted as meaning that the Moabites were so heartened and stimulated by the sacrifice that their king had offered, that they were victorious against the Israelites and drove them from their land. Any defeat in battle for the Israelites would have been described by the deuteronomists as due to the anger of God. ✻

THE PROPHET'S WIDOW

4 The wife of a member of a company of prophets appealed to Elisha. 'My husband, your servant, has died', she said. 'You know that he was a man who feared the LORD; but a creditor has come to take away my two boys
2 as his slaves.' Elisha said to her, 'How can I help you? Tell me what you have in the house.' 'Nothing at all',
3 she answered, 'except a flask of oil.' 'Go out then', he said, 'and borrow vessels from all your neighbours; get
4 as many empty ones as you can. Then, when you come home, shut yourself in with your sons, pour from the flask into all these vessels and, as they are filled, set them
5 aside.' She left him and shut herself in with her sons. As
6 they brought her the vessels she filled them. When they were all full, she said to one of her sons, 'Bring me another.' 'There is not one left', he said. Then the flow
7 of oil ceased. She came out and told the man of God, and

he said, 'Go and sell the oil and redeem your boys who are being taken as pledges,[a] and you and they can live on what is left.'

✻ This story is typical of the kind of legend that came to be attached to the name of a religious leader and was treasured by his followers and their successors. It echoes in some respects the story told in 1 Kings 17: 8–16 of Elijah's help to a widow and her son. The purpose of the editors in including it may have been to show that Elisha was the true successor of Elijah. God had endowed him with the same powers, and he used them in the same way as his master had done. It also teaches that help was to be sought from Yahweh and not from Baal. Although it is a legend, it does witness to the kind of man the followers of Elisha believed their master to be. In this way it throws light on the idea of the ideal prophet which was in the minds of the editors. The story also supports another doctrine to which the deuteronomists were deeply committed, namely that God does not allow the innocent to suffer.

1. *a creditor...slaves*: slavery was a recognized institution in Israel and all the neighbouring states. It was an essential part of the economy. Israelite law set a limit on the term of the slavery (cp. Exod. 21: 2–3). Prisoners of war provided one regular source of slaves but poor Israelites could be driven by extreme poverty to sell their children and themselves into slavery (Neh. 5: 1–5). In this instance the plight of the woman was desperate. She had been left a widow and the only bread-winners left to her were about to be removed.

7. *redeem...pledges*: the alternative translation (N.E.B. footnote) is closer to the Hebrew. The text is a paraphrase to indicate the significance of paying the debt. ✻

[a] redeem...pledges: *or* pay off your debt.

THE SON OF THE SHUNAMMITE WOMAN

8 It happened once that Elisha went over to Shunem.
There was a great lady there who pressed him to accept
her hospitality, and so, whenever he came that way, he
9 stopped to take food there. One day she said to her husband, 'I know that this man who comes here regularly is
10 a holy man of God. Why not build up the wall to make
him a little roof-chamber, and put in it a bed, a table, a
seat, and a lamp, and let him stay there whenever he
11 comes to us?' Once when he arrived and went to this
12 roof-chamber and lay down to rest, he said to Gehazi, his
servant, 'Call this Shunammite woman.' He called her
13 and, when she appeared before the prophet, he said to his
servant, 'Say to her, "You have taken all this trouble for
us. What can I do for you? Shall I speak for you to the
king or to the commander-in-chief?"' But she replied,
14 'I am content where I am, among my own people.' He
said, 'Then what can be done for her?' Gehazi said,
'There is only this: she has no child and her husband is
15 old.' 'Call her back', Elisha said. When she was called,
16 she appeared in the doorway, and he said, 'In due season,
this time next year, you shall have a son in your arms.'
But she said, 'No, no, my lord, you are a man of God
17 and would not lie to your servant.' Next year in due
season the woman conceived and bore a son, as Elisha had
foretold.

18 When the child was old enough, he went out one day
19 to the reapers where his father was. All of a sudden he
cried out to his father, 'O my head, my head!' His father
20 told a servant to carry him to his mother. He brought

40

him to his mother; the boy sat on her lap till midday, and
then he died. She went up and laid him on the bed of the 21
man of God, shut the door and went out. She called her 22
husband and said, 'Send me one of the servants and a she-
ass, I must go to the man of God as fast as I can, and come
straight back.' 'Why go to him today?' he asked. 'It is 23
neither new moon nor sabbath.'*a* 'Never mind that', she
answered. When the ass was saddled, she said to her 24
servant, 'Lead on and do not slacken pace unless I tell
you.' So she set out and came to the man of God on 25
Mount Carmel. The man of God spied her in the distance
and said to Gehazi, his servant, 'That is the Shunammite
woman coming. Run and meet her, and ask, "Is all well 26
with you? Is all well with your husband? Is all well
with the boy?"' She answered, 'All is well.' When she 27
reached the man of God on the hill, she clutched his feet.
Gehazi came forward to push her away, but the man of
God said, 'Let her alone; she is in great distress, and the
LORD has concealed it from me and not told me.' 'My 28
lord,' she said, 'did I ask for a son? Did I not beg you not
to raise my hopes and then dash them?' Then he turned 29
to Gehazi: 'Hitch up your cloak; take my staff with you
and run. If you meet anyone on the way, do not stop to
greet him; if anyone greets you, do not answer him. Lay
my staff on the boy's face.' But the mother cried, 'As the 30
LORD lives, your life upon it, I will not leave you.' So he
got up and followed her.*b*

Gehazi went on ahead of them and laid the staff on the 31
boy's face, but there was no sound and no sign of life. So
he went back to meet Elisha and told him that the boy

[*a*] *Or* full moon.   [*b*] *Or* went with her.

32 had not roused. When Elisha entered the house, there was
33 the boy dead, on the bed where he had been laid. He went
   into the room, shut the door on the two of them and
34 prayed to the LORD. Then, getting on to the bed, he lay
   upon the child, put his mouth to the child's mouth, his
   eyes to his eyes and his hands to his hands; and, as he
35 pressed*a* upon him, the child's body grew warm. Elisha
   got up and walked once up and down the room; then,
   getting on to the bed again, he pressed*a* upon him and
   breathed into him*b* seven times; and the boy opened his
36 eyes. The prophet summoned Gehazi and said, 'Call this
   Shunammite woman.' She answered his call and the
37 prophet said, 'Take your child.' She came in and fell
   prostrate before him. Then she took up her son and went
   out.

* This story is very similar to the one told of Elijah in 1 Kings
17: 17–24 where he also restored a child to life. The editors
may have included it to demonstrate again that Yahweh had
truly chosen Elisha to be the successor of Elijah. Both stories
make the same point, that life and blessing come from Yahweh
and not from Baal, and that reverence for Yahweh's prophets
and obedience to their teaching was what God wanted from
his people.

8. *Shunem* was situated near the Jezreel valley on the south-
west slopes of the hill of Moreh (see map on p. 80). It was not
far distant from the main routes used by travellers. *a great lady*:
she was a person of some wealth and standing in the local
community, probably noted for her piety. She *pressed him to
accept her hospitality* on account of her piety. Close proximity
to a prophet on the part of a sinner, or even someone only

[a] *Prob. rdg.; Heb.* crouched.
[b] *and breathed into him:* or *and the boy sneezed.*

moderately zealous for the cause of Yahweh, would have been regarded as dangerous. Yahweh would have brought some punishment on such presumption, but close and friendly association with a prophet on the part of a pious person would be expected to lead to blessing and increased prosperity.

10. *Why not build...a little roof-chamber*: the N.E.B. has paraphrased because the Hebrew is not entirely clear. The houses had flat roofs which were often used to provide extra accommodation. Tents could be pitched on the roofs or temporary wooden rooms built. The suggestion here is that a permanent rather than a temporary room should be provided. The wall of the house would be higher than the roof to provide a parapet. The N.E.B. makes the woman suggest that a part of the wall should be raised and a permanent room built against it. She may have suggested building a walled chamber anywhere on the roof (cp. the Revised Standard Version translation). The justification for this expense and for the luxurious conditions provided – travellers usually sat, ate and slept on the floor – was her acknowledgement of Elisha as 'a holy man of God'. The *lamp* would have been a pottery vessel which contained oil and was shaped to hold a wick.

12. *she appeared before the prophet*: she stood on the roof out of sight of Elisha. The fact that the conversation was carried on through the prophet's servant was a mark of her reverence for the man of God.

13. *Shall I speak...to the commander-in-chief?*: her husband was a man of property. Elisha was offering to obtain some remission of the taxes or obligation to provide or support soldiers, which would have fallen upon her husband. The woman refused such help. She was unwilling to receive special treatment. Her security lay in the closeknit loyalty of the local community. The N.E.B. has given a paraphrase of her reply, *I am content where I am, among my own people*, which implies that Elisha was offering to seek social advancement for her which would have meant her leaving Shunem. This is unlikely.

14. *she has no child*: barrenness was the greatest reproach to

a wife, and the promise of a child correspondingly the greatest blessing. Sarah (Gen. 18: 11–15) and Hannah (1 Sam. 1: 4–8) are earlier examples of the significance of such a promise.

16. *she appeared in the doorway*: she now spoke directly with Elisha. *No, no, my lord*: the general run of prophets were very willing to make promises which they thought would please their hearers; cp. the story of the prophetic opponents of Micaiah in 1 Kings 22. The woman could not believe that Elisha's promise would come true and was anxious that he should not compromise his integrity or show that her trust in him was misplaced.

19. '*O my head, my head!*': the child probably suffered an attack of sun-stroke.

21. *laid him on the bed of the man of God*: this may have been done to keep him in an atmosphere which was imbued with the spirit of Elisha. She *shut the door and went out* to keep her son's death a secret. As long as the secret could be kept, the issue was between her and Elisha. Once the death was public knowledge, the mourning rites would begin and in the general view either Elisha would be accounted a false prophet or the woman a great sinner. Even if Elisha were a true prophet, it would have been taken as a mark of the limitation of his prophetic inspiration that he could have consorted with such a woman. What was at stake was Elisha's credibility as a prophet.

23. *It is neither new moon nor sabbath*: these were the rest days when no work was done and so visits to consult a prophet were usually made on them. *sabbath* normally means the seventh day, Saturday. In earlier ages it may have referred to the day of the full moon. Some scholars think that the earliest custom, before a seven-day week was established, was to have two days in the month when all work was forbidden, new moon and full moon. So in passages where new moon is linked with sabbath, as here, the N.E.B. footnote suggests that *sabbath* may refer to an earlier meaning 'full moon'. The prohibition of work on these days may have originated in the

belief that they were unlucky, but was reinterpreted as a memorial to God's rest at creation (cp. Exod. 20: 8–11), or his deliverance of Israel from slavery in Egypt (cp. Deut. 5: 12–15).

25. *Mount Carmel*: this was the great headland overlooking the sea some 15 miles (24 km) west of Shunem. The modern city of Haifa is built below Mount Carmel. Elijah had conducted his contest with the prophets of Baal there (cp. 1 Kings 18: 17–40).

26. *Is all well with you?*: only disaster of some kind would account for such a visit. *She answered, 'All is well'* because the matter was too serious to be dealt with through a servant.

27. *the LORD has concealed it from me and not told me*: Elisha makes it clear that whatever had happened was not his doing. His goodwill towards the woman had not changed and so her fear that she was suffering because of the caprice of a prophet was not justified.

29. *take my staff with you and run*: Moses had performed miracles by the use of a staff (cp. Exod. 4: 1–4 and 17: 8–13). Running shows the urgency of the mission as does the command to ignore all normal courtesy by not exchanging greetings with other travellers. Also any speech might have dissipated the power entrusted to Gehazi, therefore *if anyone greets you, do not answer him*.

30. The woman knows that the matter is so serious that the personal presence of Elisha is essential. Whatever the outcome was to be, the prophet must be known to have exerted his powers to the utmost. *and followed her*: or as the N.E.B. footnote paraphrases 'went with her' since in the East those who walk together may in fact go one behind the other in single file.

34. *he lay upon the child*: the manner of revival is similar to that used by Elijah (1 Kings 17: 21). The life and vigour of the prophet was believed to be transferred to the child. It may have been thought that the power of Yahweh of which Elisha was the agent was counteracting the evil power which had

brought about the death of the child. *he pressed upon him*: the Hebrew verb is only found elsewhere at 1 Kings 18: 42 where it describes Elijah's posture when he waited on Mount Carmel after his contest with the prophets of Baal. There the N.E.B. translated 'he crouched'. Elisha's actions in reviving the boy have been interpreted as an example of the 'kiss of life' revival technique. This is improbable. Elisha was a Hebrew prophet not a modern doctor. His actions were intended to symbolize the transference of strength from every part of his body to the boy's body. The most that can be said is that Elisha's actions may have had the same result as the 'kiss of life' technique.

35. *walked once up and down the room*: in order to revive his physical and spiritual energy for a fresh attack upon the evil. *and breathed into him seven times*: here the N.E.B. has changed the text. The Hebrew means 'and the boy sneezed seven times' (N.E.B. footnote). In the story of Elijah's revival of the widow's son, the N.E.B. has also altered the text in a similar way; cp. 1 Kings 17: 21. *breathed into* is found in the Hexaplaric version of the Greek, a revision made by the Christian scholar Origen, but in place of 'he pressed upon him'. It is meant to echo God's creation of man in Eden (cp. Gen. 2: 7), but there is no justification for setting aside the Hebrew, which also depends upon Genesis. The boy 'sneezed' to indicate that 'the breath of life' had returned to his nostrils. The number seven may have indicated the completeness of the restoration.

37. *and fell prostrate before him*: in worship. She acknowledged that the power of Yahweh had been at work in Elisha. ✳

DEATH IN THE POT

38 Elisha returned to Gilgal at a time when there was a famine in the land. One day, when a group of prophets was sitting at his feet, he said to his servant, 'Set the big pot on the fire and prepare some broth for the company.'
39 One of them went out into the fields to gather herbs and

found a wild vine, and filled the skirt of his garment with bitter-apples.[a] He came back and sliced them into the pot, not knowing what they were. They poured it out for the 40 men to eat, but, when they tasted it, they cried out, 'Man of God, there is death in the pot', and they could not eat it. The prophet said, 'Fetch some meal.' He threw it into 41 the pot and said, 'Now pour out for the men to eat.' This time there was no harm in the pot.

* This story is another example of the kind of legend which popular tradition associated with Elisha as a leader of the prophets. It portrays him as a wonder-worker who used his powers for the good of his followers. The editors when they included it in their narrative may have wished simply to illustrate the position Elisha had come to hold in popular acclaim. They could have been pointing to him as the successor of Moses who had made the bitter waters of Marah sweet (cp. Exod. 15: 23-5).

38. *Gilgal*: this may be one of several places (see note on 2: 1). It may be that *Gilgal* here simply means a sanctuary where prophetic schools met. *famine*: in 8: 1 there is a reference to a 'seven years' famine' which could be the context of this incident. The prophets were *sitting at his feet* for instruction.

39. The *wild vine* could have been the plant *citrullus colocynthus* which grows in the Jordan valley. This is a plant of the gourd family which produces yellow fruits like small melons which have been called 'bitter-apples'. They are purgative and in large quantities have been known to be fatal.

40. *there is death in the pot*: are these words meant to be taken literally, or are they exaggerated metaphor? We, at times, refer to food which is unpleasant as 'poisonous'. It may be that words which were originally spoken as metaphor were later understood as being literal. Then the significance of the

[a] *Or* poisonous wild gourds.

incident, as a miracle, would have been heightened. However that may be, later generations of disciples certainly understood the incident in its literal sense, and it is included here to support the portrait of Elisha as a wonder-worker. ✳

BREAD FOR THE HUNGRY

42 A man came from Baal-shalisha, bringing the man of God some of the new season's bread, twenty barley loaves, and fresh ripe ears of corn.*a* Elisha said, 'Give this
43 to the people to eat.' But his disciple protested, 'I cannot set this before a hundred men.' Still he repeated, 'Give it to the people to eat; for this is the word of the LORD:
44 "They will eat and there will be some left over."' So he set it before them, and they ate and left some over, as the LORD had said.

✳ The last story showed Yahweh through his prophet providing food from the wild vines of Canaan. This story continues the theme by showing Yahweh providing a superabundance of bread for his people. It is Yahweh not Baal who is the Lord of Canaan, and to whom the people are to look for their material well-being. The story is clearly echoed in the New Testament where Jesus is described as feeding great crowds in a similar fashion (cp. Matt. 14: 13–21).

42. *Baal-shalisha* was the village now known as Kefr Tilt (see map on p. 80). Was the name of the village deliberately chosen to indicate Yahweh's superiority to Baal? *the new season's bread*: this translation makes the bread a personal gift, but the gift may have been the ritual offering of the firstfruits of the harvest as ordered in Lev. 23: 17 (the Revised Standard Version translates 'bread of the first fruits'). In that case the

[a] fresh...corn: *prob. rdg.; Heb. unintelligible.*

man had brought his firstfruits to the sanctuary and offered them to Elisha as the leader of the prophets there.

43. *and there will be some left over*: God provides in abundance for his people. ✶

NAAMAN CURED FROM LEPROSY

Naaman, commander of the king of Aram's army, was **5** a great man highly esteemed by his master, because by his means the LORD had given victory to Aram; but he was a leper.[a][b] On one of their raids the Aramaeans **2** brought back as a captive from the land of Israel a little girl, who became a servant to Naaman's wife. She said to **3** her mistress, 'If only my master could meet the prophet who lives in Samaria, he would get rid of the disease for him.' Naaman went in and reported to his master word **4** for word what the girl from the land of Israel had said. 'Very well, you may go,' said the king of Aram, 'and I **5** will send a letter to the king of Israel.' So Naaman went, taking with him ten talents of silver, six thousand shekels of gold, and ten changes of clothing. He delivered the **6** letter to the king of Israel, which read thus: 'This letter is to inform you that I am sending to you my servant Naaman, and I beg you to rid him of his disease.' When **7** the king of Israel read the letter, he rent his clothes and said, 'Am I a god[c] to kill and to make alive, that this fellow sends to me to cure a man of his disease? Surely you must see that he is picking a quarrel with me.' When **8** Elisha, the man of God, heard how the king of Israel had rent his clothes, he sent to him saying, 'Why did you rend

[a] he was a leper: *or* his skin was diseased.
[b] *So Luc. Sept.; Heb. adds* a mighty warrior.   [c] *Or* Am I God.

your clothes? Let the man come to me, and he will know
9 that there is a prophet in Israel.' So Naaman came with
his horses and chariots and stood at the entrance to Elisha's
10 house. Elisha sent out a messenger to say to him, 'If you
will go and wash seven times in the Jordan, your flesh
11 will be restored and you will be clean.' Naaman was
furious and went away, saying, 'I thought he would at
least have come out and stood, and invoked the LORD his
God by name, waved his hand over the place and so rid
12 me of the disease. Are not Abana and Pharpar, rivers of
Damascus, better than all the waters of Israel? Can I not
wash in them and be clean?' So he turned and went off
13 in a rage. But his servants came up to him and said, 'If the
prophet had bidden you do something difficult, would
you not do it? How much more then, if he tells you to
14 wash and be clean?' So he went down and dipped himself in the Jordan seven times as the man of God had told
him, and his flesh was restored as a little child's, and he was
clean.

15 Then he and his retinue went back to the man of God
and stood before him; and he said, 'Now I know that
there is no god anywhere on earth except in Israel. Will
16 you accept a token of gratitude from your servant?' 'As
the LORD lives, whom I serve,' said the prophet, 'I will
accept nothing.' He was pressed to accept, but he refused.
17 'Then if you will not,' said Naaman, 'let me, sir, have
two mules' load of earth. For I will no longer offer whole-
18 offering or sacrifice to any god but the LORD. In this one
matter only may the LORD pardon me: when my master
goes to the temple of Rimmon to worship, leaning on my
arm, and I worship in the temple of Rimmon when he

worships*ª* there, for this let the LORD pardon me.' And 19
Elisha bade him farewell.

Naaman had gone only a short distance on his way, 20
when Gehazi, the servant of Elisha the man of God, said
to himself, 'What? Has my master let this Aramaean,
Naaman, go scot-free, and not accepted what he brought?
As the LORD lives, I will run after him and get something
from him.' So Gehazi hurried after Naaman. When 21
Naaman saw him running after him, he jumped down
from his chariot to meet him and said, 'Is anything
wrong?' 'Nothing,' said Gehazi, 'but my master sent me 22
to say that two young men of the company of prophets
from the hill-country of Ephraim have just arrived. Could
you provide them with a talent of silver and two changes
of clothing?' Naaman said, 'By all means; take two 23
talents.' He pressed*ᵇ* him to take them; so he tied up the
two talents of silver in two bags, and the two changes of
clothing, and gave them to his two servants, and they
walked ahead carrying them. When Gehazi came to the 24
citadel*ᶜ* he took them from the two servants, deposited
them in the house and dismissed the men; and they
departed. When he went in and stood before his master, 25
Elisha said, 'Where have you been, Gehazi?' 'Nowhere',
said Gehazi. But he said to him, 'Was I not with you*ᵈ* in 26
spirit when the man turned back from his chariot to meet
you? Is it not true that you have the money? You may buy
gardens with it,*ᵉᶠ* and olive-trees and vineyards, sheep

[a] *So Sept.; Heb.* I worship.   [b] *Prob. rdg.; Heb.* broke out on.
[c] *Or* hill.   [d] with you: *so Sept.; Heb. om.*
[e] gardens with it: *prob. rdg.; Heb.* garments.
[f] Is it not...with it: *or* Was it a time to get the money and to get
garments?

27 and oxen, slaves and slave-girls; but the disease of Naaman will fasten on you and on your descendants for ever.' Gehazi left his presence, his skin diseased, white as snow.

* In this story Elisha appears as a solitary prophet. We hear nothing of any group of prophets with him. He occupies a house in Samaria. This gives a different impression of the life of a prophet from that which we were given in 4: 1–7 and will meet again in chapter 6. It seems unlikely that the stories have been set out in chronological sequence. Rather they are each meant to illustrate some facet of the prophet's life and teaching. Here the point is made that Yahweh by the hand of the prophet shows that he is Lord not only of Canaan but also of the whole earth. Men in any place are to look to him for assistance in their troubles. Naaman paid his true token of gratitude by his recognition of the source of his healing (cp. verse 15), and it was Gehazi's failure to recognize this which led to the disease being transferred to him. There are many stories in Kings which seem to show that Israel was meant to hate and fear all foreigners – the story of Elijah's contest on Mount Carmel is an obvious example (1 Kings 18: 17–40) – but this story goes some way to redress the balance. It takes its place with the teaching given in Isa. 40–55 and in Jonah, namely that God cares for all men. It was man as such, and not just the Israelite, who was made in the image of God (Gen. 1: 27).

1. Neither the name of the *king of Aram* nor that of the king of Israel is given. It may be that the Ben-hadad who is mentioned in 8: 7 is the king of Aram, but we cannot be certain. The incident must have happened during one of those periods when there was a truce between the two enemies Aram and Israel. *Aram* was the state on the northern border of Israel whose capital was Damascus (see map on p. xii). *the LORD had given victory to Aram*: all victories whether for Israel or for

52

her enemies were accepted as given by Yahweh. He is shown as Lord of the whole earth and not just the national God of Israel. *a leper*: we cannot be sure exactly what this means. The word was used in the Old Testament to describe a far wider range of diseases than it does today. Some might have been skin complaints which were not contagious and were curable. It was the duty of the priests to recognize leprosy (cp. Lev. 13). In some cases a leper had to live apart from society (Lev. 13: 45–6). In other cases, as here, the disease was recognized as one which did not require such extreme measures. Most scholars agree with the N.E.B. in accepting the shorter text and regarding the phrase 'a mighty warrior' as an editorial addition.

5. We cannot be sure of the exact value of *talents* and *shekels*. The value was related to the weight of metal which varied in different systems and in different places. It is clear though that Naaman took with him a very large sum of money which indicated the strength of his desire to rid himself of his complaint.

6. The king of Aram took it for granted that a prophet with such powers would be a member of the royal household, hence his letter. On the other hand the king of Israel seems to be quite ignorant of Elisha's powers.

7. *he rent his clothes*: a sign of sorrow and mourning. For the king of Israel the letter was a prelude to war. *Am I a god*: the N.E.B. seems to present the king as a polytheist, i.e. one who believed in a group or family of gods each of whom directed one of the controlling forces in life; though *god* here could mean no more than 'someone with access to supernatural powers'. The alternative reading, 'Am I God' (N.E.B. footnote), means that such powers belong to Yahweh alone. The Hebrew can be understood in either way. 'Am I God' is the preferable translation. It makes a dramatic contrast between the king and the prophet. Many kings did claim to be sons of gods or at least their vice-regents on earth, and the policy of the house of Ahab in Israel was to strengthen and

extend the power of the kings. Here the editors make it plain that kings have not the power of God. They need to seek help from God's servants the prophets and accept their authority just as other men.

8. *a prophet in Israel*: one with access to the very powers which kings claimed and the king of Israel clearly did not possess. A prophet was one who by his words and actions made God's presence in a situation clear and his will known.

10. *Elisha sent out a messenger*: he and Naaman did not meet. The great soldier came in considerable state and was treated as the humblest of suppliants. *wash seven times*: seven was regarded by many ancient peoples as a holy or magic number. For the Hebrews it may particularly have had the significance of wholeness or completeness. God rested from his work of creation on the seventh day which was commemorated in the weekly sabbath. The number also occurs in the story of the healing of the child at Shunem (4: 35).

11. Naaman expected to be treated with the deference he considered due to his position, and with the kind of ritual which was in use by healers.

12. *Abana*: the name was corrected to Amana by the Massoretes. The Assyrians named a mountain near Damascus Amanus. It was probably the Anti-lebanon, north-west of Damascus. If so, then the Abana was the river now called the Barada. The Pharpar is probably the river now known as the A'waj which rises on Mount Hermon. Both rivers flow into the swamps to the south-east of Damascus.

15. *Now I know...except in Israel*: this confession of faith by a non-Israelite and servant of a foreign king goes far beyond any claim made previously. Yahweh is Lord not only of Canaan but of the whole world. All other gods are false. Here as in verse 7 *god* could be translated 'God'.

17. *two mules' load of earth*: it has often been claimed that the transporting of this earth to Damascus showed that Yahweh's writ was not believed to extend beyond Israel, where he was regarded as the national God. In view of the confession of

verse 15 this can hardly be so. Naaman probably wished to have the earth as a visible reminder of his visit to Elisha, much as pilgrims today return from their pilgrimages with visible mementoes of the places they have visited. *whole-offering*: this was the kind of sacrifice which was completely burned on the altar as an offering to God. In other sacrifices the priests and the worshippers also ate a part of the sacrifice.

18. *Rimmon*: Ramman was a title of Hadad, the storm god of Damascus who was the equivalent of the Canaanite god, Baal. Several kings of Damascus were named Ben-hadad, i.e. son of Hadad. The Hebrew text was first written without vowels. When at a later time vowels were added to the consonants, the editors not infrequently added vowels to the names of pagan gods which turned the names into some commonplace Hebrew word. It was a form of mockery. Here *Rimmon* means 'pomegranate'. *he worships*: the Hebrew 'I worship' (N.E.B. footnote) is probably the result of careless copying due to confusion with the earlier part of the sentence.

21. *he jumped down from his chariot*: this was a remarkable act of deference from a man of Naaman's rank to a servant.

22. *Ephraim* meant originally the territory in which the tribe of that name settled. It had in course of time become one of the most powerful of the northern tribes, and the name had come to mean all the hill-country around Samaria.

23. *He pressed*: the Hebrew word used here means 'to break out' as when a great force of water broke down a wall. This is quite inappropriate here. The N.E.B. has based its translation on a suggestion that the verb has been confused with a similar verb which gives the meaning suggested.

24. *the citadel*: the Hebrew has 'the ophel' which may mean 'the hill'. The hill at Jerusalem upon which the first city was built is called Mount Ophel. On the other hand 'Ophel' may have become a proper name for the higher part of a city, the inner city in which the king and his officials lived, comparable to the keep in a mediaeval castle. The N.E.B. has understood the word in this sense. It does not seem likely though that

Gehazi's house would be situated in that part of Samaria. The reference may simply be to approaching the city of Samaria which stood upon a hill.

26. *in spirit*: this is a paraphrase. The Hebrew has 'in heart'. The paraphrase is necessary because the physical organs have different associations in the two languages. In English the heart is regarded as the seat of the emotions, while for the Hebrews it was associated with the intellect and the will. Elisha has been given second sight by God. *Is it not...with it*: the alternative translation given in the N.E.B. footnote accurately translates the Hebrew. If it is original, then Elisha is castigating Gehazi for sullying the occasion of Naaman's encounter with the power of Yahweh with mercenary considerations. The N.E.B. translation is based upon an emendation of the Hebrew which has some support from the Greek versions. It gives the lie to Gehazi's denial in verse 25.

27. *white as snow*: this is the same description as was given of Moses' leprosy (cp. Exod. 4: 6). *

THE LOST AXE-HEAD

6 A company of prophets said to Elisha, 'You can see that this place where our community is living, under you
2 as its head, is too small for us. Let us go to the Jordan and each fetch a log, and make ourselves*a* a place to live in.'
3 The prophet agreed. Then one of them said, 'Please, sir,
4 come with us.' 'I will', he said, and he went with them. When they reached the Jordan, they began cutting down
5 trees; but it chanced that, as one man was felling a trunk, the head of his axe flew off into the water. 'Oh, master!'
6 he exclaimed, 'it was a borrowed one.' 'Where did it fall?' asked the man of God. When he was shown the

[a] *So Pesh.; Heb. adds* there.

place, he cut off a piece of wood and threw it in and made
the iron float. Then he said, 'There you are, lift it out.' So 7
he stretched out his hand and took it.

∗ This story is a legend. It is the kind of miraculous story
which came to be attached by tradition to the persons of
religious leaders. Though to say this is not to dismiss it as
being pointless. Almost all religious leaders of the ancient
world had stories of miraculous happenings associated with
them, but the kind of story and, indeed, the kind of miracle
would differ according to the image of the person to whom it
was attributed. So by studying the kind of miracle that was
linked with Elisha we can learn something of the kind of
person he was believed to be. We are given a picture in this
story of power being used not for personal aggrandisement,
but with compassion and in service to people. Iron was scarce
and valuable. An iron axe-head was a valuable implement. Its
loss, particularly since it had been borrowed, would involve
the loser in considerable hardship. Elisha is shown as using
miraculous powers to relieve such hardship and that, however
we may interpret the miracle, tells us something about Elisha.

1. *A company of prophets*: Elisha is here once more shown as
living in a community of prophets and not alone as in the
story preceding. *this place*: the location is never given but it is
likely to have been near the Jordan, perhaps near Jericho or
Gilgal.

2. *and make ourselves*: 'there' (N.E.B. footnote) which is in
the Hebrew text has been omitted. It is unlikely that the
prophets would have made a new settlement by the Jordan
which was semi-tropical, the home of wild beasts and
malarial. The word is not found in the Peshitto, the Syriac
Authorized Version. It may have been added by a scribe.

6. *and threw it in*: it has been suggested that Elisha poked
about in the water with a stick until he managed to push his
stick through the socket in the axe-head prepared for the shaft.

The 'miracle' may have developed from such an incident, but may equally well have not. It is our age rather than Elisha's which seeks always to find justification for stories of the miraculous. The throwing of the wood into the water could easily have been understood as a piece of imitative magic. ✻

A BLIND ARMY

8 Once, when the king of Aram was making war on Israel, he held a conference with his staff at which he said, 9 'I mean to attack in such and such a direction.' But the man of God warned the king of Israel: 'Take care to avoid this place, for the Aramaeans are going down that 10 way.' So the king of Israel sent to the place about which the man of God had given him this warning; and the king took special precautions every time he found him- 11 self near that place. The king of Aram was greatly per- turbed at this and, summoning his staff, he said to them, 'Tell me, one of you, who has betrayed us*a* to the king of 12 Israel?' 'None of us, my lord king,' said one of his staff; 'but Elisha, the prophet in Israel, tells the king of Israel 13 the very words you speak in your bedchamber.' 'Go and find out where he is,' said the king, 'and I will send and seize him.' He was told that the prophet was at Dothan, 14 and he sent a strong force there with horses and chariots. They came by night and surrounded the city.

15 When the disciple of the man of God rose early in the morning and went out, he saw a force with horses and chariots surrounding the city. 'Oh, master,' he said, 16 'which way are we to turn?' He answered, 'Do not be afraid, for those who are on our side are more than those

[a] who...us: *so Luc. Sept.; Heb.* who of ours.

on theirs.' Then Elisha offered this prayer: 'O LORD, 17
open his eyes and let him see.' And the LORD opened the
young man's eyes, and he saw the hills covered with
horses and chariots of fire all round Elisha. As they came 18
down towards him, Elisha prayed to the LORD: 'Strike
this host, I pray thee, with blindness'; and he struck them
blind as Elisha had asked. Then Elisha said to them, 'You 19
are on the wrong road; this is not the city. Follow me and
I will lead you to the man you are looking for.' And he
led them to Samaria. As soon as they had entered Samaria, 20
Elisha prayed, 'O LORD, open the eyes of these men and
let them see again.' And he opened their eyes and they
saw that they were inside Samaria. When the king of 21
Israel saw them, he said to Elisha, 'My father, am I to
destroy them?' 'No, you must not do that', he answered. 22
'You may destroy*a* those whom you have taken prisoner
with your own sword and bow, but as for these men, give
them food and water, and let them eat and drink, and
then go back to their master.' So he prepared a great feast 23
for them, and they ate and drank and then went back to
their master. And Aramaean raids on Israel ceased.

✲ No date can be given to this story. As in chapter 5 the king
of Aram is not named. In fact, although verse 8 sets the story
within the context of a full-scale war, it is more likely to be a
story of the kind of border raiding that went on most of the
time, cp. verse 23. Possibly the account of the capture by a
ruse of such a band of raiders has been used as the basis for a
story which further expands our understanding of the function and character of Elisha. The various elements in the story
are linked by the contrast between vision and blindness.

[a] *Prob. rdg.; Heb.* Would you destroy.

Elisha is first shown as a man with second sight who uses his powers to frustrate the plans of the enemies of Israel. Then his disciple is shown as needing his eyes to be opened to the true realities of the situation. Finally the enemy army is blinded and captured. In 2: 12 Elisha saw Elijah, his departing master, as Israel's cavalry. The point of this story may be to show that Elisha has truly become the successor of Elijah, and is acting as the protector of Israel.

8. *when the king of Aram was making war on Israel*: this may be an editorial addition to a story of border raiding. '*I mean to attack in such and such a direction*': this translation has emended the Hebrew. The Revised Standard Version translates, 'At such and such a place shall be my camp.' The Hebrew noun translated 'camp' is otherwise unknown. It may have been misread from a verb. The N.E.B. translates as a verb as some of the Versions did. That the king was annoyed because his attacks were foreknown, rather than the site of his camps, is much more likely.

9. *going down that way*: in order to attack.

11. *who has betrayed us*: these words are based upon an emendation of the Hebrew (see the N.E.B. footnote). The Hebrew has different words, 'Who of us is for the king of Israel?', but the meaning is the same.

12. *the very words you speak in your bedchamber*: this probably means that Elisha had second sight, though it has been interpreted as meaning that he received information from Israelite captives who were servants in the houses of the king and his officials (cp. 5: 2 above). In either case it was such service which led to him being described as the cavalry of Israel (cp. 13: 14).

13. Dothan was a strategic point (see map on p. 80). It was situated about 9 miles (14½ km) north of Samaria controlling a valley which led into the hill-country of Ephraim from the plain of Jezreel. If the king of Aram was able to control territory as far south as Dothan then this must have been a time of Israelite weakness; but this was probably no more than a raid.

Such raids bear some resemblance to the rapid movement, and attacks against strategic objects, of mechanized formations in modern warfare.

17. '*O LORD, open his eyes and let him see*': the prayer is that the disciple should be granted for a short time the same insight into the activity of God as Elisha himself had been given (see note on 2: 11).

19. That a stronger enemy should be tricked and ridiculed in this way points to the fact that the story as we have it is a folk-tale.

21. *My father*: the king, very unusually in these stories, acknowledges the authority of the prophet.

22. *You may destroy*: the Hebrew underlying these words is not easy to interpret (see the N.E.B. footnote), but the general sense is clear. Prisoners taken captive in battle were at the disposal of the captor, to be killed, or ransomed, or sold into slavery. In this case these men were God's prisoners. The king may have accepted this, and then the question would have been asked whether or not they should have been killed in sacrifice. In the early days of Israel when the tribes had been called together in the name of Yahweh to fight a holy war, the spoils of victory had commonly been offered in sacrifice. This practice has been referred to as 'putting to the ban' or 'devoting to Yahweh'. In this instance to treat a raiding party with such clemency and to feast them would have created a bond of obligation which would severely limit their raiding in the future. ✶

SAMARIA UNDER SIEGE

But later, Ben-hadad king of Aram called up his entire 24
army and marched to the siege of Samaria. The city was 25
near starvation, and they*a* besieged it so closely that a
donkey's head was sold for eighty shekels of silver, and a

[a] they: *so some MSS.; others om.*

26 quarter of a kab of locust-beans for five shekels. One day, as the king of Israel was walking along the city wall, a
27 woman called to him, 'Help, my lord king!' He said, 'If the LORD will not[a] bring you help, where can I find any
28 for you? From threshing-floor or from winepress? What is your trouble?' She replied, 'This woman said to me, "Give up your child for us to eat today, and we will eat
29 mine tomorrow." So we cooked my son and ate him; but when I said to her the next day, "Now give up your
30 child for us to eat", she had hidden him.' When he heard the woman's story, the king rent his clothes. He was walking along the wall at the time, and when the people looked, they saw that he had sackcloth underneath, next
31 to his skin. Then he said, 'The LORD do the same to me and more, if the head of Elisha son of Shaphat stays on his shoulders today.'

32 Elisha was sitting at home, the elders with him. The king had dispatched one of his retinue but, before the messenger arrived, Elisha said to the elders, 'See how this son of a murderer has sent to behead me! Take care, when the messenger comes, to shut the door and hold it fast against him. Can you not hear his master following on
33 his heels?' While he was still speaking, the king[b] arrived and said, 'Look at our plight! This is the LORD's doing.
7 Why should I wait any longer for him to help us?' But Elisha answered, 'Hear this word of the LORD: By this time tomorrow a shekel will buy a measure[c] of flour or
2 two measures of barley in the gateway of Samaria.' Then the lieutenant on whose arm the king leaned said to the

[a] If the LORD will not: *so Targ.; Heb.* Let not the LORD.
[b] *Prob. rdg.; Heb.* messenger.   [c] *Heb.* seah.

man of God, 'Even if the LORD were to open windows in the sky, such a thing could not happen!' He answered, 'You will see it with your own eyes, but none of it will you eat.'

At the city gate were four lepers.[a] They said to one 3 another, 'Why should we stay here and wait for death? If we say we will go into the city, there is famine there, 4 and we shall die; if we say we will stay here, we shall die just the same. Well then, let us go to the camp of the Aramaeans and give ourselves up: if they spare us, we shall live; if they put us to death, we can but die.' And so 5 in the twilight they set out for the Aramaean camp; but when they reached the outskirts, they found no one there; for the Lord had caused the Aramaean army to hear a 6 sound like that of chariots and horses and of a great host, so that the word went round: 'The king of Israel has hired the kings of the Hittites and the kings of Egypt to attack us.' They had fled at once in the twilight, aban- 7 doning their tents, their horses and asses, and leaving the camp as it stood, while they fled for their lives. When the 8 four men came to the outskirts of the camp, they went into a tent and ate and drank and looted silver and gold and clothing, and made off and hid them. Then they came back, went into another tent and rifled it, and made off and hid the loot. Then they said to one another, 'What 9 we are doing is not right. This is a day of good news and we are keeping it to ourselves. If we wait till morning, we shall be held to blame. We must go now and give the news to the king's household.' So they came and called 10 to the watch at the city gate and described how they had

[a] *Or* men suffering from skin-disease.

gone to the Aramaean camp and found not a single man
in it and had heard no sound: nothing but horses and
11 asses tethered, and the tents left as they were. Then the
watch called out and gave the news to the king's house-
12 hold in the palace. The king rose in the night and said to
his staff, 'I will tell you what the Aramaeans have done.
They know that we are starving, and they have left their
camp to go and hide in the open country, expecting us to
come out, and then they can take us alive and enter the
13 city.' One of his staff said, 'Send out a party of men with
some of the horses that are left; if they live, they will be
as well off as all the other Israelites who are still left; if
they die,*a* they will be no worse off than all those who
have already perished. Let them go and see what has
14 happened.' So they picked two mounted men,*b* and the
king dispatched them in the track of the Aramaean army
with the order to go and find out what had happened.
15 They followed as far as the Jordan and found the whole
road littered with clothing and equipment which the
Aramaeans had flung aside in their haste. The messengers
16 returned and reported this to the king. Then the people
went out and plundered the Aramaean camp, and a
measure of flour was sold for a shekel and two measures
of barley for a shekel, so that the word of the LORD came
17 true. Now the king had appointed the lieutenant on
whose arm he leaned to take charge of the gate, and the
people trampled him to death there, just as the man of
18 God had foretold*c* when the king visited him. For when

[*a*] if they live...if they die: *prob. rdg.; Heb. obscure.*
[*b*] two mounted men: *so Sept.; Heb.* two horse-chariots.
[*c*] *So Pesh.; Heb. adds* which he had foretold.

the man of God said to the king, 'By this time tomorrow a shekel will buy two measures of barley or one measure of flour in the gateway of Samaria', the lieutenant had answered, 'Even if the LORD were to open windows in the sky, such a thing could not happen!' And the man of God had said, 'You will see it with your own eyes, but none of it will you eat.' And this is just what happened to him: the people trampled him to death at the gate. 19 20

* Again, we cannot date this story. The name of the king of Israel is not given. The point of the story seems to be to contrast the faithlessness of the king with the faithfulness of Elisha. The king had lost all hope and blamed Elisha for failing to save the situation. In the meantime, unknown to the king, deliverance was being worked out by God, and Elisha's confidence in God was vindicated. Once again Elisha has been shown to be 'the cavalry of Israel'.

24. *Ben-hadad*: several kings of Aram had this name. If historical, this must refer to Ben-hadad the son of Hazael who is usually counted Ben-hadad III. It may be that an editor has used *Ben-hadad* as being the usual name for a king of Aram of the period.

25. *near starvation*: it has been suggested that this indicates that the incident must have taken place during the years of famine that Elisha prophesied (cp. 8: 1), but the obvious explanation is that the words refer to the famine conditions created in the city by the siege. *eighty shekels of silver* was a vast amount of money to pay. It was an indication of the straits to which the people had been brought. *a kab* was the equivalent of 3½ pints (2 litres). *locust-beans*: the Hebrew is 'dove's dung'. This has caused much conjecture among commentators. It has been suggested that such dung was sold for fuel or as a substitute for salt. There is a herb which is called in Arabic 'sparrow's dung' and, on this analogy, 'dove's dung' may have

been a popular name for some poor food. Locust-beans are the fruit of the carob tree. This translation is based upon an emendation of the Hebrew.

26. *wailing along the city wall*: this was a public place so that what transpired would quickly be known throughout the city. This may account for some of the fierceness of the king's anger against Elisha.

27. *If the LORD will not*: the Hebrew may also be translated, 'No, let the LORD bring you help.' *From threshing-floor or from winepress*: all the stores were empty.

28–9. Cannibalism in such circumstances was well known; cp. Deut. 28: 53 and Ezek. 5: 10.

30. The wearing of *sackcloth* was a sign of sorrow and penitence. The king looked upon the siege as a punishment sent from God for the nation's sin and had lost all hope for the outcome. He regarded Elisha as God's agent who had actively brought about the state of affairs or, at the least, done nothing to prevent it. Hence his oath. If there is any link with the preceding chapter, the object of the siege may have been to bring about Elisha's death.

31. *The LORD do the same to me and more*: these words translate the Hebrew phrase which regularly introduces a solemn oath.

32. *before the messenger arrived*: Elisha is shown once more to have the gift of second sight. *son of a murderer*: some scholars have sought to identify the king on the basis of this phrase, but the task is pointless. *son of* is idiomatic Hebrew for 'one who has the characteristics of'.

33. *the king*: the Hebrew words for 'king' and 'messenger' are very similar. *This is the LORD's doing*: both Elisha and the king were agreed on this fact. They disagreed on the conclusions they drew from it. For the king it meant despair; for Elisha hope.

7: 1. *a measure*: a seah (N.E.B. footnote) is usually taken as being a third of an ephah. There is no certainty about the modern equivalent of Hebrew measures, but it has been reckoned as being approximately one-sixth of a bushel. *the gateway*: the open space within the gate of a city where much of the commercial and social life of the city took place.

2. *to open windows in the sky*: the lieutenant may have visualized God pouring down grain from the sky on the besieged city, but the most likely thought is of rain which would cause grain to grow and end the famine (cp. Gen. 7: 11).

3. *lepers*: see the note on 5: 1. As with Naaman, the disease had not led to the sufferers being banished from the life of the city so the alternative translation of the N.E.B. footnote is more accurate. Disease was believed to be a punishment for sin and so there is irony in 'sinners' bringing the news of salvation while the king waited in despair.

6. *a sound like that of chariots and horses and of a great host*: this is not unlike the means of deliverance in the preceding story; cp. 6: 17. (See note on 2: 11.) *the kings of the Hittites*: there had once been, in the latter part of the second millennium B.C., a great Hittite empire with its capital in Asia Minor. This had collapsed with the rise to power of the Assyrians but some small kingdoms from the old empire still remained. *the kings of Egypt* would have made a distinctly odd coalition with the kings of the Hittites. An area in Asia Minor to the north of the Taurus mountains is often referred to in Assyrian texts as 'Musri' which is very similar to the Hebrew name for Egypt. It may be that it was kings from this area who were thought to be in league with the kings of the Hittites. Another suggestion which has been made is that the reference to Egypt is correct but that the two groups should be regarded as alternatives. The Hebrew word translated *and* can sometimes mean 'or'.

12. *expecting us to come out*: the Israelites had used such a ruse themselves against the inhabitants of Ai when they first entered Canaan; cp. Josh. 8: 1–28.

13. *some of the horses*: the Hebrew is specific. It has 'five of the horses'.

67

14. *mounted men*: the difference in Hebrew between this and 'horse-chariots' (N.E.B. footnote) depends upon different vowels being used with the same consonants, as in the English 'pear' and 'pair'. Since the first manuscripts were written without vowels, the Septuagint may have preserved the true reading. Mounted men would be much more mobile than chariots and, therefore, more effective as scouts.

16. It was a part of the teaching of the deuteronomic code that the words of a true prophet were always fulfilled (cp. Deut. 18: 21–2). So here the editors note particularly the fulfilment of Elisha's prophecy.

17. 'which he had foretold' (N.E.B. footnote). These words were probably added to the Hebrew text by the error of a scribe who copied twice what only appeared once in the manuscript he was copying. This is called dittography.

18–20. This is to emphasize that Elisha was a true prophet (see note on verse 16). ✽

THE PROPERTY OF THE SHUNAMMITE WOMAN

8 Elisha said to the woman whose son he had restored to life, 'Go away at once with your household and find lodging where you can, for the LORD has decreed a seven
2 years' famine and it has already come upon the land.' The woman acted at once on the word of the man of God and went away with her household; and she stayed in the
3 Philistine country for seven years. When she came back at the end of the seven years, she sought an audience of the
4 king to appeal for the return of her house and land. Now the king was questioning Gehazi, the servant of the man
5 of God, about all the great things Elisha had done; and, as he was describing to the king how he had brought the dead to life, the selfsame woman began appealing to the king for her house and her land. 'My lord king,' said

Gehazi, 'this is the very woman, and this is her son whom Elisha brought to life.' The king asked the woman about 6 it, and she told him. Then he entrusted the case to a eunuch and ordered him to restore all her property to her, with all the revenues from her land from the time she left the country till that day.

* This continues the story whose first part was told in 4: 8–37. Once again the king is not named so that no identification is possible. This is the last of the independent stories of Elisha. The ones which follow are concerned with his involvement with Hazael's becoming king of Aram, and Jehu becoming king of Israel. This narrative seems to deal with an incident which took place after the death of Elisha. This would account for its having been separated from the earlier part of the story and put in its present position. There is an account of the death of Elisha later at 13: 14–20. King Joash was present at his death-bed so the story has been placed within the account of his reign.

In the earlier part of the story, the Shunammite woman had dealt with the problem that her kindness and generosity to the prophet had led to very unhappy consequences for herself. The son who had been born to her as Elisha had prophesied died, and his death seemed to be a punishment for her sin. Elisha restored both her son's life and her own reputation. This sequel is designed to show that the blessings which followed from her association with Elisha were continued even after his death.

1–2. The woman, seemingly now a widow, obeyed Elisha and left her home for seven years. This meant that she lost her claim to her husband's lands which reverted to the crown. This could have meant that the prophet's advice, which saved her from one famine, only involved her in the end in a greater famine because she was left destitute. *a seven years' famine* would be of abnormal length; the figure 'seven' has a symbolic sense here as in the story of Joseph in Gen. 41. Seven years' absence was the period of time which lost the woman her claim on the land.

6. *a eunuch*: the Hebrew noun used here may have come to have had a wider meaning than the English allows. It may have been used for all officials of the palace. The same word is used of Potiphar (Gen. 39: 1) who was an official of Pharaoh, but he was a married man! So here 'official' would be a better translation. ✻

ELISHA PROPHESIES THAT HAZAEL WILL BE KING OF ARAM

7 Elisha came to Damascus, at a time when Ben-hadad king of Aram was ill; and when he was told that the man 8 of God had arrived, he bade Hazael take a gift with him and go to the man of God and inquire of the LORD through him whether he would recover from his illness. 9 Hazael went, taking with him as a gift all kinds of wares of Damascus, forty camel-loads. When he came into the prophet's presence, he said, 'Your son Ben-hadad king of Aram has sent me to you to ask whether he will 10 recover from his illness.' 'Go and tell him that he will recover,' he answered; 'but the LORD has revealed to me 11 that in fact he will die.' The man of God stood there with set face like a man stunned, until he could bear it no 12 longer; then he went. 'Why do you weep, my lord?' said Hazael. He answered, 'Because I know the harm you will do to the Israelites: you will set their fortresses on fire and put their young men to the sword; you will dash their children to the ground and you will rip open their 13 pregnant women.' But Hazael said, 'But I am a dog, a mere nobody; how can I do this great thing?' Elisha

answered, 'The LORD has revealed to me that you will be king of Aram.' Hazael left Elisha and returned to his 14 master, who asked him what Elisha had said. 'He told me that you would recover', he replied. But the next day he 15 took a blanket and, after dipping it in water, laid it over the king's face, and he died; and Hazael succeeded him.

* The last story told of something that happened after the death of Elisha. Here we are back with events during his life-time. This is a further indication that the stories are not set out in chronological order but follow another pattern. Here the purpose seems to be to return the narrative of 2 Kings, which since 3: 3 has been concerned with personal stories describing the various wonders worked by Elisha, to the history of the kingdom of Israel. Much of the history of the coming years will be concerned with the rivalry between Israel and her northern neighbour Aram, and the new turn taken in the relationship between the two states with the accession of Jehu as king of Israel and the end of the house of Ahab. So we are now shown Elisha's part in bringing about the changes both in Damascus and in Samaria. The editors were concerned to show that kings rise and fall by the will of God, as expressed by his servant the prophet Elisha. The same point had already been made about the same kings in 1 Kings 19: 15–16. There it is reported that Elijah was commanded by God to anoint Hazael and Jehu as kings of Aram and Israel respectively at the same time as he was to anoint Elisha as prophet in his place. Elijah's action may have been repeated by Elisha but that is unlikely. It is much more likely that the two narratives are duplicates from variant traditions. Both traditions were concerned to make the point that God announced his will to kings by the agency of prophets, but in the one tradition Elijah was God's spokesman while in the other it was Elisha. It has been suggested that Elisha had become known in

71

Damascus after the healing of Naaman and might even have been summoned there by King Ben-hadad.

7. *Ben-hadad king of Aram*: there was more than one king of Aram with the name Ben-hadad. The king who led the coalition of allies against the Assyrians at Qarqar in 853 B.C. was named Ben-hadad, as was the king to whom Asa of Judah sent for help when his territory was invaded by Baasha of Israel (1 Kings 15: 18). Whether these two incidents refer to the same person is not certain. However, the king mentioned here is the one who was at Qarqar and is mentioned as an enemy of Ahab in 1 Kings 20. Some scholars think that the same king also attacked Baasha. Others suggest that this Ben-hadad was the father of Baasha's enemy. So we cannot be certain whether the king mentioned here was Ben-hadad I or Ben-hadad II. Hazael had a son who followed him as king of Aram. He also was called Ben-hadad.

8. *Hazael*: in the annals of Shalmanezer III of Assyria it is noted that Hazael seized the throne of Aram, probably in 842 B.C. There Hazael is said to have been 'the son of a nobody', i.e. he was a self-made man like Omri who had earlier made himself king of Israel.

9. *forty camel-loads*: the number seems exaggerated. It may have been a conventional number for a very large amount.

10. *he will recover*: the Hebrew word can mean 'recover' or 'live'. It may be that as in so many oracular utterances, the apparent meaning and the true meaning are quite different, each depending upon a particular interpretation of a word or phrase. Ben-hadad asks whether he will live. The answer is that he will recover, and Elisha's awareness of the difference in meaning leads him to further prophecy.

11. *with set face like a man stunned*: Elisha was silent and still as other communications became articulate within himself. On this interpretation the words describe a moment of ecstasy such as many prophets at that time experienced. It was from such moments that it was believed that a word from God was given to the prophet. But the Hebrew is difficult and may

be understood in a different way, 'he set his face and stared at him'. If this meaning is accepted, then the set face of the prophet is directed at and against Hazael because of the harm Elisha knows he will do to Israel. It shows Elisha's attitude to the words he must speak. The following phrase, *until he could bear it no longer*, is equally difficult. The subject is not stated. It could be Elisha. Then the meaning is that when the full meaning of the word he had received became clear to him, he wept. However, the subject could be Hazael. Then the meaning is that his conscience was moved by Elisha's gaze. Hazael knew what ambitions he had in his heart. This meaning is supported by a literal translation of the Hebrew which would be, 'until he was ashamed', but must face the difficulty that Hazael's shame made no difference to his conduct. This lends support to the N.E.B. translation which implies simply that he found the direct meeting with a prophet in a moment of ecstasy uncomfortable.

12. *I know the harm you will do to the Israelites*: did Elisha incite Hazael to murder his master? The thought that a man of God could so act will be abhorrent to us, but we must not import our moral standards into Elisha's age. Men of God believed it right then to do things which we would now condemn (cp. 1 Sam. 15: 33), and their intervention in political affairs led to their speaking words without qualification, which implied God's approval for acts of violence (cp. Isa. 10: 5). So Elisha could have incited Hazael, but did he? The objection is that if he did, he created the strongest and most determined enemy on the throne of Aram that Israel was to know during the whole period. Would a true prophet of Israel act so? Yet a true prophet could regard the hostile actions of a strong enemy as a lesson sent from God; Isaiah interprets the Assyrian attack thus (Isa. 10: 5) and Jeremiah the Babylonian conquest (Jer. 25: 9), though it is noteworthy that divine judgement is also pronounced on the alien power. The issue remains open, and our judgement on it will depend to some degree on our understanding of the nature of the words

Elisha spoke here. Did the prophet's word simply declare what was inevitably going to happen in the near future, or was it spoken in order that the word itself might become a decisive factor in determining what would happen in the near future? *you will set their fortresses on fire...rip open their pregnant women*: such barbarities were commonly practised then in warfare (cp. 15: 16). ✳

THE REIGN OF JORAM OF JUDAH

16 In the fifth year of Jehoram son of Ahab king of Israel,[a]
17[b] Joram son of Jehoshaphat king of Judah became king. He was thirty-two years old when he came to the throne, and
18 he reigned in Jerusalem for eight years. He followed the practices of the kings of Israel as the house of Ahab had done, for he had married Ahab's daughter; and he did
19 what was wrong in the eyes of the LORD. But for his servant David's sake the LORD was unwilling to destroy Judah, since he had promised to give him and[c] his sons a flame, to burn for all time.

20   During his reign Edom revolted against Judah and set
21 up its own king. Joram crossed over to Zair with all his chariots. He and his chariot-commanders set out by night, but they were surrounded by the Edomites and defeated,[d]
22 whereupon the people fled to their tents. So Edom has remained independent of Judah to this day; Libnah also
23 revolted at the same time. The other acts and events of Joram's reign are recorded in the annals of the kings of
24 Judah. So Joram rested with his forefathers and was

[a] *So some Sept. MSS.; Heb. adds* and Jehoshaphat king of Judah.
[b] *Verses 17–22: cp.* 2 Chr. 21: 5–10.
[c] *So many MSS.; others om.*
[d] and defeated: *prob. rdg.; Heb.* and he defeated Edom.

buried with them in the city of David, and his son
Ahaziah succeeded him.

✻ The narrative now turns from Elisha to the stories of the
kings. This is the first reference to a king since 3: 1, where it
was noted that Jehoram followed Ahab as king of Israel. Here
the record of Joram of Judah is given and this is immediately
followed by the account of the accession of his son Ahaziah.
The editors are preparing the scene for the next great event in
the history of the two kingdoms, the revolt of Jehu, at the
prompting of Elisha, against the two kings of Israel and Judah.

16. The words 'and Jehoshaphat king of Judah' (N.E.B.
footnote) have been rightly omitted. They are found in the
Hebrew but are clearly a mistake made by an earlier editor.

18. *he had married Ahab's daughter*: this was a dynastic
marriage. It shows that Judah had become an ally of Israel and
was, in effect, little more than a vassal. For the royal house of
David to contract a marriage with a rival dynasty which had
come into existence by an act of rebellion against itself must
have been humiliating. It indicates how weak Judah had
become. *he did what was wrong in the eyes of the LORD*: this is
the judgement of the deuteronomic editors. It means that he
allowed religious practices in the temple and elsewhere which
had been copied from Canaanite neighbours.

19. This verse is also the work of the same editors. It
reflects their interest in Judah, which they regarded as the one
legitimate Hebrew monarchy. The promise referred to is that
recorded in 2 Sam. 7: 16. The word *and* before *his sons* is
better omitted. The promise was given to David. The sons
were, as future kings, the object of the promise and themselves, therefore, the *flame*.

20. *Edom revolted*: Judah had always tried to dominate Edom
in order to control the route to the port of Ezion-geber which
was situated at the head of the Gulf of Aqaba, the tongue of
the Red Sea lying to the east of the Sinai peninsula. Ezion-

geber was well situated for trade by sea with southern Arabia and the coast of East Africa. David had first conquered Edom, and Solomon had developed trade (cp. 1 Kings 9: 26). We have already met at 3: 9 a reference to a king of Edom who was a vassal of Judah. If that reference is correct, then the king mentioned here must have been a usurper, as Jehu was to be in Israel.

21. Zair has not been identified with certainty. It must have been in the Arabah or southern Judah. *and defeated*: these words express the outcome of the battle, but they are not what the Hebrew means (see N.E.B. footnote). Most scholars have understood the Hebrew to mean that, after the army of Judah had been surrounded by the Edomites, Joram and his chariot-commanders broke through the Edomites and escaped. *fled to their tents*: this is the usual Hebrew phrase to indicate the conclusion of a battle and a war which had ended in defeat. It originally referred to an army made up of tribesmen who slipped away to their homes after they had been defeated.

22. *to this day*: i.e. in perpetuity. Libnah has not been certainly identified. It is generally thought to have been a Philistine city on the western border of Judah. *

THE REIGN OF AHAZIAH OF JUDAH

25[a] In the twelfth year of Jehoram son of Ahab king of Israel, Ahaziah son of Joram king of Judah became king.
26 Ahaziah was twenty-two years old when he came to the throne, and he reigned in Jerusalem for one year; his mother was Athaliah granddaughter[b] of Omri king of
27 Israel. He followed the practices of the house of Ahab and did what was wrong in the eyes of the LORD like the house of Ahab, for he was connected with that house by
28 marriage. He allied himself with Jehoram son of Ahab to

[a] Verses 25–9: cp. 2 Chr. 22: 1–6.   [a] Lit. daughter.

fight against Hazael king of Aram at Ramoth-gilead; but
King Jehoram was wounded by the Aramaeans, and re- 29
turned to Jezreel to recover from the wounds which were
inflicted on him at Ramoth*a* in battle with Hazael king of
Aram; and because of his illness Ahaziah son of Joram
king of Judah went down to Jezreel to visit him.

✻ 26. *granddaughter*: Athaliah was Ahab's daughter; cp. verse
18. The Hebrew word *bath* usually means daughter but can
have the wider meaning of 'female descendant'.

28. *He allied himself*: he may have had little option since he
was more like a vassal than an independent ally (cp. the
relationship between Ahab and Jehoshaphat; 1 Kings 22).
Hazael was king of Aram from 844 to 798 B.C. (cp. note at
8: 8). Ramoth-gilead was an important border town on the
east side of the Jordan (see map on p. 30). Its possession by
Israel was frequently disputed by the Aramaeans (cp. 1 Kings
22).

29. Jezreel was situated in the northern part of Israel on the
west side of the Jordan in the valley which separated the
central hill-country from Galilee. The kings of Israel had a
palace there which Ahab had extended by confiscating the
vineyard of Naboth (cp. 1 Kings 21: 1). *Ramoth*: the Hebrew
(N.E.B. footnote) has become confused with another place
whose name sounds much the same. The confusion was probably due to the error of a scribe in copying manuscripts. It is
not stated whether Joram *went down to Jezreel* from Ramoth-
gilead or Jerusalem. If he had been fighting alongside Jehoram,
then he would have gone down from Ramoth-gilead, but it is
not clear how active Ahaziah had been in the alliance. His
support may have been little more than token. In this case he
may well have gone down from Jerusalem. At all events, the
enemies of the two kings saw this meeting as an opportunity

[a] *So Sept.; Heb*. Ramah.

to assassinate both of them and thus remove what they considered to be the evil influence of the house of Ahab from both Israel and Judah. *

THE PROPHETIC REVOLT

* The story of the assassination of Jehoram king of Israel and Ahaziah king of Judah by Jehu, an army commander, at the instigation of the prophet Elisha, is clearly regarded by the editors as a most important turning-point in the history of the kingdoms. With the death of these two kings, the house of Omri and Ahab came to an end. The kings of that house had pursued for political reasons policies of alliance with their Canaanite neighbours, the kings of the cities of the Phoenician seaboard. These policies had led to their being sympathetic to the spread of the influence of Canaanite religious practices in their kingdoms. Elijah and Elisha had rightly seen such practices as being destructive of the distinctive character of Israel's religion, and had therefore opposed the alliances and made themselves enemies of the house of Omri and Ahab. It was concern for the religious future of the people of Israel and Judah as the covenant people of God which led Elisha to encourage Jehu's ambitions. Jehu acted as a traitor against his king, but the support which he received from Elisha enabled him to present his action as being inspired by patriotism rather than personal ambition. The countries were taking a new direction in politics and religion, or rather were reverting to the older traditional ideas and ideals which had been set aside by Omri and Ahab. The prophets Elijah and Elisha stood for these older ideals and this was the prophetic revolt.

It was at best only partially successful. Jehu proved to be, in practice, little different from the kings he had replaced. However, in the eyes of the deuteronomic editors, the revolt was an attempt to bring back the people to their true vocation. They gave it, therefore, great prominence in their story. Indeed, they seem to have inserted into their narrative an account

78

of the revolt as they received it without alteration. It is much more detailed than the accounts of other events and repeats some of the things that have already been told in the accounts of the reign of Ahaziah. All this indicates the importance that the editors felt belonged to these events. God in them was showing that he was unwilling to allow his people to be seduced lightly from their loyalty to him. He sent prophets to influence the kings and people, and bring them back to their true religious allegiance. Only after every attempt at such persuasion had been made and failed would he allow the kingdoms to be destroyed by military enemies. *

JEHU IS ANOINTED AND PROCLAIMED KING

Elisha the prophet summoned one of the company **9** of prophets and said to him, 'Hitch up your cloak, take this flask of oil with you and go to Ramoth-gilead. When 2 you arrive, you will find Jehu son of Jehoshaphat, son of Nimshi; go in and call him aside from his fellow-officers, and lead him through to an inner room. Then take the 3 flask and pour the oil on his head and say, "This is the word of the LORD: I anoint you king over Israel"; then open the door and flee for your life.' So the young pro- 4 phet went to Ramoth-gilead. When he arrived, he found 5 the officers sitting together and said, 'Sir, I have a word for you.' 'For which of us?' asked Jehu. 'For you, sir', he said. He rose and went into the house, and the prophet 6 poured the oil on his head, saying, 'This is the word of the LORD the God of Israel: "I anoint you king over Israel, the people of the LORD. You shall strike down the house 7 of Ahab your master, and I will take vengeance on Jezebel for the blood of my servants the prophets and for the blood of all the LORD's servants. All the house of Ahab 8

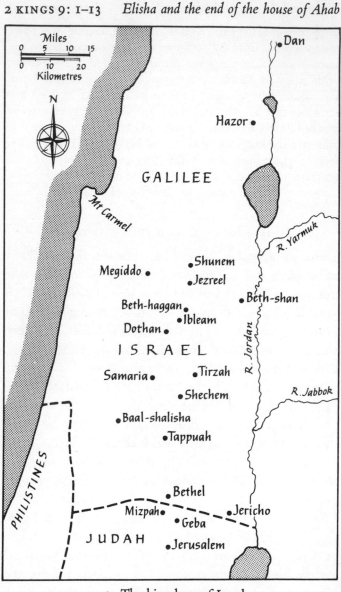

3. The kingdom of Israel

shall perish and I will destroy every mother's son of his
house in Israel, whether under the protection of the family
or not. And I will make the house of Ahab like the house 9
of Jeroboam son of Nebat and the house of Baasha son of
Ahijah. Jezebel shall be devoured by dogs in the plot of 10
ground at Jezreel and no one will bury her."' Then he
opened the door and fled. When Jehu rejoined the king's 11
officers, they said to him, 'Is all well? What did this crazy
fellow want with you?' 'You know him and the way his
thoughts run', he said. 'Nonsense!' they replied; 'tell us 12
what happened.' 'I will tell you exactly what he said:
"This is the word of the LORD: I anoint you king over
Israel."' They snatched up their cloaks and spread them 13
under him on the stones*a* of the steps, and sounded the
trumpet and shouted, 'Jehu is king.'

* According to the story in 1 Kings, Elijah at Mount Horeb
was commanded by God to anoint Jehu (1 Kings 19: 16).
That account conflicts with the story of the anointing as told
here. It was probably the work of an editor who wrote it and
added it to the story of Elijah at Horeb in order to connect
Elijah and his authority with the events of the prophetic
revolt. There is a true sense in which Jehu's coming to the
throne grew out of Elijah's work – it was Elijah who first
made the protest which led to the revolt – but historically it
must have been Elisha and not Elijah who anointed Jehu.

1. *Ramoth-gilead*: Jehu was fighting with the army which
King Jehoram had had to leave because of his wounds. In
political terms he raised a rebellion against the ruler whose
servant he was. There must have been disaffection in the army,
possibly because of earlier defeats. The archaeological evidence
at Samaria, Megiddo and elsewhere shows that Ahab, like

[a] *Prob. rdg.; Heb. obscure.*

Solomon, had been a great builder, and again as with Solomon, this must have placed a great burden of taxes on the people. The army had become all-powerful in the state and could make and break kings. Omri had been made king by the army (1 Kings 16: 16) and now his grandson was to be deposed by the army.

2. *Jehu*: the name means 'Yahweh is He', i.e. Yahweh is the true God. With such a name Jehu must have come from a family which was sympathetic to the ideals of Elisha. However, the fact that as king he did little to further those ideals (cp. 10: 30–1) points to the conclusion that he was chiefly motivated by political ambition. Certainly the prophet Hosea did not think highly of Jehu (cp. Hos. 1: 4). *an inner room*: because there was need for secrecy until Jehu had declared himself.

3. The prophet Samuel had anointed Saul to be king and then David to be his successor. So such anointing could be taken as the guarantee of success, and provided the stimulus which Jehu needed to declare himself. Anointing signified that the spirit of God had come to rest upon a man and had empowered him with the gifts which were necessary for kingship. Kings came to be referred to as 'the Anointed of God', and the Hebrew word for 'Anointed One', *Messiah*, came to be used of the perfect king whom God would send to his people at some future time. *flee for your life*: in case the anointing should be received by Jehu or some other of the officers as a treacherous invitation to rebellion, and punished accordingly.

6. *the people of the LORD*: the call from God by the hand of the prophet was more than political. It was to lead the people back to a way of life which would give first priority to their vocation as the covenant people of God.

7–10. The rest of the words set out as spoken by the young prophet in these verses are generally considered to have been added by an editor. They contradict the instructions given earlier to the prophet to say as little as possible and then flee for his life (cp. verses 1–3). The editor who added them was concerned that the reader should not miss what he considered to be the significance of what had been done, and the consequences that followed from it. The words reflect the interests of the deuteronomists who were concerned to portray Jehu as one raised up by God to exterminate the house of Ahab. The real Jehu was probably more prompted by political motives and ambitions.

In the law as set out in Deuteronomy a true prophet could be distinguished from a false one in that his prophecies came true. In line with this teaching the editors of Kings are careful to show that the prophecies of the true prophets did come true. In 1 Kings 21: 21–3 Elijah, after the murder of Naboth, prophesied that God would destroy the house of Ahab and Jezebel. The words of the young prophet here repeat the words of Elijah and thus show that Elijah was a true prophet and that God punished those who flouted his law.

7. Jezebel sought to kill Elijah (1 Kings 19: 2) and incited Ahab to arrange the murder of Naboth (1 Kings 21: 1–14).

9. The attitude of the editors was that all the kings inevitably went to the bad and became religiously corrupt, and as such an evil influence on the people. This was a judgement formed in the light of a succession of bad kings. The prophet Hosea came to the same judgement (Hos. 13: 11) as did one of the editors of Samuel (1 Sam. 8: 6–18).

11. *crazy fellow*: this is usually taken to be the officers' contemptuous attitude to one given to periods of ecstasy, when he would speak and act in ways which seemed near to madness.

13. *They snatched...and spread them under him*: they were showing symbolically that they were willing to serve under him as king. Similarly on Palm Sunday the people laid down their cloaks on the Mount of Olives for Jesus to ride over them. *stones*: the meaning of the Hebrew is uncertain. The translation depends upon the suggestion that the word meant that the steps were bare. Another suggestion is that the word is an architectural term whose precise meaning has been lost. *sounded the trumpet*: this was a part of the coronation rite (cp. 1 Kings 1: 34). ✳

83

THE ASSASSINATION OF THE KINGS OF
ISRAEL AND JUDAH

14 Then Jehu son of Jehoshaphat, son of Nimshi, laid his
plans against Jehoram, while Jehoram and the Israelites
were defending Ramoth-gilead against Hazael king of
15 Aram. King Jehoram had returned to Jezreel to recover
from the wounds inflicted on him by the Aramaeans when
he fought against Hazael king of Aram. Jehu said to them,
'If you are on my side,[a] see that no one escapes from the
16 city to tell the news in Jezreel.' He mounted his chariot
and drove to Jezreel, for Jehoram was laid up there, and
Ahaziah king of Judah had gone down to visit him.

17   The watchman standing on the watch-tower in Jezreel
saw Jehu and his troop approaching and called out, 'I see
a troop of men.' Then Jehoram said, 'Fetch a horseman
18 and send to find out if they come peaceably.' The horseman went to meet him and said, 'The king asks, "Is it
peace?"' Jehu said, 'Peace? What is peace to you? Fall in
behind me.' Thereupon the watchman reported, 'The
19 messenger has met them but he is not coming back.' A
second horseman was sent; when he met them, he also
said, 'The king asks, "Is it peace?"' 'Peace?' said Jehu.
20 'What is peace to you? Fall in behind me.' Then the
watchman reported, 'He has met them but he is not
coming back. The driving is like the driving of Jehu son[b]
21 of Nimshi, for he drives furiously.' 'Harness my chariot',
said Jehoram. They harnessed it, and Jehoram king of
Israel and Ahaziah king of Judah went out each in his own

[a] on my side: *so Sept.; Heb. om.*
[b] *Or* grandson (*cp. verse 2*).

chariot to meet Jehu, and met him by the plot of Naboth
of Jezreel. When Jehoram saw Jehu, he said, 'Is it peace, 22
Jehu?' But he replied, 'Do you call it peace while your
mother Jezebel keeps up her obscene idol-worship and
monstrous sorceries?' Jehoram wheeled about and fled, 23
crying out to Ahaziah, 'Treachery, Ahaziah!' Jehu 24
seized his bow and shot Jehoram between the shoulders;
the arrow pierced his heart and he sank down in his
chariot. Then Jehu said to Bidkar, his lieutenant, 'Pick 25
him up and throw him into the plot of land belonging to
Naboth of Jezreel; remember how, when you and I were
riding side by side behind Ahab his father, the LORD pronounced this sentence against him: "It is the very word 26
of the LORD: as surely as I saw yesterday the blood of
Naboth and the blood of his sons, I will require you in
this plot." So pick him up and throw him into it and thus
fulfil the word of the LORD.' When Ahaziah king of 27
Judah saw this, he fled by the road to Beth-haggan. Jehu
went after him and said, 'Make sure of him too.' They
shot him down*a* in his chariot on the road up the valley*b*
near Ibleam, but he escaped to Megiddo and died there.
His servants conveyed his body to Jerusalem and buried 28
him in his tomb with his forefathers in the city of David.

✻ The emphasis in this passage upon the swiftness of Jehu's
coup d'état seems to imply that there was a real possibility of
strong opposition to him if Jehoram had had time to rally his
supporters. This contrasts with the over-all impression that
the editors wish to give, that Jehu had been chosen by God
and anointed by God's prophet in order to bring back the

[a] They...down: *so Pesh.; Heb. om.*
[b] the valley: *prob. rdg.; Heb.* to Gur.

people to their religious obedience. From this point of view the editors portray Jehu as being overwhelmingly successful and meeting no real opposition. In this passage they appear to have taken an existing account of the revolt and adapted it to their purposes. Verses 14–15 repeat information which has already been given (8: 28–9) and this seems to point to two original sources, but the way that the narrative emphasizes that Jehu is God's agent sent to punish those who connived at Naboth's murder is typical of the editors' use of events to teach religious lessons.

14–15. *while Jehoram...against Hazael king of Aram*: this explains why Jehu chose this time to make his move. The words interrupt the flow of the story and could well be placed in parenthesis as in the Revised Standard Version. The words *were defending* are confusing. Jehu *laid his plans* after the king had left Ramoth-gilead. The tense in the Hebrew is ambiguous but a pluperfect would be clearer, i.e. 'Jehoram and the Israelites had been defending Ramoth-gilead...but King Jehoram had returned to Jezreel.' Ramoth-gilead was last mentioned as the place where King Ahab had died in battle in a vain attempt to recover the city from the Aramaeans. The Israelites must have recaptured the city at some later time since Jehoram is here defending it. The recapture has not been mentioned in Kings since the editors ignored even important military and political events when they did not fit in with their purposes. It may be that they wished to link the events that led to the end of the house of Ahab and the death of Jezebel with the death of Ahab by showing that both began at Ramoth-gilead. *on my side*: this phrase represents one Hebrew word which could have been easily omitted accidentally from manuscripts. The king had supporters even in Ramoth-gilead.

16. *Jezreel*: see note on 8: 29. It dominates the valley which leads down to the city of Beth-shan and the Jordan. It was on a main high road to the territory east of the Jordan (see map on p. 80).

17. *they come peaceably*: the king was anxious in case the

86

troop meant that all was not going well with the army at Ramoth-gilead. The Hebrew word for peace, *shalom*, was, and is, the greeting exchanged when men met. It means a great deal more than mere absence of hostility. Peace for the Hebrew was the description of a life in which the community and all its members were living in full harmony together and were able to express and develop fully every aspect of their corporate and individual life. In the whole passage, verses 17–22, there is here a play on the various meanings of 'peace'. The king is asking, 'Is the kingdom secure?', meaning 'Are we holding the Aramaeans at bay?' Jehu's reply means, 'How can a kingdom be secure when its own chief defender is pursuing policies which must lead to disaster by corrupting its very being?'

18. *Fall in behind me*: so that the king should not know Jehu's purpose until it was too late to defend himself.

21. Jehoram went out to meet Jehu to hear his news in private. He understood Jehu's not allowing the messengers to return as meaning that he was the bearer of news which would dismay the people of the town if they were allowed to hear it. *by the plot of Naboth of Jezreel*: this was the land that King Ahab, prompted by his queen Jezebel, had taken from Naboth in circumstances which showed that he had no regard for God or his laws (1 Kings 21).

22. *Do you call it peace*: see note on verse 17 above. *obscene idol-worship*: this is a paraphrase. The Hebrew means 'harlotries'. Many of the prophets used this image of false worship. They looked upon Israel as a bride who had been married to Yahweh by the covenant which he had made with Moses at Mount Sinai. The covenant demanded loyalty expressed by exclusive worship. Hence all worship of the gods or goddesses of Canaan was condemned as 'harlotry' (cp. Jer. 3: 1–20). This particular image was doubtless chosen because the religion of Canaan, in which so many Israelites dabbled, was a fertility cult which made much use of sexual imagery. *monstrous sorceries*: magical practices of various kinds

were widely indulged in by the Canaanites. The law of Deuteronomy totally forbade all such practices to Israelites (Deut. 18: 9–14) as it did idolatry (Deut. 17: 2–7). It held that God would provide through his priests and prophets all the help and guidance his people required. Therefore an Israelite by turning to sorcery was declaring his lack of faith in his God, and doubting his sovereign control over the forces of nature.

24. Is the editor hinting at a similarity with the death of Ahab (1 Kings 22: 34–5)?

25. *the plot of land belonging to Naboth of Jezreel*: this is emphasized to show that the prophecy of Elijah came true (1 Kings 21: 19–21). The editors were always concerned to show that the words of the prophets were fulfilled. This indicated that they were true and not false prophets (cp. Deut. 18: 21–2).

27. *Beth-haggan* means 'Garden House'. It was probably the same place as En-gannim, 'Garden Spring', which is mentioned in Josh. 19: 21. The name of the modern town on this site is Jenin. It is some 7 miles (11 km) south of Jezreel. Ahaziah was thus making for Judah. *They shot him down*: the Hebrew has lost a verb by scribal error. The same verb occurs twice in slightly different forms. Literally, 'he said "Shoot him"', and they shot him'. This kind of error, in which a word very similar in form to the one preceding it was accidentally omitted, is fairly common. *the road up* 'to Gur' (N.E.B. footnote): no place called Gur is otherwise known. 'Gur' may have come from a corruption of *gai*, a word meaning 'valley'. Ahaziah was hurrying up the road into the hill-country. Ibleam is mentioned in Josh. 17: 11. Its modern name is Tel Bel'ameh. Once Ahaziah had been wounded, he knew he would never reach Judah and so turned westwards to the sanctuary of the nearest fortress city, Megiddo. *

A CORRECTED DATING

In the eleventh year of Jehoram son of Ahab, Ahaziah 29
became king over Judah.

* This verse is out of order. Such statements are placed at the
introduction to a reign not at its end. Neither does it agree
with the statement made at the beginning of Ahaziah's reign
(8: 25). It seems to be a very early attempt to correct the dating
of the king. In 3: 1 it was stated that Jehoram reigned twelve
years, and in 8: 25 that Ahaziah became king in the twelfth
year of Jehoram and reigned one year. This 'one year' may
have been only a few months. Here an editor has taken it
literally and corrected, as he thought, the regnal year of
Jehoram from twelve to eleven in order to allow Ahaziah to
reign a full year. *

THE END OF JEZEBEL

Jehu came to Jezreel. Now Jezebel had heard what had 30
happened; she had painted her eyes and dressed her hair,
and she stood looking down from a window. As Jehu 31
entered the gate, she said, 'Is it peace, you Zimri, you
murderer of your master?' He looked up at the window 32
and said, 'Who is on my side, who?' Two or three
eunuchs looked out, and he said, 'Throw her down.' 33
They threw her down, and some of her blood splashed on
to the wall and the horses, which trampled her underfoot.
Then he went in and ate and drank. 'See to this accursed 34
woman', he said, 'and bury her; for she is a king's
daughter.' But when they went to bury her they found 35
nothing of her but the skull, the feet, and the palms of the
hands; and they went back and told him. Jehu said, 'It is 36

the word of the LORD which his servant Elijah the Tishbite spoke, when he said, "In the plot of ground at
37 Jezreel the dogs shall devour the flesh of Jezebel, and
Jezebel's corpse shall lie like dung upon the ground in the
plot at Jezreel so that no one will be able to say: This is
Jezebel."'

* The death of Jezebel is described not only because of her
position and influence in the country, but also because it had
been predicted by Elijah (1 Kings 21: 23). To the editors it
vindicated the claim of Elijah to be a true prophet and showed
how God dealt with the wicked.

30. Jezebel was the queen mother and as such influential in
the affairs of the kingdom. In many kingdoms, including
Judah, the mother of the reigning king had an official position
at court and could become a powerful person in the kingdom
with considerable influence on the policies the state pursued.
Jezebel was a Phoenician princess who had married Ahab
(1 Kings 16: 31) and was regarded by the editors as having
exercised a disastrously strong influence over her husband in
that she encouraged him both to rule in the despotic manner
of the Canaanite kings (1 Kings 21), and also to introduce
practices from the Canaanite cults into the religious practices
of Israel (1 Kings 19: 1–2). Thus she epitomized for them all
that was corrupt and evil in Israelite society. *she had painted her
eyes*: probably with kohl, a powder usually made with anti-
mony which is still used as a cosmetic by Arab women to
darken the eyes. Jezebel prepared to meet her enemy as a
queen. She may have thought that by so doing she could
frighten him and arouse support in the kingdom. Her greeting
to Jehu was meant to express her scorn and her conviction that
his revolt would be short-lived.

31. *Is it peace*: i.e. how can the nation be prosperous when
its future is threatened by ambitious army commanders (see
note at 9: 17)? *you Zimri*: this was a shrewd blow. Zimri was

an army commander who had rebelled and assassinated his king. His triumph was short-lived. He only reigned for seven days and had been brought to destruction by Omri, Jezebel's father-in-law.

32. *Two or three eunuchs*: Jezebel's prestige must have sunk very low when slaves of her own household turned against her.

34. *he went in and ate and drank*: this indicates that some considerable period of time elapsed before Jehu grew concerned about the disposal of Jezebel's remains. *and bury her*: the Hebrews did not regard death as meaning the separation of the spirit and the body. The spirit was still linked with the body, and its existence in the afterworld of Sheol was dependent upon the continuing existence of the body or at least the bones. Hence proper burial was a matter of great importance, and for a body to be left unburied and, therefore, a prey for birds and wild beasts, was regarded as being the greatest curse that could fall upon any person or family.

35. *the skull, the feet, and the palms of the hands*: i.e. the parts of the body that were inedible.

36. The reference is to the prophecy of Elijah at 1 Kings 21: 23. *the dogs* were the scavengers of the towns and as such regarded as impure and looked upon with disgust. ✳

THE DESTRUCTION OF AHAB'S FAMILY AND COURT

Now seventy sons of Ahab were left in Samaria. Jehu **10** therefore sent a letter to Samaria, to the elders, the rulers of the city,[a] and to the tutors of Ahab's children,[b] in which he wrote: 'Now, when this letter reaches you, 2 since you have in your care your master's family as well as his chariots and horses, fortified cities[c] and weapons,

[a] *So Luc. Sept.; Heb.* of Jezreel.
[b] children: *so some Sept. MSS.; Heb. om.*
[c] *So some MSS.; others* city.

3 choose the best and the most suitable of your master's family, set him on his father's throne, and fight for your
4 master's house.' They were panic-stricken and said, 'The two kings could not stand against him; what hope is there
5 that we can?' Therefore the comptroller of the household and the governor of the city, with the elders and the turors, sent this message to Jehu: 'We are your servants. Whatever you tell us we will do; but we will not make
6 anyone king. Do as you think fit.' Then he wrote them a second letter: 'If you are on my side and will obey my orders, then bring the heads of[a] your master's sons to me at Jezreel by this time tomorrow.' Now the royal princes, seventy in all, were with the nobles of the city who were
7 bringing them up. When the letter reached them, they took the royal princes and killed all seventy; they put their heads in baskets and sent them to Jehu in Jezreel.
8 When the messenger came to him and reported that they had brought the heads of the royal princes, he ordered them to be put in two heaps and left at the entrance of the
9 city gate till morning. In the morning he went out, stood there and said to all the people, 'You are fair judges. If I conspired against my master and killed him, who put all
10 these to death? Be sure then that every word which the LORD has spoken against the house of Ahab shall be fulfilled, and that the LORD has now done what he spoke
11 through his servant Elijah.' So Jehu put to death all who were left of the house of Ahab in Jezreel, as well as all his nobles, his close friends, and his priests, until he had left not one survivor.

[a] *So Luc. Sept.; Heb. adds* the men of.

✷ The story has been included by the editors to show how Ahab's family was completely obliterated. For them this was a just punishment inflicted by God for the sins of Ahab and his house in seducing the Israelites from their loyalty to their God. When read without the theological ideas of the deuteronomists in mind, it tells a somewhat different story. Then it shows, as some of the earlier incidents have also hinted, that Jehu was far less secure than the editors believed or want us to believe. There were strong forces in the country which could have ranged themselves against him and his *coup* might well have failed. So far we have seen Jehu succeeding by his courage, confidence, and vigour. To these qualities there is also added in this incident political astuteness, even craftiness, of a high order. The success of Jehu was brought about by the exercise of all these qualities. The editors portray him simply as a willing instrument in the hand of God. The sources they used show us glimpses of the human, full-blooded character who was mostly concerned with the fulfilment of his own ambitions. The latter picture need not make us doubt the conclusions of the deuteronomists – God did use Jehu – but it does warn us once again that they did not look at history as we do.

1. *seventy sons*: this means the whole family of Ahab, all his descendants. 'son' in Hebrew can be used in a wider sense than in English. They may have numbered seventy but it is more likely that this number is used as the customary way of expressing a large number. Jacob went to Egypt with seventy (Gen. 46: 27) and Gideon had seventy sons (Judg. 8: 30). Samaria was the capital of Israel and a very strong fortress. With courageous and determined leadership it could have held out for a long time and allowed time for the opposition to Jehu to rally. *a letter*: the Hebrew has 'letters'. *the elders* represented and led the citizens of Samaria. *the rulers* were probably the military leaders, the governor and his officers. *of the city*: the Hebrew has 'of Jezreel' (N.E.B. footnote) but this is clearly wrong. *the tutors* were the guardians of the royal

family. *Ahab's children*: the Hebrew reads 'of Ahab' but a word must have been lost from the text.

2–3. The letter was a challenge, and maybe even a bluff. It said, in effect, that if they really believed that Jehu was a Zimri, an impious rebel, then they had only to gather their forces and fight. God in those circumstances must give them victory. On the other hand, only one who fought with the help of God could prevail over such strength as was at their disposal. *fortified cities*: most Hebrew manuscripts read the singular. Either 'city' or *cities* fits the context, the reference being to Samaria alone, or to all the fortresses of the kingdom. The plural is to be preferred because it is read by the Versions and is more in keeping with the point that Jehu was making.

6. Jehu's second letter contained a deliberate ambiguity. He certainly wanted all the family of Ahab to be killed. Every usurper in those days always killed all the members of the former royal family. As long as any remained alive, they were a possible focus for rebellion and therefore a menace to his security. The leaders of Samaria understood this, and rightly read his letter in that sense, but the ambiguity of the letter allowed Jehu to disclaim responsibility for the murders. The Hebrew word translated 'head', *rosh*, has, like its English equivalent, a wide range of meaning. Jehu's words could have been understood literally as referring to the heads of Ahab's sons. They could also have been taken as meaning the leading figures among those sons. In this latter sense Jehu was asking that the most important members of Ahab's family should be delivered to him as hostages on the following day. In the Hebrew a word has been inserted which is translated 'the men of' (N.E.B. footnote). This, if original, would remove the ambiguity from the letter. *Rosh* could then only mean 'chief'. For this reason it is rightly taken by N.E.B. as a scribal addition to the text.

8. It seems to have been a regular custom of conquerors to place heaps of human heads, or baskets full of them, at the entrance to cities as a deterrent to would-be rebels. In

mediaeval English cities the heads of traitors were impaled on pikes over the gates for the same purpose.

9. *You are fair judges*: *fair* translates the Hebrew *tsaddiq*, which is often translated as 'righteous'. It was a word used in the law courts and there signified innocence. Jehu is here inviting all the citizens to come to a judgement on him. They can judge him a rebel against his master. If so, then God ought to have punished him. But God has in fact given the kingdom into his hand since the very guardians of Ahab's family have removed from the scene every possible rival for the throne. Jehu is claiming that this can only mean that he did what he did as the instrument of God.

10. Jehu made his claim for political reasons, to gain the kingdom without protracted warfare. The editors, seeing him as the one who removed the corrupting influence of the house of Ahab from Israel, accepted his claim for religious reasons. It fitted in well with the way they understood the history of their people. Verse 10 is probably a comment which they added to the story to make their point of view more explicit.

11. Jehu now felt strong enough to remove all the possible sources of opposition and future disaffection. ✻

THE DESTRUCTION OF THE FAMILY OF AHAZIAH

Then he set out for Samaria, and on the way there, 12 when he had reached a shepherds' shelter,*a* he came upon 13 the kinsmen of Ahaziah king of Judah and said, 'Who are you?' 'We are kinsmen of Ahaziah,' they replied; 'and we have come down to greet the families of the king and of the queen mother.' 'Take them alive', he said. So they 14 took them alive; then they slew them and flung them into the pit that was there, forty-two of them; they did not leave a single survivor.

[a] a shepherds' shelter: *or* Beth-eker of the Shepherds.

✻ By this chance meeting Jehu was given the opportunity to eliminate all those who might have organized opposition to him in Judah in the same way as he had just eliminated his opponents from Israel. For the editors this was also a part of that cleansing of the covenant people from the evil influence of false religion. But did it happen quite as set out here? Samaria is no great distance from Jezreel and the kinsmen of Ahaziah would surely not have set out for Jezreel after the massacre of Ahab's family. It has been suggested that the kinsmen of Ahaziah were returning south after having paid their visit to the king's family at Jezreel, but, if that were the case, they must have known of the deaths of Jehoram and Ahaziah. Another suggestion is that the incident never happened but was invented by the editors to complete their picture of Jehu as a religious reformer who rid both Israel and Judah of the bad influence of the former royal families. It seems unnecessary to charge the editors with such invention. Jehu was quite capable of such slaughter. What they probably did was to take the narrative out of its original context and set it here so that it would add to the religious point they were making.

12. *a shepherds' shelter*: a place where shepherds gathered with their flocks. The place may have had a proper name (cp. N.E.B. footnote) and the place called Bait Qad some 3 miles (nearly 5 km) north-east of Jenin has been suggested.

13. *the queen mother* was Jezebel. The queen mother was always an influential person at the royal court and none more so than Jezebel (see note at 9: 30).

14. *forty-two of them*: the she-bears mauled a similar number of small boys who had mocked Elisha (2: 24). The number may have been traditional. Those who think that the editors invented this massacre point to this number as support for their view, but it may have been a traditional way of indicating that a great number were killed. ✻

THE ELIMINATION OF BAAL WORSHIP FROM
SAMARIA

When he had left that place, he found Jehonadab son 15
of Rechab coming to meet him. He greeted him and said,
'Are you with me heart and soul, as I am with you?'
'I am', said Jehonadab. 'Then if you are,' said Jehu,*a*
'give me your hand.' He gave him his hand and Jehu
helped him up into his chariot. 'Come with me,' he said, 16
'and you will see my zeal for the LORD.' So he*b* took him
with him in his chariot. When he came to Samaria, he 17
put to death all of Ahab's house who were left there and
so blotted it out, in fulfilment of the word which the
LORD had spoken to Elijah. Then Jehu called all the people 18
together and said to them, 'Ahab served the Baal a little;
Jehu will serve him much. Now, summon all the prophets 19
of Baal, all his ministers and priests; not one must be
missing. For I am holding a great sacrifice to Baal, and no
one who is missing from it shall live.' In this way Jehu
outwitted the ministers of Baal in order to destroy them.
So Jehu said, 'Let a sacred ceremony for Baal be held.' 20
They did so, and Jehu himself sent word throughout 21
Israel, and all the ministers of Baal came; there was not a
man left who did not come. They went into the temple of
Baal and it was filled from end to end. Then he said to the 22
person who had charge of the wardrobe, 'Bring out
robes for all the ministers of Baal'; and he brought them
out. Then Jehu and Jehonadab son of Rechab went into 23
the temple of Baal and said to the ministers of Baal, 'Look

[a] said Jehu: *so Sept.; Heb. om.*
[b] *So Sept.; Heb.* they.

carefully and make sure that there are no servants of the LORD here with you, but only the ministers of Baal.'

24 Then they went in to offer sacrifices and whole-offerings. Now Jehu had stationed eighty men outside and said to them, 'I am putting these men in your charge, and any man who lets one escape shall answer for it with his life.'

25 When he had finished offering the whole-offering, Jehu ordered the guards and the lieutenants to go and cut them all down, and let not one of them escape; so they slew them without quarter. The escort and the lieutenants

26 then rushed into the keep of the temple of Baal and brought out the sacred pole[a] from the temple of Baal

27 and burnt it; and they pulled down the sacred pillar of the Baal and the temple itself and made a privy of it – as it is today.

* The temple of Baal at Samaria had been built by Ahab (1 Kings 16: 32). It was a part of his policy of alliance with the Phoenicians and may have even been provided as a chapel for his queen Jezebel. Jehu's attack upon it was based upon political motives. He wished to remove a feature of the life of the city which was particularly associated with the family of Ahab, and in murdering the leaders of the Baal cult he was removing from the kingdom those who had most reason to be loyal to the house of Ahab. The editors have chosen to interpret Jehu's act as being primarily religious in purpose. They portray it as part of a religious reformation and to that end they have associated with Jehu in the destruction of the Baal temple Jehonadab the Rechabite leader. He and his group were fervent supporters of Yahweh and opponents of Canaan so there is nothing improbable in an alliance between Jehu and Jehonadab. But it can hardly have taken place just as it has

[a] *Prob. rdg.; Heb.* sacred pillars.

been described here. If Jehu had ridden to Samaria with Jehonadab in his chariot he would have alarmed the supporters of Baal rather than lulled them into a false sense of security as he seems to have done. The alliance with Jehonadab must have been made at some time after the destruction of the temple of Baal. It may be that the destruction of the temple was the act which caused Jehonadab to give whole-hearted support to Jehu. Once again the editors have taken narratives which were originally principally concerned with political issues and re-ordered them, in order to make the political issues which are being described serve the religious purposes which provided the motive of their history.

15. *Jehonadab son of Rechab* was the founder of a sect of Israelites who led a particularly strict life. Details of their customs are given in Jer. 35: 1–11. From these details it seems that Jehonadab insisted that his followers should continue to live in Canaan by the pattern of life which all Israelites had lived by in the wilderness days before they had settled in Canaan. The purpose of this 'puritanism' was to avoid all the influences of Canaan by rejecting its culture. The Rechabites thus stood for the religious and cultural purity of Israel's earliest days. *He greeted him*: the Hebrew literally means 'he blessed him'. Every greeting was meant to be a blessing in which peace was given, but here more than normally in that the two leaders were ratifying an alliance to work together in the service of their God. *said Jehu*: these words are not in the Hebrew but their inclusion makes the sense much clearer. They were probably omitted by scribal error.

16. *he took him*: the plural subject of the Hebrew (N.E.B. footnote) is due to a scribal error. It is inconsistent with the singular adjective which follows in *his chariot*.

17. *the word which the LORD had spoken to Elijah* as given in 1 Kings 21: 20–4. This is a further example of the editors' concern to demonstrate that the prophecies of a true prophet were fulfilled.

18. This is the beginning of the original story of the

99

destruction of the temple of Baal to which the editors have added the story of Jehu's alliance with Jehonadab. *Ahab served the Baal a little*: Ahab's devotion to the Baal was probably perfunctory, a political necessity in view of his alliances. For *Baal* see notes at 1: 2 and 3: 2. *Jehu will serve him much*: Jehu's strategy was to lull the Baal worshippers into a false sense of security by making them believe that he was making a bid for their allegiance. There may have been a pun in his words in that the Hebrew words for 'serve' and 'destroy' are very similar. *serve him much* could become with only a slight change of consonants 'destroy him'.

22. *Bring out robes*: to change one's clothes was a part of the purification rites which were considered necessary before taking part in an important religious ceremony (cp. Gen. 35: 2, N.E.B. footnote). In later times the high priest in the temple at Jerusalem completely changed all his clothing twice on the Day of Atonement. Muslim pilgrims to Mecca still wear a special garment while they are in the precincts of the holy place.

23. *and Jehonadab the son of Rechab*: these words have been added to the story by the editors. It is not difficult to think of Jehu offering sacrifice to Baal, but a rigorist, such as Jehonadab was, would hardly have done so. The words '*Look carefully...*' would have come very oddly from him, and his presence would have been bound to create suspicion and alarm among the adherents of Baal.

24. *sacrifices and whole-offerings*: the difference between these two was that a part of the sacrifices were eaten by the priests and worshippers while the whole-offerings were totally burnt as an offering to God.

25. *When he had finished offering the whole-offering*: Jehu, as king, acted as chief priest. Solomon had similarly offered sacrifice at the dedication of the Jerusalem temple (1 Kings 8: 62–4). The Baal worshippers would have thought that by this act Jehu had irrevocably committed himself to their cause. *rushed into the keep of the temple of Baal*: the Hebrew word

underlying *rushed* is difficult. The Revised Standard Version gives the sense of the Hebrew better with 'cast them out and went into'. *the keep of the temple* clearly means the inner sanctuary where the idols of the god stood. The usual Hebrew word for shrine is not used. In fact the word used, *'ir*, always elsewhere means 'city', hence the N.E.B. translation *keep* rather than 'shrine'.

26–7. What was *brought out* from the keep of the temple, and what was *burnt*? The Hebrew is in some confusion. It has *sacred pillar* in both instances, the only difference being that the plural is used at the first occurrence and the singular at the second. This is clearly wrong. A sacred pillar, *mazzebah*, was a well-known cultic object widely used in Canaan and elsewhere. It was a large stone set upright in or near a sanctuary. It was regarded as the symbol of the presence of a god or spirit and was treated with great reverence. Offerings of oil, wine or even blood were made to it by being poured upon it, and offerings of wheat and other food were placed by it. Another cultic object which was widely used in Canaanite sanctuaries was the sacred pole, *asherah*. In open-air shrines this could be a tree planted in the shrine. In other shrines, it was a wooden pole which represented a living tree. Asherah was the name of the mother goddess in the Canaanite pantheon of gods. The sacred pole seems to have had a considerable significance for the fertility rites which were practised at Canaanite shrines. Quite what its function was, other than representing life, growth and fertility, is not clear. It may have been the symbol of the tree of life of the creation myths.

The N.E.B. has emended the first occurrence of 'sacred pillars' to *sacred pole* since a wooden object was more likely to have been burnt. But this may not be correct. A sacred pillar may have been burnt, since the easiest way of destroying a stone object was to heat it with fire and then pour cold water over it so that the stone broke into pieces. If the stone pillar was burnt, then the altar of Baal would have been pulled down. This is likely in that a reference to the altar is to be expected, and also because the Hebrew word for altar, *mizbeah*, could much more easily have been mistaken for *mazzebah*, sacred pillar, by a careless scribe, than the word for sacred pole, *asherah*.

27. *made a privy of it*: in order to desecrate it and prevent it ever being used as a place of worship again. *privy* is rather an old-fashioned word for modern English; 'public lavatory' is a clearer translation. *as it is today*: i.e. in perpetuity. The judgements of God are never reversed. *

THE VERDICT ON JEHU

28, 29 Thus Jehu stamped out the worship of Baal in Israel. He did not however abandon the sins of Jeroboam son of Nebat who led Israel into sin, but he maintained the worship of the golden calves of Bethel and Dan.

30 Then the LORD said to Jehu, 'You have done well what is right in my eyes and have done to the house of Ahab all that it was in my mind to do. Therefore your sons to 31 the fourth generation shall sit on the throne of Israel.' But Jehu was not careful to follow the law of the LORD the God of Israel with all his heart; he did not abandon the sins of Jeroboam who led Israel into sin.

32 In those days the LORD began to work havoc on Israel, and Hazael struck at them in every corner of their terri- 33 tory eastwards from the Jordan: all the land of Gilead, Gad, Reuben, and Manasseh, from Aroer which is by the gorge of the Arnon, including Gilead and Bashan.

34 The other events of Jehu's reign, his achievements and his exploits, are recorded in the annals of the kings of 35 Israel. So Jehu rested with his forefathers and was buried in Samaria; and he was succeeded by his son Jehoahaz. 36 Jehu reigned over Israel in Samaria for twenty-eight years.

✻ There are two summaries of the reign of Jehu, verses 28–9 being one, and verses 30–1 the other. The latter is probably the original, but we cannot be sure. It summarizes all that has been told about Jehu; his destruction of the house of Ahab, rather than the destruction of the temple of Baal alone. Verses 28–9 could have been inserted by an editor who thought that too favourable an impression was being given of Jehu in the narrative of the destruction of the temple of Baal. This editor was at pains to point out that the temple of Baal was not the only pagan shrine in use in Israel.

29. *Jeroboam son of Nebat* revolted successfully against Rehoboam, Solomon's son, and thus created the kingdom of Israel. *the worship of the golden calves*: the editors regarded this as the sign that the northern kingdom had from its inception abandoned its loyalty to Yahweh. In fact the judgement displays the bias of the editors towards the southern kingdom. They regarded the temple at Jerusalem as the only legitimate Israelite shrine and condemned all others as idolatrous. Jeroboam's calves may only have been thrones upon which the invisible Yahweh was believed to sit. In this case Jeroboam's purpose was not as disloyal to the tradition of Israel as the editors imply. He was concerned to set up shrines for the worship of Yahweh at two centres in his kingdom, Bethel in the south and Dan in the north, so that his subjects would not need to visit the temple in Jerusalem which was the capital city of the king against whom he had revolted. The two shrines may have marked the northern and southern limits of the kingdom (cp. 1 Kings 12: 25–31 and the comment on that passage in the commentary in this series).

30. *to the fourth generation*: Jehu's dynasty did reign for four generations after him until his descendant Zechariah was murdered by a usurper (15: 12).

31. The deuteronomists believed that God dealt with both nations and individuals according to strict and rigid principles of retributive justice, rewarding the good and punishing the wicked, and it was one of the purposes of their history to

demonstrate the working out of this principle so that their readers would be encouraged to do good and deterred from doing evil. For them the fact that Jehu's family kept the throne for four generations was the mark of God's approval of what Jehu had done. Yet that approval was not complete as was shown in the fact that the dynasty did not keep the throne for ever. To account for this limited approval for Jehu, they point out that Jehu destroyed Baal worship but did not remove the 'idolatries' introduced into the northern kingdom by Jeroboam I.

32. Here the editors offer further evidence that God did not wholly approve of Jehu's work. Clearly Jehu's revolt and the change of political policy which it involved left Israel considerably weakened. Hazael, the king of Damascus, Israel's strong rival, took full advantage of this situation. He particularly coveted the Transjordan territories because they were very fertile.

33. *all the land of Gilead...Manasseh*: this seems to have been added by an editor, probably during the period of the exile, for the benefit of readers who, he thought, would not know the full extent of the *territory eastwards from the Jordan*. *the Arnon* is a river which empties itself into the east side of the Dead Sea. For much of its course it flows in a steep gorge. It was accepted as the southern border of Israel on the east side of the Jordan, and the northern border of Moab (see map on p. 30).

34–6. Jehu has been presented by the deuteronomists as a king raised up by God to reform the religious life of the people. This view is an oversimplification. Jehu was probably a military adventurer who saw in the sickness of King Jehoram an opportunity for seizing the throne for himself. Since the reigning dynasty of Ahab was so closely linked with the Phoenician states (Jezebel being a Phoenician princess) an attempt to overthrow them was bound to involve an attack upon the Baal cult and its supporters. This cult had been imported by Ahab from Phoenicia. It is doubtful whether

Jehu had any genuine interest in religious reform for its own sake, but his attitude made him a natural ally of Elisha. His revolt and the new policies which developed from it led to a period of political weakness. Israel was isolated from former allies and at the mercy of the strong northern neighbour, Hazael of Damascus. When Shalmanezer III, the Assyrian emperor, attacked Damascus in 841 B.C. Jehu paid tribute. Either he was not strong enough to join in an alliance against the Assyrians as Omri had done, or considered Damascus the greater enemy. Shalmanezer recorded details of his victories on an obelisk of black limestone which he erected in the main square of Nimrud his capital city. It was discovered by A. H. Layard in 1846 and presented by him to the British Museum. The Black Obelisk, as it is called, has a picture carved in bas-relief of Jehu doing homage to the Assyrian emperor. It records, 'I received the tribute of the people of Tyre, Sidon, and of Jehu, son of Omri.' The description of Jehu as 'son of Omri' is ironic! It indicates the impact Omri had made upon the Assyrians in that later kings were called sons of Omri. More details of the Black Obelisk can be found in *Old Testament Illustrations* in this series, pp. 85–6.

All this might seem to detract from the deuteronomists' favourable view of Jehu in that he was not very successful, and therefore by their yardstick of retributive justice could not have been blessed by God. On a longer view, they could claim justification for their judgement in that the reign of Jeroboam II, Jehu's greatgrandson, was perhaps the most prosperous in the whole history of the northern kingdom. ✶

Kings of Israel and Judah

✻ In this section of the narrative, chapters 11–15, the story is told of the two kingdoms to the accession of Ahaz to the throne of Judah in 735 B.C. During this period, Israel for a short time under Jeroboam II (786–746 B.C.) grew strong and powerful again, but after his death the country quickly declined. The kingdom was then ruled by a succession of short-lived usurpers and the country fell into ever greater decay. The cause of this was the pressure of Assyria upon Israel and her neighbours. Assyria was able to isolate the kingdoms from each other and prevent any grand alliance such as had earlier successfully opposed her at Qarqar in 853 B.C. So one by one the kingdoms were defeated. At first when the Assyrian pressure was on Aram, Israel's northern neighbour and rival, Israel had a time of prosperity. The territory along the border which Aram had taken was recovered and Israel seemed superficially to be recovering her old strength. But it was only for a time. Once Damascus had fallen and Aram been annexed as a province of the Assyrian Empire, then pressure was exerted against Israel. Prosperity disappeared and the kingdom of Israel began to decline. Such are the facts of the political history, but the deuteronomists did not write their history from this point of view. They gave almost too little attention to Jeroboam II, as they had done to Omri, but they had their own understanding of history and just how they presented the story is the important thing to notice. ✻

THE REIGN OF QUEEN ATHALIAH AND HER
ASSASSINATION

As soon as Athaliah mother of Ahaziah saw that **11** 1[a]
her son was dead, she set out to destroy all the royal
line. But Jehosheba daughter of King Joram, sister of 2
Ahaziah, took Ahaziah's son Joash and stole him away
from among the princes who were being murdered; she
put[b] him and his nurse in a bedchamber where he was
hidden from Athaliah and was not put to death. He 3
remained concealed with her in the house of the LORD for
six years, while Athaliah ruled the country. In the seventh 4
year Jehoiada sent for the captains of units of a hundred,
both of the Carites and of the guards, and he brought
them into the house of the LORD; he made an agreement
with them and put them on their oath in the house of the
LORD, and showed them the king's son, and gave them 5
the following orders: 'One third of you who are on duty
on the sabbath are to be on guard[c] in the palace; the rest 6
of you are to be on special duty in the house of the LORD,
one third at the Sur Gate and the other third at the gate
with[d] the outrunners. Your two companies who are off 7
duty on the sabbath shall be on duty for the king in the
house of the LORD. So you shall be on guard round the 8
king, each man with his arms at the ready, and anyone
who comes near the ranks is to be put to death; you must
be with the king wherever he goes.'

The captains carried out the orders of Jehoiada the 9

[a] *Verses 1–20: cp. 2 Chr. 22: 10 – 23: 21.*
[b] she put: *prob. rdg., cp. 2 Chr. 22: 11; Heb. om.*
[c] are to be on guard: *so Pesh.; Heb.* who keep guard.
[d] *Or* behind.

priest to the letter. Each took his men, both those who
came on duty on the sabbath and those who came off, and
10 came to Jehoiada. The priest handed out to the captains
King David's spears[a] and shields, which were in the house
11 of the LORD. Then the guards took up their stations, each
man carrying his arms at the ready, from corner to corner
of the house to north and south,[b] surrounding the king.
12 Then he brought out the king's son, put the crown on his
head, handed him the warrant and anointed him king.
The people[c] clapped their hands and shouted, 'Long live
13 the king.' When Athaliah heard the noise made by the
guards and[d] the people, she came into the house of the
14 LORD where the people were and found the king standing,
as was the custom, on the dais,[e] amidst outbursts of song
and fanfares of trumpets in his honour, and all the populace rejoicing and blowing trumpets. Then Athaliah rent
15 her clothes and cried, 'Treason! Treason!' Jehoiada the
priest gave orders to the captains in command of the
troops: 'Bring her outside the precincts and put to the
sword anyone in attendance on her'; for the priest said,
'She shall not be put to death in the house of the LORD.'
16 So they laid hands on her and took her out by the entry
for horses to the royal palace, and there she was put to
death.

17   Then Jehoiada made a covenant between the LORD and
the king and people that they should be the LORD's
18 people, and also between the king and the people. And
all the people went into the temple of Baal and pulled it

[a] *So Sept., cp. 2 Chr. 23: 9; Heb.* spear.
[b] *Prob. rdg.; Heb. adds* of the altar and the house.
[c] *So Luc. Sept.; Heb. om.*
[d] *So Pesh.; Heb. om.*   [e] *Or* by the pillar.

down; they smashed to pieces its altars and images, and they slew Mattan the priest of Baal before the altars. Then Jehoiada set a watch over the house of the LORD; he took 19 the captains of units of a hundred, the Carites and the guards and all the people, and they escorted the king from the house of the LORD through the Gate of the Guards to the royal palace, and seated him on the royal throne. The 20 whole people rejoiced and the city was tranquil. That is how Athaliah was put to the sword in the royal palace.

* Although Athaliah ruled Judah for six years, we are given no details of her reign other than the manner of her accession. The story concentrates on her death, and gives considerable detail about its circumstances. The reason for this is that Athaliah was a daughter of Ahab and Jezebel, and with the description of her death, the editors were indicating how all the consequences of that marriage were removed from Judah as well as Israel. For them her murder was an act of purification. By it Judah showed that she was ready to cleanse herself from the influence of Canaan. It was this interest which probably led to the inclusion of verses 13–18a, originally a separate account of Athaliah's death. (Some scholars have thought that verses 1–12 and 18b–20 are an account derived from the priests in Jerusalem, and 13–18a a popular account of the event.) They emphasize that the whole people approved of Athaliah's death, rededicated themselves to the service of Yahweh and destroyed the alien temple of Baal. Thus the whole narrative presents Athaliah's death as a part of a religious reform which foreshadowed the even greater reform of Josiah which was to come later.

1. Athaliah's destruction of *all the royal line* was aimed at protecting her own position. Jehu as king of Israel would be an enemy who could easily incite a king of Judah to murder her. She thought that by making herself queen, and removing all possible rivals she would protect her life.

2. Jehosheba must have been a daughter of Joram by another wife. The Chronicler claims that she was wife of Jehoiada (2 Chron. 22:11) which would account for Joash being securely hidden in the temple for six years. *she put*: a Hebrew word has been omitted probably through the error of a scribe.

4. Jehoiada was the priest (verse 9); probably the leader of the temple priests if he was in fact the son-in-law of the late king. *the Carites* were foreign mercenaries. They may be the Kerethites of 2 Sam. 20:23. Both groups were probably recruited from the Philistines.

5. *the following orders*: the orders are not easy to understand, though their general meaning is clear. The whole guard was to assemble in the temple, both to protect the king and to show their loyalty to him. The third who were carrying out their normal duty of 'guarding the palace' (which included the temple) were to be joined by the rest of the guard acting as a special guard in the temple itself. All were to guard the king against enemies.

6. This verse is probably an addition to the text added to give details about the positions of the extra guards. The position of *the Sur Gate* is not known. The Hebrew, translated *the gate with the outrunners*, is difficult. It refers to another unknown gate. The precise meaning of the name is lost to us.

10. *King David's spears and shields*: we have no other record of David having left such weapons for the temple. They may have been made from the metal David captured from Hadadezer, king of Zobah (2 Sam. 8:7-8). Solomon had given 'shields of gold' to the temple, but these were pillaged by Pharaoh Shishak and replaced by Rehoboam with bronze copies (1 Kings 14:26-8). These weapons were ceremonial ones, carried in the presence of the king, and their use here was to demonstrate Joash's legitimacy and the guards' loyalty to him. The N.E.B. has the plural, *spears*. There may have been one spear only (see the N.E.B. footnote) which had the same symbolism as a military standard.

11. The words in the N.E.B. footnote, 'of the altar and the

house', which are a part of the Hebrew text, give a detail whose precise meaning is not clear to us. We have no full or clear description of the temple.

12. This is one of the clearest descriptions in the Old Testament of a king's coronation. Joash was *brought out* from the temple on to the great open space before it where sacrifices were offered. The *crown* was the symbol of consecration, and in the Hebrew has that meaning. It was some object worn on the head to mark that significance. It may have been a crown, or a band of gold, or even, as has been suggested, a golden flower worn in the hair. Saul had such a 'crown' which was removed from his body by the Amalekite who killed him, and handed to David (2 Sam. 1: 10). Saul also had an 'armlet' which marked his royal status. It has been suggested that Jehoiada handed such an armlet to Joash here rather than *the warrant*. Such a change of the text is unjustifiable. The consecration of the king meant that he undertook to rule his people in accordance with God's will. The warrant, or 'testimony' (Revised Standard Version), could have been a copy of the law by which the king would conduct his reign. The kings of Judah were thus not absolute monarchs. They were not regarded as divine beings whose every word conveyed the authority of the gods. Rather, they were Yahweh's anointed, and as such wielded his authority, but his word was also revealed to other servants, to priests and prophets, and their work placed a limit on the authority of the king. It is that limit, the obligation to rule in accordance with God's will, which is symbolized by the giving of the warrant. Anointing signified the endowment with the spirit, a gift of energy from God to ensure the completion of the work which had been laid on the king. Since the kings of Judah were not absolute monarchs, it was appropriate that the people should witness the coronation and assent to it. The words, *the people*, are absent in the Hebrew but have been added on the authority of the Versions quoted in the N.E.B. footnote.

13–18a. This is a second description of the coronation

added to the official account from a lay source. There seems to be a slight difference between the two sources regarding the place where Athaliah was actually killed, cp. verses 16 and 20.

14. Athaliah, when alerted by the noise, realized immediately from what she saw that a coronation was in progress. *she came into the house of the LORD* must mean that she entered the temple precincts. The ceremony took place in the open in front of the temple where all could see. There was a particular place where kings were crowned and it may have been a raised platform. The Hebrew can mean 'a standing place', hence *dais*, but it is more likely that the king was crowned near one of the two great pillars which flanked the entrance to the temple. In this case, 'by the pillar' (N.E.B. footnote) should be read. (The Hebrew word can mean 'pillar'.) It is not stated which pillar was associated with coronations, but it was probably the pillar on the right hand, Jachin. This name means, 'It shall stand' (cp. 1 Kings 7: 21). *populace* translates a Hebrew phrase *'am ha'arets* whose exact meaning is uncertain. In much later times it was used by the Pharisees as a term of contempt to describe the great mass of the ordinary Jewish population who had not acquired the zeal and knowledge which the Pharisees considered essential for a proper devotion to the law. It has been suggested that in the period before the exile it described a particular social class, free-born Israelites who lived off their own land. If this is so, that class may have had the right by long-standing custom to take part in a coronation. Their assent to it could have been necessary, though there is no evidence for such a practice.

15. *She shall not be put to death*: a violent death would defile the holiness of the temple, which was a place of sanctuary.

16. *the entry for horses*: this may have been the same as the Horse Gate mentioned by Jeremiah (31: 40).

17. *Jehoiada made a covenant*: two covenants are mentioned here, the one religious in purpose, the other political. There is a clear similarity in the case of the first covenant with that made

later by Josiah as a part of his reform; cp. 23: 1–3. That reform was so important to the editors, and so normative in their eyes for all that the relations between God and his people should be, that the editors may have modelled a similar covenant here on the Josianic pattern. On the other hand, this may be plain description of what happened and some scholars, viewing it so, have seen it as an example of the covenant-making that they believe was the foundation of Israelite kingship. In their view all kings of Judah from David onwards entered into covenant with God and the people that the nation should be the people of God, and being the people of God involved living out the terms of the covenant. It was this view of kingship which was challenged by Omri and the Canaanite influences which he and his successors brought into Israel, and through Israel into Judah. There is little direct evidence for such covenant-making, though Deut. 27 and Josh. 24 have been claimed as examples. On the other hand, it can be argued that such covenant-making was normally taken for granted and only specifically mentioned in special cases such as this one, when the apostasy of Athaliah called for a particular intense renewal of the covenant. The political covenant, *between the king and the people*, has called forth less comment. Some scholars, who have accepted the historicity of the religious covenant, have viewed this as unhistorical, an expression of the covenant idea in later times when the religious and the political were separated. Yet it may be that the political covenant was the earlier and original one, and the religious covenant an attempt to restate it in terms more acceptable to the theology of the editors.

18. *the temple of Baal*: this would have been the temple of the cult imported into Jerusalem from Samaria by Athaliah as a part of her marriage settlement. She and her followers probably did not consider such worship to involve disloyalty to Yahweh as the deuteronomists did. The destruction of this temple, as in the case of the destruction of the similar temple in Samaria (10: 17–28), was at least in part inspired by political

motives. *Then Jehoiada set a watch*: here the original story is resumed from verse 12. The purpose of the watch may have been to prevent Athaliah taking possession of the temple. There was no mention of her death in this source until verse 20.

19. *seated him on the royal throne*: this was a part of the coronation. One of the chief functions of the king was to dispense justice and thus ensure that society was just and righteous. The making of the covenant, and the handing over of 'the warrant', both symbolized that. Once the king had sworn so to rule, he was seated on the throne from which he daily dispensed justice to his people. ✷

THE REIGN OF JOASH IN JUDAH

21;*ab* **12** Joash was seven years old when he became king. In the seventh year of Jehu, Joash became king, and he reigned in Jerusalem for forty years; his mother was Zibiah of 2 Beersheba. He did what was right in the eyes of the LORD 3 all his days, as Jehoiada the priest had taught him. The hill-shrines, however, were allowed to remain; the people still continued to sacrifice and made smoke-offerings there.

4   Then Joash ordered the priests to take*c* all the silver brought as holy-gifts into the house of the LORD, the silver for which each man was assessed,*d* the silver for the persons assessed under his name, and any silver which any 5 man brought voluntarily to the house of the LORD. He ordered the priests, also, each to make a contribution from his own funds, and to repair the house wherever it

[a] *12: 1 in Heb.*
[b] *11: 21 – 12: 15: cp. 2 Chr. 24: 1–14.*
[c] to take: *so Sept.; Heb. om.*
[d] the silver...assessed: *prob. rdg.; Heb. obscure.*

was found necessary. But in the twenty-third year of the 6
reign of Joash the priests had still not carried out the
repairs to the house. King Joash summoned Jehoiada the 7
priest and the other priests and said to them, 'Why are
you not repairing the house? Henceforth you need not
contribute from your own funds for the repair of the
house.' So the priests agreed neither to receive money 8
from the people nor to undertake the repairs of the house.
Then Jehoiada the priest took a chest and bored a hole in 9
the lid and put it beside the altar on the right side going
into the house of the LORD, and the priests on duty at the
entrance put in it all the money brought into the house of
the LORD. And whenever they saw that the chest was well 10
filled, the king's secretary and the high priest came and
melted down the silver found in the house of the LORD
and weighed it. When it had been checked, they gave the 11
silver to the foremen over the work in the house of the
LORD and they paid the carpenters and the builders
working on the temple and the masons and the stone- 12
cutters; they used it also to buy timber and hewn stone
for the repairs and for all other expenses connected with
them. They did not use the silver brought into the house 13
of the LORD to make silver cups, snuffers, tossing-bowls,
trumpets, or any gold or silver vessels; but they paid it to 14
the workmen and used it for the repairs. No account was 15
demanded from the foremen to whom the money was
given for the payment of the workmen, for they were
acting on trust. Money from guilt-offerings and sin- 16
offerings was not brought into the house of the LORD: it
belonged to the priests.

Then Hazael king of Aram came up and attacked Gath 17

18 and took it; and he moved on against Jerusalem. But Joash king of Judah took all the holy-gifts that Jehoshaphat, Joram, and Ahaziah his forefathers, kings of Judah, had dedicated, and his own holy-gifts, and all the gold that was found in the treasuries of the house of the LORD and in the royal palace, and sent them to Hazael king of Aram; and he withdrew from Jerusalem.

19 　The other acts and events of the reign of Joash are
20*a* recorded in the annals of the kings of Judah. His servants revolted against him and struck him down in the house of
21 Millo on the descent to Silla. It was his servants Jozachar*b* son of Shimeath and Jehozabad son of Shomer who struck the fatal blow; and he was buried with his forefathers in the city of David. He was succeeded by his son Amaziah.

⁎ We are only told two things about the long reign of Joash. First, he caused the temple to be repaired. This mattered to the editors because of the importance they attached to the temple and its wellbeing. Secondly, he bought off Hazael of Aram who had attacked some of his territory. The fact that Hazael could attack Judah makes very plain the weakness of Israel. The two incidents are unrelated to each other but are included because they were considered to be significant by the editors. They may have viewed the repair of the temple as something of a cleansing after the apostasy of Athaliah's reign, and Joash's assassination may have been to them a punishment for his denuding the temple of its treasure to buy off Hazael.

21. *Joash*: there is a variant spelling of the king's name here in the Hebrew which has sometimes been put into English as

[a] *Verses 20, 21: cp. 2 Chr. 24: 25–7.*
[b] *So some MSS.; others* Jozabad.

Jehoash. The N.E.B. has ignored this so as not to confuse the reader.

12: 1. *forty years*: this may be a conventional number. Forty years was used in this way in Judg. 5: 31 and 8: 28, but there is nothing inherently improbable in a child who becomes king at seven years old reigning for forty years.

3. The editorial approval is only partial. No kings are totally approved of by the editors with the exception of Hezekiah and Josiah, both of whom instigated reforms of the temple. *smoke-offerings*: the carcases of sacrificial animals were burned as an offering to God.

4. A quite different account of the repair of the temple is given in Chronicles (2 Chron. 24). It would be surprising if this was the first which the temple had needed. Previous kings had probably financed necessary repairs from their own revenues. Joash instituted a new method of financing them. He may have been too poor to support the work himself. *the silver for which each man was assessed*: this may be a reference to the duty of each adult male to pay a half-shekel tax to the temple. The law is given in Exod. 30: 13. This refers to the practice after the exile but the custom may have been started by Joash. *the silver for the persons assessed under his name*: this seems to refer to the practice of redeeming a vow made on the life of some other person (cp. Lev. 27: 2). In earlier times such a vow would have involved human sacrifice, Jephthah's daughter being an example (Judg. 11: 30–40). Later it was commuted for a money payment.

5. *each to make a contribution from his own funds*: the Revised Standard Version translates, 'each from his acquaintance'. There is a Hebrew word here which in post-biblical Hebrew means 'acquaintance'. But that sense does not fit here. On the basis of a similar word in an Ugaritic text, it has been suggested that here it refers to some kind of cultic official, i.e. that each priest had an assistant whose duty it was to receive and value the offerings given to the priest. The king is now ordering that each priest should set aside a portion of such

offerings for the repair of the temple. This 'income tax' proved to be as unpopular then as it has been since.

7. *Henceforth you need not...*: the Hebrew is not clear, but even so the N.E.B. seems to have missed the sense. The king commanded, 'Henceforth you shall not make a contribution but you shall hand over all the money for the repair of the house.'

8. This could only have referred to the priest's share of a particular kind of offering and not to every offering made (see verse 16 below).

9. *beside the altar*: this must refer to the altar of sacrifice which stood in the court in front of the temple (cp. 16: 14), but the description is not clear. It has been suggested that the Hebrew word for altar is a mistake. There may be the same confusion between *mizbeaḥ*, 'altar', and *mazzebah*, 'sacred pillar', as in 10: 26 (see p. 102). *Mazzebah* is usually used of those stone pillars which the Canaanites used as cultic objects. That association may have led to its being changed here. If the original word was 'pillar', then the box was placed beside the standing pillar 'Jachin' on the right side of the entrance to the temple.

10. *high priest* was only used as a title in the second temple, which was built after the exile. Some scholars would omit *high* as a scribal error, but there must have been a chief priest. *melted down...weighed it*: there was no coinage at this time, so the silver was melted down and made into ingots on which the temple mark would be stamped. The verb translated *melted down* has traditionally been linked with another similar verb which means 'bundled up'. Other translations have maintained this link, e.g. the Revised Standard Version's 'counted and tied up in bags the money', but archaeological evidence, which has shown that some temples had foundries attached to them, supports the N.E.B.

13. The vessels were all used in the religious ceremonies of the temple. The *tossing-bowls* were used for pouring the blood of the sacrifices on the altar. Details about the vessels are given

in the description of the building of the temple in 1 Kings 7: 49–50. The priests could have used the silver to make new vessels and then taken those that had been replaced for themselves, thus using the gift for themselves rather than the upkeep of the temple.

16. *guilt-offerings* were offerings made to atone for offences against God that the offerer had committed. Such offences could be deliberate or unconscious, moral or ritual. The way in which the ancient Israelites made no distinction as to motive or intention but were concerned only with acts, and made no distinction as to the moral quality of an act, is one of the greatest differences between their view of religion and more modern ways of thinking. *sin-offerings* were very like guilt-offerings. The regulations governing the former are set out in Lev. 4, and for the latter in Lev. 5, though these regulations as they stand refer to the period of the second temple after the exile.

17. *Gath*: the name means 'wine press'. There was more than one place with this name, but by far the best known was the Gath which was one of the five cities of the Philistines. Goliath was a native of this Gath (1 Sam. 17: 4). Its site is uncertain but it was the nearest Philistine city to Judah. According to Chronicles Rehoboam fortified it (2 Chron. 11: 8) and, if this report is accurate, the city from that time may have been regarded as Judaean. But it is strange that Hazael should attack a city so far from his own border, and so the Gath referred to here may be another city further to the north.

20. *revolted against him*: no reason is given. His policies could have so antagonized the priests that they encouraged his assassination. The site of Silla is unknown. It may have been a suburb of Jerusalem. Solomon built 'the Millo' at Jerusalem (1 Kings 9: 15) though we are not sure what it was. It may have been a fortress or the filling-in of a hollow to make an area of level ground, or terracing to allow houses to be built on the steep slopes of the hill-side. This last suggestion would fit best here; though we cannot be completely certain that the Millo here is Solomon's. The word means 'a filling'.

21. *Jozachar*: or 'Jozabad' (N.E.B. footnote). The manuscript difference is due to the similarity of the Hebrew letters. ✳

THE REIGN OF JEHOAHAZ IN ISRAEL

13 In the twenty-third year of Joash son of Ahaziah king of Judah, Jehoahaz son of Jehu became king over Israel in 2 Samaria and he reigned seventeen years. He did what was wrong in the eyes of the LORD and continued the sinful practices of Jeroboam son of Nebat who led Israel into 3 sin, and did not give them up. So the LORD was roused to anger against Israel and he made them subject for some years to Hazael king of Aram and Ben-hadad son of 4 Hazael. Then Jehoahaz sought to placate the LORD, and the LORD heard his prayer, for he saw how the king of 5 Aram oppressed Israel. The LORD appointed a deliverer for Israel, who rescued them from[a] the power of Aram, and the Israelites settled down again in their own homes. 6 But they did not give up the sinful practices of the house of Jeroboam who led Israel into sin, but continued[b] in 7 them; the goddess Asherah[c] remained in Samaria. Hazael had left Jehoahaz no armed force except fifty horsemen, ten chariots, and ten thousand infantry; all the rest the king of Aram had destroyed and made like dust under foot.

8 The other events of the reign of Jehoahaz, and all his achievements and his exploits, are recorded in the annals 9 of the kings of Israel. So Jehoahaz rested with his fore-

[a] who rescued them from: *so Luc. Sept.; Heb.* they came out of.
[b] *So Sept.; Heb.* he continued.
[c] the goddess Asherah: *or* the sacred pole.

fathers and was buried in Samaria; and he was succeeded
by his son Jehoash.

✶ Jehoahaz reaped the political consequences of his father's
work. The break with the Phoenician allies left Israel even
more at the mercy of her northern neighbour Aram. Israel's
weakness continued through the reign of Jehoahaz and his son
Jehoash, and the situation was only changed by renewed
pressure on Aram by the Assyrians, which took place during
the reign of Jeroboam II, the son of Jehoash.

2. *So the LORD was roused to anger*: as always the editors
accounted for political and military defeat by religious
apostasy. The surprising thing is that defeat should have happened so quickly after the reformation inspired by Jehu. The
answer given here is that the reformation did not go far
enough, cp. the references to 'the goddess Asherah' in verse 6.
There is a memory of this time in the oracle of the prophet
Amos against Damascus (Amos 1: 3–5) written some fifty
years after the events.

4–6. Many scholars have thought that these three verses are
an addition to the original text. Verse 7 follows naturally
after verse 3 and indicates just how weak Jehoahaz became as
a result of the attacks of Aram. In the light of verse 7 it seems
difficult to believe that any *deliverer* was appointed during the
reign of Jehoahaz. One suggestion is that the deliverer referred
to was King Jeroboam II, Jehoahaz's grandson, in whose
reign Israel became strong again. If this is so, the reference here
is out of order but was inserted by the editors to show that
even in the worst times, God did not abandon his people. His
wrath had for its purpose their discipline and not their destruction (cp. 14: 27). Another suggestion is that the deliverer
was Elisha who was always able and ready to show the people
the way to deliverance but was impeded by feeble kings. The
verses then are to be linked with the story of the death of
Elisha which follows later in the chapter.

A further possibility is that they referred to someone who curbed the power of Aram for a time. Adadnirari III of Assyria has been suggested since he invaded Syria in 806 B.C., but, if we are to take verse 7 seriously, no attack upon Aram at this time made any difference to the fortunes of Jehoahaz. The work of the deliverer is described in much the same way as that of the Judges (cp. Judg. 2: 16–23) and so may well be an editorial reference to Jeroboam II. *Asherah* was the name of a Canaanite goddess and also of the pole which was erected in sanctuaries to symbolize her presence (see comment at 10: 26). Ahab had set up such a pole in the temple of Baal which he built in Samaria (1 Kings 16: 33) but this had been destroyed by Jehu (10: 26). Either Jehoahaz set up a second pillar, or this is an editorial comment which uses Asherah as a symbol of Canaanite influence.

7. *Hazael*: in the Hebrew the subject of the verb is not specified. 'He' can refer to Hazael as the N.E.B. suggests or to God. If this verse follows verse 3 then Hazael is clearly the subject of the verb. According to Assyrian records Ahab had taken 2000 chariots and 10,000 footmen to the battle at Qarqar. ✳

THE REIGN OF JEHOASH IN ISRAEL

10 In the thirty-ninth[a] year of Joash king of Judah, Jehoash son of Jehoahaz became king over Israel in
11 Samaria and reigned sixteen years. He did what was wrong in the eyes of the LORD; he did not give up any of the sinful practices of Jeroboam son of Nebat who led Israel
12 into sin, but continued in them. The other events of the reign of Jehoash, all his achievements, his exploits and his war with Amaziah king of Judah, are recorded in the
13 annals of the kings of Israel. So Jehoash rested with his

[a] *So some Sept. MSS.; Heb.* thirty-seventh.

forefathers and was buried in Samaria with the kings of
Israel, and Jeroboam sat upon his throne.

Elisha fell ill and lay on his deathbed, and Jehoash king 14
of Israel went down to him and wept over him and said,
'My father! My father, the chariots and the horsemen of
Israel!' 'Take bow and arrows', said Elisha, and he took 15
bow and arrows. 'Put your hand to the bow', said the 16
prophet. He did so, and Elisha laid his hands on those of
the king. Then he said, 'Open the window toward the 17
east'; he opened it and Elisha told him to shoot, and he
shot. Then the prophet said, 'An arrow for the LORD's
victory, an arrow for victory over Aram! You will defeat
Aram utterly at Aphek'; and he added, 'Now take up 18
your arrows.' When the king had taken them, Elisha
said, 'Strike the ground with them.' He struck three times
and stopped. The man of God was furious with him and 19
said, 'You should have struck five or six times; then you
would have defeated Aram utterly; as it is, you will strike
Aram three times and no more.'

Then Elisha died and was buried.   20

Year by year Moabite raiders used to invade the land. 21
Once some men were burying a dead man when they
caught sight of the raiders. They threw the body into the
grave of Elisha and made off;[a] when the body touched
the prophet's bones, the man came to life and rose to his
feet.

All through the reign of Jehoahaz, Hazael king of Aram 22
oppressed Israel. But the LORD was gracious and took 23
pity on them; because of his covenant with Abraham,
Isaac, and Jacob, he looked on them with favour and was

[a] *So Luc. Sept.; Heb.* and he made off.

unwilling to destroy them; nor has he even yet banished
24 them from his sight. When Hazael king of Aram died
25 and was succeeded by his son Ben-hadad, Jehoash son of
Jehoahaz recaptured the cities which Ben-hadad had taken
in war from Jehoahaz his father; three times Jehoash
defeated him and recovered the cities of Israel.

* The conventional formula which sums up the king's reign
is given at 14: 15–16 following an account of the reign of
Amaziah of Judah – the two kings went to war and Amaziah
was defeated – but the material directly relating to the reign
of Jehoash is given in the following verses. It is a collection of
originally independent pieces of information whose connect-
ing link is the king's partial success against Aram.

10. *the thirty-ninth year*: from the information given in
13: 1, this is what we should expect, and so it appears in some
Greek manuscripts; but others and the Hebrew have 'thirty-
seventh' (N.E.B. footnote), and this should be read, since the
datings in Kings are difficult (see p. 12).

12–13. These verses are out of place. They duplicate the
ending given at 14: 15–16 and they are not written in the
conventional phraseology. They were probably added by a
scribe.

14. *Elisha fell ill*: this is the first reference to Elisha since 9: 1
where he was said to have sent a disciple to anoint Jehu, which
was forty-five years before Jehoash became king. The story is
given here to account for Jehoash's three victories against
Aram. *the chariots and the horsemen of Israel*: Elisha himself had
used these words of his master Elijah (2: 12). The meaning is
not completely clear, but the words seem to imply that the
possession of a true prophet gave such protection to the
country as other kings looked for from cavalry and chariotry.
The king is distressed because with the death of the prophet
such a force will be lost to him (see note on 2: 11).

15–19. Elisha was trying to show the king that he was

handing over power to him to defend Israel against her chief enemy. Such actions are often described as prophetic symbolic acts and many of the prophets seem to have used them. They believed that the words they spoke or the actions they performed as God's prophet must be fulfilled. It was not that the prophet was setting out to compel God to act in a particular way, which was advantageous to him or his clients, but that God was allowing his servants through his prophet to understand more fully his will and his purposes and bring their own purposes into accordance with it. Here *Elisha laid his hands on those of the king* to show that the king's action and God's action were one, but then afterwards, when the king struck the ground with the arrows, the feebleness of his resolution became apparent. He must have known that the striking was symbolic and showed that he had not the will or the character to be God's instrument for the task that was being laid upon him.

21. This is a legend which has been inserted here. It indicates the reverence in which Elisha was held by his contemporaries and successors, and the spiritual power that they believed to have been in him. The Hebrews at this time believed that life after death was a weak and feeble affair to be postponed as long as possible. So one of the greatest blessings that God could confer was a long life, and great age, as here of Elisha, was a sign of special blessing from God. That power to revive a corpse should still be in the bones of Elisha long after death was an indication of the intensity of the power that was believed to have been in him during his lifetime.

23. This may have been added to the narrative in the final revision during the exile. It was only then that the idea of a covenant with the patriarchs became prominent. If so, the purpose of this verse is to offer comfort to those who were reading the book in the Babylonian exile. The editor understood foreign oppression as being used by God to change his people rather than destroy them, and so it was in the circumstances of the readers, *nor has he even yet banished them from his sight*.

24–5. This is the fulfilment of Elisha's word. ✶

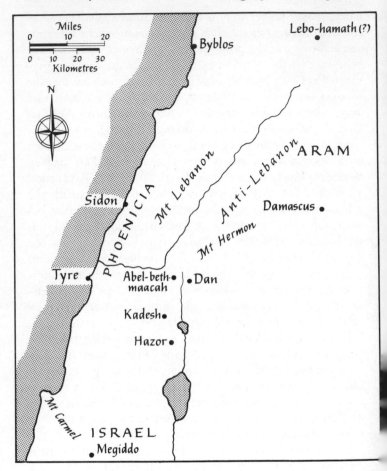

4. The kingdoms of Aram and Phoenicia

THE REIGN OF AMAZIAH IN JUDAH

In the second year of Jehoash son of Jehoahaz king of **14** 1*ᵃ*
Israel, Amaziah son of Joash king of Judah succeeded his
father. He was twenty-five years old when he came to the 2
throne, and he reigned in Jerusalem for twenty-nine
years; his mother was Jehoaddin of Jerusalem. He did 3
what was right in the eyes of the LORD, yet not as his
forefather David had done; he followed his father Joash
in everything. The hill-shrines were allowed to remain; 4
the people continued to slaughter and burn sacrifices
there. When the royal power was firmly in his grasp, he 5
put to death those of his servants who had murdered the
king his father; but he spared the murderers' children in 6
obedience to the LORD's command written in the law of
Moses: 'Fathers shall not be put to death for their children,
nor children for their fathers; a man shall be put to death
only for his own sin.' He defeated ten thousand Edomites 7
in the Valley of Salt and captured Sela; he gave it the
name Joktheel, which it still bears.

Then Amaziah sent messengers to Jehoash son of 8*ᵇ*
Jehoahaz, son of Jehu, king of Israel, to propose a meeting.
But Jehoash king of Israel sent this answer to Amaziah 9
king of Judah: 'A thistle in Lebanon sent to a cedar in
Lebanon to say, "Give your daughter in marriage to my
son." But a wild beast in Lebanon, passing by, trampled
on the thistle. You have defeated Edom, it is true; and it 10
has gone to your head. Stay at home and enjoy your
triumph. Why should you involve yourself in disaster

[a] *Verses 1–6: cp. 2 Chr. 25: 1–4.*
[b] *Verses 8–14: cp. 2 Chr. 25: 17–24.*

and bring yourself to the ground, and Judah with you?'

11 But Amaziah would not listen; so Jehoash king of Israel marched out, and he and Amaziah king of Judah met one 12 another at Beth-shemesh in Judah. The men of Judah 13 were routed by Israel and fled to their homes. But Jehoash king of Israel captured Amaziah king of Judah, son of Joash, son of Ahaziah, at Beth-shemesh. He went to Jerusalem and broke down the city wall from the Gate of Ephraim to the Corner Gate, a distance of four hundred 14 cubits. He also took all the gold and silver and all the vessels found in the house of the LORD and in the treasuries of the royal palace, as well as hostages, and returned to Samaria.

15 The other events of the reign of Jehoash, and all his achievements, his exploits and his wars with Amaziah king of Judah, are recorded in the annals of the kings of 16 Israel. So Jehoash rested with his forefathers and was buried in Samaria with the kings of Israel; and he was succeeded by his son Jeroboam.

17^a Amaziah son of Joash, king of Judah, outlived Jehoash 18 son of Jehoahaz, king of Israel, by fifteen years. The other events of Amaziah's reign are recorded in the annals of 19 the kings of Judah. A conspiracy was formed against him in Jerusalem and he fled to Lachish; but they sent after 20 him to Lachish and put him to death there. Then his body was conveyed on horseback to Jerusalem, and there he 21 was buried with his forefathers in the city of David. The people of Judah took Azariah, now sixteen years old, and 22 made him king in succession to his father Amaziah. It was

[a] *Verses 17–22: cp. 2 Chr. 25: 25 – 26: 2.*

he who built Elath and restored it to Judah after the king rested with his forefathers.

✻ Because of the war which Amaziah provoked with Israel a large part of this section deals as much with Jehoash as with Amaziah and an editor has included the formal summary of the end of Jehoash's reign in it.

2. A reign of *twenty-nine years* does not agree with the information given in 13: 10 and 15: 1. This kind of disagreement occurs in several places in Kings (see p. 12).

6. In earlier times a man's family were regarded as being implicated in his actions. The responsibility and blame for them was thought to rest upon the family rather than the individual and punishment was meted out accordingly (cp. Josh. 7: 16-25). The putting to death of a man's children destroyed such hope of his name being preserved as a man might have since death was thought to be the end of all effective life. The deuteronomic law forbade the execution of children for this reason (Deut. 24: 16). This is in line with the general humanitarian tendencies of Deuteronomy. It is the law which is referred to here as *the law of Moses*.

7. David and Solomon had controlled Edom. It opened up the route to the Red Sea and made trade with Arabia possible. But the Edomites took every opportunity of re-asserting their independence, not least because the trade was so valuable. Solomon's successor, Joram, lost control over Edom (8: 20) and so Amaziah's re-assertion of Judah's authority in that region was a mark of strength. It was this strength and his success against Edom which led Amaziah to challenge Israel. *the Valley of Salt* has not been certainly identified. It was probably the Arabah, the part of the great rift valley which lay south of the Dead Sea. The site of Sela, the capital of Edom, is also uncertain. The name means 'rock' but it seems that it was not the place later known as Petra, which derives from the Greek word for 'rock'. *Joktheel*: to rename a place implied claiming control over it.

8. *to propose a meeting*: the N.E.B. has paraphrased the Hebrew. The Revised Standard Version translates more literally, 'Come, let us look one another in the face.' This was an idiomatic way of speaking which may well have implied much more than a meeting. The idiom is used again in verse 11 where the N.E.B. translates 'met'. There it clearly refers to a battle. So Amaziah may have thrown down a gauntlet rather than proposed a meeting.

9. *A thistle in Lebanon*...: a similar parable was used by Jotham against the men of Shechem (Judg. 9: 7–15).

11. *Beth-shemesh in Judah*: so described to avoid confusion with a place of the same name to the south of the Sea of Galilee. This Beth-shemesh was situated in the valley of Sorek some 24 miles (38½ km) west of Jerusalem (see map on p. 30). The reason why the battle took place here rather than on the northern border of Judah is not clear.

13. Jehoash *broke down the city wall* to make Jerusalem vulnerable to attack for some years to come and therefore no longer a threat to him. We no longer know the exact sites of the two gates mentioned, but *the Gate of Ephraim* was almost certainly the principal exit from the city to the north as the Damascus gate is now.

14. Jehoash seems to have had no respect for the temple at Jerusalem. He acted much as a king of any of the neighbouring states would have done. *hostages* are only mentioned in the Old Testament here and in the parallel passage in Chronicles (2 Chron. 25: 24). They may have been taken to ensure Amaziah's good behaviour in future, or against payment of further gold and silver.

15–16. The summary of the reign of Jehoash would be more appropriate at the end of chapter 13. It has been inserted here after the last mention of events that happened in the king's reign.

19. *A conspiracy was formed against him*: the people of Judah throughout the whole period of the kingdom remained loyal to the house of David so that there were no changes of

dynasty in Judah as there were in Israel. Unpopular kings were assassinated, as in the cases of Amaziah and his father, but the rightful heir was always allowed to succeed to the throne. Lachish was a Judaean city sited approximately 30 miles (48 km) south-west of Jerusalem on the road to Gaza (see map on p. 30). The site is now known as Tel ed-Duweir. It was excavated between 1932 and 1938. The most important finds were a series of letters written in Hebrew on pottery dating from the time of Jeremiah.

22. *It was he who built Elath*: it is not clear to whom *he* refers. If Azariah, then he must have continued his father's uncompleted conquest of Edom. Alternatively, *he* may refer to Amaziah and in that case this sentence has been added to make clear that the conquest of Edom mentioned earlier was complete. The king who *rested with his forefathers* then must have been Joash and the meaning is that Amaziah mounted his campaign against Edom as soon as he had full and complete control of the army. Previously he had probably acted as regent in the last years of his father's reign. Elath was a port on the Red Sea near Ezion-geber at the head of the Gulf of Aqaba from which the merchant ships sailed to Arabia (see map on p. xii). ✳

THE REIGN OF JEROBOAM II IN ISRAEL

In the fifteenth year of Amaziah son of Joash king of 23 Judah, Jeroboam son of Jehoash king of Israel became king in Samaria and reigned for forty-one years. He did what 24 was wrong in the eyes of the LORD; he did not give up the sinful practices of Jeroboam son of Nebat who led Israel into sin. He re-established the frontiers of Israel from 25 Lebo-hamath to the Sea of the Arabah, in fulfilment of the word of the LORD the God of Israel spoken by his servant the prophet Jonah son of Amittai, of Gath-hepher. For 26 the LORD had seen how bitterly Israel had suffered; no one

was safe, whether under the protection of his family or
27 not, and Israel was left defenceless. But the LORD had
made no threat to blot out the name of Israel under
heaven, and he saved them through Jeroboam son of
28 Jehoash. The other events of Jeroboam's reign, and all his
achievements, his exploits, the wars he fought and how he
recovered Damascus and Hamath in Jaudi for*a* Israel, are
29 recorded in the annals of the kings of Israel. So Jeroboam
rested with his forefathers the kings of Israel; and he was
succeeded by his son Zechariah.

* This brief reference to the reign of one of the most powerful and successful of the kings of Israel is further evidence that
the editors of Kings had a very different point of view from
that of modern historians. From their point of view the reign
of Jeroboam was lacking in incident and in interest and therefore they devoted to it only the minimum of space and attention. The fact that Jeroboam was in political terms an
important and successful king who extended his frontiers and
brought peace and prosperity to his subjects, was of no
importance to the editors except that they had to explain it in
terms of their own understanding of the meaning of history
(verses 26-7). If there had not been available to us other
material describing Israel in Jeroboam's time, we should have
known as little about it as we do of the reign of Omri. However, the prophet Amos lived and worked in Israel during the
reign of Jeroboam and from his oracles we can learn something of the power and affluence that existed in Israel at that
time. The success of Jeroboam's reign was ensured by a
combination of character and good fortune; he must have
possessed great powers of leadership and strength of character
to do what he did, but he was also lucky. His father and grandfather had both had to spend much of their time warding off

[a] in Jaudi for: *prob. rdg.; Heb.* to Judah in.

the attacks of their powerful and aggressive northern neighbour Aram. Jeroboam was spared this problem. During his
reign the Assyrians again began to move against the west and
this time their pressure fell upon Aram. In 773 B.C. Shalmaneser IV attacked Damascus, and after that it was only a
question of time before Aram was completely defeated and
absorbed into the Assyrian Empire. During that time the
pressure of Aram was removed from Israel and she could
expand once more. To many it seemed like a rebirth of former
glory. God had once more smiled on Israel and declared openly
by the might he had given to the Israelites that they were his
own chosen people. A few were more discerning and saw that
this time of prosperity was not the beginning of the millennium but the lull before the storm. What was happening in
Damascus could also soon happen in Samaria. In this period of
ease Israel was being given a warning; was being allowed an
opportunity to show her own true nature; and to learn a
lesson so that destruction should not also overtake her. But if
Israel's fate was to be different from that of Aram, then she
must exhibit a different character. Unfortunately the happenings of the reign of Jeroboam showed plainly that Israel was in
character and purposes to all intents identical with her neighbour. So Israel used the time of her respite to weave the rope
with which she was soon to be hanged. Amos condemned his
contemporaries for their refusal to accept the obligations of
the covenant. He preached the need for a justice which would
radically alter the whole structure of the greed-ridden society
which he saw around him, and confidently but sadly expected
a national destruction which would be God's judgement on a
disobedient people.

The editors of Kings in many ways shared Amos' view, but
they make no mention of it with reference to the reign of
Jeroboam. They simply record in the baldest way that Jeroboam's reign was the Indian summer of the northern kingdom.
For a short time Israel was as strong and powerful again as ever
she had been. Both they, and their readers who were living as

exiles in the Babylonian Empire, knew that the prosperity of Jeroboam's reign had no lasting political consequences. It disappeared as quickly as it had come. They saw its purpose as being to comfort their readers. 'The LORD had made no threat to blot out the name of Israel under heaven' (verse 27). This thought was inspired by Jeroboam's reign but it was directed as a word of comfort to their own contemporaries. They wrote their history to show that all things were under God's control. They believed that they knew God, and so could interpret his nature and his will. To a disobedient people he spoke in judgement, but his judgement was directed not to their destruction but to repentance and renewal, so the final message was hope and not despair.

25. *Lebo-hamath* was the traditional northern limit of Canaan. According to tradition Solomon's kingdom had reached that far (1 Kings 8: 65) and Amos spoke of it as the nation's most northerly point (Amos 6: 14). We are not quite sure where it was. Obviously since *Lebo* means 'entrance', it is likely to have been on the border of Hamath, perhaps at the northern, narrow end of the valley between the Lebanon and Anti-Lebanon mountains (see map on p. 126). *the Sea of the Arabah* was the Dead Sea. We know nothing other than this of *the prophet Jonah*. Clearly he was an enthusiast for national prosperity. It may be this characteristic which caused the anonymous author of the book of Jonah, written after the exile, to choose *Jonah son of Amittai* as the subject of his story. Gath-hepher was a village in Galilee a little to the north of Nazareth. It is now called Al-Meshed, and the reputed tomb of the prophet Jonah is still to be seen there.

26-7. This editorial comment is meant as a comfort to the readers living in exile in Babylon.

28. *he recovered Damascus*: this is exaggeration unless some words have been lost from the text and the meaning is that he recovered some territory from Damascus. The Hebrew of the following phrase is corrupt (see the N.E.B. footnote). *Hamath in Jaudi*: this also is an exaggeration. The Hebrew has 'Judah'

for *Jaudi*. The N.E.B. thinks *Jaudi*, a name for an area in north Syria known from Assyrian texts, has been changed to 'Judah' by a scribe who did not know what *Jaudi* meant. *

THE DECLINE OF ISRAEL

* Jeroboam II was the last effective king of Israel. His son Zechariah, who succeeded him, was very soon murdered by a usurper, and then in a space of twenty years there were five more kings, four of whom gained the throne by murdering his predecessor. The peace and prosperity that had marked Jeroboam's reign came to an end with his death and was succeeded by ever growing anarchy. The prophet Hosea was active in Israel at this time and many of his oracles provide vivid pictures of the political, social and moral disintegration of the community. Hosea was sure that this state of affairs was the result of the spiritual corruption of the people. They had abandoned their God and as a consequence lost all sure guidelines for social and political life. This was true so far as it went but it did not indicate the pressure which had been exerted on the national life and had brought these weaknesses to light. This pressure was the Assyrian ambition to control all the states of Syria and Palestine. While this pressure had been exerted against Aram, Israel had had a period of relative calm and prosperity, but shortly before Jeroboam's reign ended, a new Assyrian ruler appeared on the scene, Tiglath-pileser III, who was to pursue Assyrian objectives in Syria with even greater vigour than his predecessors. He took Damascus in 732 B.C. and incorporated Aram into his empire. From that time the full force of Assyrian pressure was exerted against Israel with the results that we have noted. *

THE REIGN OF AZARIAH IN JUDAH

In the twenty-seventh year of Jeroboam king of Israel, **15** Azariah[a] son of Amaziah king of Judah became king. He

[a] Uzziah *in verses 13, 30, 32, 34.*

2^a was sixteen years old when he came to the throne, and he
reigned in Jerusalem for fifty-two years; his mother was
3 Jecoliah of Jerusalem. He did what was right in the eyes
4 of the LORD, as Amaziah his father had done. But the
hill-shrines were allowed to remain; the people still con-
5^b tinued to slaughter and burn sacrifices there. The LORD
struck the king with leprosy,^c which he had till the day of
his death; he was relieved of all duties and lived in his
own house, while his son Jotham was comptroller of the
6 household and regent. The other acts and events of
Azariah's reign are recorded in the annals of the kings of
7 Judah. So he rested with his forefathers and was buried
with them in the city of David; and he was succeeded by
his son Jotham.

✴ 1. *Azariah* is sometimes in Kings called Uzziah (see the
N.E.B. footnote) and always referred to by that name in the
prophetic books. It has been suggested that one of the names
was that given to him at birth and the other a name that he
assumed when he became king. He had a very long reign of
which the editors give us no details. It is reasonable to suppose,
and such details as are given in Chronicles agree, that Judah
during this time shared the peace and prosperity that Israel
enjoyed.

4. The editors looked upon the worship of *the hill-shrines* as
being a dangerous source of Canaanite influence. Hence they
were always critical of their use. This verse may be intended
as a simple statement of fact, but it is more likely that it has
been introduced by the editors to explain why a king who
'did what was right in the eyes of the LORD' was struck with
leprosy. 'Hill-shrine' translates a Hebrew word, *bamah*, which

[a] *Verses 2, 3: cp. 2 Chr. 26: 3, 4.*
[b] *Verses 5–7: cp. 2 Chr. 26: 21–3.*
[c] *Or a skin-disease.*

has two different meanings depending on whether it is used in a secular or cultic sense. When used in a cultic sense the word would be describing some place or object used in religious worship. In its secular use the word means 'hill-side', and from this meaning the translation 'hill-shrine' has been derived for the cultic sense. Originally the cultic use may have grown up because of the use of hill-tops as shrines but by this time the word *bamah* was used cultically in a much more general sense. It is very unlikely that there were hill-shrines in cities (cp. 17: 9). The word really seems to be used to describe a raised structure or platform which was used for cultic purposes. It can at times mean 'altar' or 'sanctuary'. Normally the word refers to such platforms as they were used for alien religious practices. Examples of such 'hill-shrines' have been discovered by archaeologists at Megiddo and other places (see *Old Testament Illustrations* in this series, pp. 152–3).

5. *leprosy*: see comment on 5: 1. *in his own house*: it is not necessary to believe that the king was put into isolation as some commentators and translations have suggested. Naaman was allowed to move freely in the royal court when he was a leper. But the king was regarded as ritually unclean and therefore could not perform the duties of his office.

7. *he rested with his forefathers*: the prophet Isaiah received his call in this year (Isa. 6: 1). ✳

FIVE KINGS OF ISRAEL

In the thirty-eighth year of Azariah king of Judah, 8 Zechariah son of Jeroboam became king over Israel in Samaria and reigned six months. He did what was wrong 9 in the eyes of the LORD, as his forefathers had done; he did not give up the sinful practices of Jeroboam son of Nebat who led Israel into sin. Shallum son of Jabesh 10 formed a conspiracy against him, attacked him in Ibleam,*

[a] *So Luc. Sept.; Heb.* before people.

11 killed him and usurped the throne. The other events of
   Zechariah's reign are recorded in the annals of the kings
12 of Israel. Thus the word of the LORD spoken to Jehu was
   fulfilled: 'Your sons to the fourth generation shall sit on
   the throne of Israel.'

13 Shallum son of Jabesh became king in the thirty-ninth
   year of Uzziah king of Judah, and he reigned one full
14 month in Samaria. Then Menahem son of Gadi came up
   from Tirzah to Samaria, attacked Shallum son of Jabesh
15 there, killed him and usurped the throne. The other
   events of Shallum's reign and the conspiracy that he
   formed are recorded in the annals of the kings of Israel.

16 Then Menahem, starting out from Tirzah, destroyed
   Tappuah*a* and everything in it and ravaged its territory;
   he ravaged it because it had not opened its gates to him,
   and he ripped open all the pregnant women.

17 In the thirty-ninth year of Azariah king of Judah,
   Menahem son of Gadi became king over Israel and he
18 reigned in Samaria for ten years. He did what was wrong
   in the eyes of the LORD; he did not give up the sinful
   practices of Jeroboam son of Nebat who led Israel into
19 sin. In his days*b* Pul king of Assyria invaded the country,
   and Menahem gave him a thousand talents of silver to
   obtain his help in strengthening his hold on the kingdom.
20 Menahem laid a levy on all the men of wealth in Israel,
   and each had to give the king of Assyria fifty silver
   shekels. Then the king of Assyria withdrew without
21 occupying the country. The other acts and events of
   Menahem's reign are recorded in the annals of the kings

[a] *So Luc. Sept.; Heb.* Tiphsah.
[b] In his days: *so Sept.; Heb.* All his days.

of Israel. So Menahem rested with his forefathers; and he 22
was succeeded by his son Pekahiah.

In the fiftieth year of Azariah king of Judah, Pekahiah 23
son of Menahem became king over Israel in Samaria and
reigned for two years. He did what was wrong in the eyes 24
of the LORD; he did not give up the sinful practices of
Jeroboam son of Nebat who led Israel into sin. Pekah son 25
of Remaliah, his lieutenant, formed a conspiracy against
him and, with the help of fifty Gileadites, attacked him in
Samaria in the citadel of the royal palace,*a* killed him and
usurped the throne. The other acts and events of Peka- 26
hiah's reign are recorded in the annals of the kings of Israel.

In the fifty-second year of Azariah king of Judah, 27
Pekah son of Remaliah became king over Israel in Samaria
and reigned for twenty years. He did what was wrong in 28
the eyes of the LORD; hc did not give up the sinful practices of Jeroboam son of Nebat who led Israel into sin. In 29
the days of Pekah king of Israel, Tiglath-pileser king of
Assyria came and seized Iyyon, Abel-beth-maccah,
Janoah, Kedesh, Hazor, Gilead, and Galilee, with all the
land of Naphtali, and deported the people to Assyria.
Then Hoshea son of Elah formed a conspiracy against 30
Pekah son of Remaliah, attacked him, killed him and
usurped the throne in the twentieth year of Jotham son
of Uzziah. The other acts and events of Pekah's reign are 31
recorded in the annals of the kings of Israel.

✻ 8–12. Zechariah.

10. Jehu had killed King Ahaziah of Judah near Ibleam
(9: 27). It was situated just south of Jenin. The Hebrew words

[a] *Prob. rdg.; Heb. adds* Argob and Arieh.

for 'before people' (N.E.B. footnote) sound rather like *in Ibleam*. They must be the mistake of a scribe.

12. *the word of the LORD* was given at 10: 30. The editors are always careful to point out a fulfilment of prophecy.

13–16. Shallum.

14. Tirzah had for a time been the capital of Israel before Omri built Samaria and transferred the capital there. It is the present Tcl el Far'ah some 8 miles (nearly 13 km) north of Shechem. Perhaps Menahem was governor there.

16. This is detail added by an editor. Tiphsah (N.E.B. footnote) was the city later known as Thapsakis on the Euphrates at that river's most western point. 1 Kings 4: 24 claims that it marked the northern limit of Solomon's empire. It is clearly out of place here. The site of Tappuah is not certain but it was a city in Israel. Present-day Sheikh Abu-Zarad, some 10 miles (16 km) south of Shechem, has been suggested. Menahem had to establish his authority decisively over the whole kingdom. Tappuah may have resisted because it was the birthplace of Shallum. At all events civil war of this severity is never elsewhere recorded of Israel. *he ripped open all the pregnant women*: such conduct is noted of the Ammonites as an exceptional act of barbarism by Amos (see Amos 1: 13 in the Revised Standard Version's translation. The N.E.B. prefers a different interpretation of that verse). Hosea sees this as the fate of the women of Samaria of his day (Hos. 13: 16).

17–22. Menahem.

19. *Pul* is Tiglath-pileser III. He assumed the name Pul as a throne name when he became king of Babylon in 729 B.C. This tribute of Menahem was recorded by Tiglath-pileser in his official records (quoted in *Documents from Old Testament Times*, p. 54).

20. *men of wealth*: the Hebrew is *gibbore ḥayil* which usually describes military leaders. It was so used of Naaman in 5: 1. At this time the great men of Israel were the wealthy which indicates just how accurate is the description of the state of the country given by Amos and Hosea. There were 3000 shekels

to the talent, so 60,000 men must have contributed to the levy.

23–6. Pekahiah.

25. The words in the Hebrew which have been omitted (see N.E.B. footnote) are probably names of places in Transjordan which belong to the list of Tiglath-pileser's conquests in verse 29. They may have been added here by a careless scribe following the reference to *Gileadites*. The central authority of the country was growing weaker and weaker, and local leaders who exploited sectional interests and prejudices were making bids for power. Menahem may have been governor of Tirzah (verse 14). Here Pekah gains the support of Gileadites from the eastern bank of the Jordan.

27–31. Pekah.

27. *and reigned for twenty years*: the number twenty cannot be correct. From the information given in Assyrian records it has been calculated that Pekah could not have reigned more than five years at most. The reference to 'the twentieth year of Jotham' in verse 30 is also incorrect. It is contradicted by the official numbering of verse 33. Perhaps 'twenty' has been added incorrectly in both places.

29. The first five places which Tiglath-pileser seized were all in northern Galilee. The first two are named in 1 Kings 15: 20 as places which Ben-hadad of Aram attacked when he went to war with King Baasha. Archaeological evidence at Hazor has shown that the city was devastated with fire during this period. Gilead, Galilee, and Naphtali were all districts, Gilead being east of the Jordan. *deported the people to Assyria*: this is the first mention of a custom practised both by the Assyrians and also by the Babylonians who followed them. After a new territory had been conquered and annexed to the empire as a province, all the leading families of that territory were forcibly deported and resettled in another part of the empire. The purpose of this was to remove all the natural leaders of the people and thus prevent future rebellion. The place of the deportees was taken by groups of foreigners imported into the district by the new authority. In later years

the remainder of Israel and then Judah would be dealt with in this way.

30. *in the twentieth year of Jotham*: see comment on verse 27. According to the Assyrian record Hoshea was an Assyrian nominee. This is quite likely to have been the case. 'They overthrew their king Pekah and I placed Hoshea as king over them. I received from them 10 talents of gold, 1,000 (?) talents of silver as their tribute and I brought them to Assyria' (from the Annals of Tiglath-pileser III translated in *Ancient Near Eastern Texts* (2nd ed.), p. 284). ✱

THE REIGN OF JOTHAM IN JUDAH

32 In the second year of Pekah son of Remaliah king of Israel, Jotham son of Uzziah king of Judah became king.
33[a] He was twenty-five years old when he came to the throne, and he reigned in Jerusalem for sixteen years; his mother
34 was Jerusha daughter of Zadok. He did what was right in
35 the eyes of the LORD, as his father Uzziah had done;[b] but the hill-shrines were allowed to remain and the people continued to slaughter and burn sacrifices there. It was he who constructed the upper gate of the house of the LORD.
36 The other acts and events of Jotham's reign are recor-
37 ded in the annals of the kings of Judah. In those days the LORD began to make Rezin king of Aram and Pekah son
38 of Remaliah attack Judah. And Jotham rested with his forefathers and was buried with them in the city of David his forefather; and he was succeeded by his son Ahaz.

✱ 32. The Chronicler adds that Jotham built fortifications throughout Judah, and was successful in a war against Ammon (2 Chron. 27: 4–5). It was probably these signs of strength

[a] *Verses 33–5: cp. 2 Chr. 27: 1–3.*
[b] *So some MSS.; others repeat* had done.

which caused Rezin and Pekah to attempt to force Jotham into an alliance with them.

33. The *sixteen years* would include the period during which he ruled as co-king owing to his father's leprosy.

35. *the upper gate of the house of the LORD* is probably that which is referred to in Jer. 20: 2 and Ezek. 9: 2.

37. This was the beginning of the war which took place in the reign of Ahaz. Rezin and Pekah were trying to create a coalition to ward off further attacks by Tiglath-pileser. Rezin, who is called 'Razon' in Akkadian and Greek, was the last king of Aram. *

Downfall of the northern kingdom

* Although this heading is given to chapters 16–20, only chapter 17 describes the reign of a king of Israel. The other chapters describe the reigns of two kings of Judah, Ahaz and Hezekiah, and to the reign of Hezekiah three whole chapters, 18–20, are devoted. When we remember the brief treatment which important and powerful kings of Israel such as Omri and Jeroboam II have received, this expansive treatment of the reign of Hezekiah seems all the more remarkable. Hezekiah saved Jerusalem from the Assyrians, but otherwise he was not politically a particularly successful king. Judah was saved from the fate of Israel at this time because Jerusalem was a very difficult city to capture, and also because Judah was so weak and insignificant that the Assyrians did not consider the effort needed to be justified by the results. Judah, they believed, could be kept under sufficient control without the effort of a conquest. So Hezekiah's continued independence was due largely to Judah's comparative insignificance. Why then this great emphasis in Kings upon the reign of Hezekiah? He was a king of Judah and all deuteronomists always favoured Judah.

God, they believed, had placed his one true temple in Jerusalem and so the kings who ruled Jerusalem were to them the true guardians of the tradition. Among them Hezekiah was given a particular place of honour by the deuteronomists because he had carried out a reform of the worship of the temple. In fact they regarded this reform as being so important even though they described it with extreme brevity, that they placed it second only to the reform later carried out by Josiah who was their greatest hero. A further point in Hezekiah's favour was that one of his principal advisers was the prophet Isaiah. Stories about Isaiah together with his teaching were collected together and treasured by the prophet's disciples so that there was abundant material from the reign of Hezekiah available. In fact almost all of the account of the reign of Hezekiah in 2 Kings is also to be found in the book of Isaiah as chapters 36–9, acting there as an historical appendix to those chapters of the book which give the teaching of the prophet himself. Isa. 40–66 is the work of later prophets.

All the material in these chapters concerns the attacks of the Assyrians upon Samaria and Jerusalem. This is what gives them their unity. They tell how Samaria was captured and destroyed in 721 B.C. and the northern kingdom of Israel brought to an end. Judah alone was left to maintain the covenant tradition. She survived for a century and a half, and by so doing ensured that the history of the period, when it came to be written, would be written from a Judaean point of view. The deuteronomists, as has already been said, were bound to favour Hezekiah, but it may be that they gave such great prominence to his reign to show that at this decisive moment in the history of the nation, when the northern kingdom of Israel was reaping the rewards of its apostasy in defeat and extermination, Judah was undergoing a religious reform to remove from its life those elements which had led Israel astray. *

THE REIGN OF AHAZ IN JUDAH

IN THE SEVENTEENTH YEAR of Pekah son of Remaliah, **16**
Ahaz son of Jotham king of Judah became king. Ahaz 2[a]
was twenty years old when he came to the throne, and he
reigned in Jerusalem for sixteen years. He did not do what
was right in the eyes of the LORD his God like his forefather David, but followed in the footsteps of the kings 3
of Israel; he even passed his son through the fire, adopting
the abominable practice of the nations whom the LORD
had dispossessed in favour of the Israelites. He slaughtered 4
and burnt sacrifices at the hill-shrines and on the hill-tops
and under every spreading tree.

Then Rezin king of Aram and Pekah son of Remaliah 5
king of Israel attacked Jerusalem and besieged Ahaz but
could not bring him to battle. At that time the king of 6
Edom[b] recovered Elath and drove the Judaeans out of it;
so the Edomites entered the city and have occupied it to
this day. Ahaz sent messengers to Tiglath-pileser king of 7
Assyria to say, 'I am your servant and your son. Come
and save me from the king of Aram and from the king of
Israel who are attacking me.' Ahaz took the silver and 8
gold found in the house of the LORD and in the treasuries
of the royal palace and sent them to the king of Assyria
as a bribe. The king of Assyria listened to him; he advan- 9
ced on Damascus, captured it, deported its inhabitants to
Kir and put Rezin to death.

When King Ahaz went to meet Tiglath-pileser king of 10
Assyria at Damascus, he saw there an altar of which he

[a] *Verses 2–4: cp. 2 Chr. 28: 1–4.*
[b] *the king of Edom: prob. rdg.; Heb. Rezin king of Aram.*

145

sent a sketch and a detailed plan to Uriah the priest.
11 Accordingly, Uriah built an altar, following all the instructions that the king had sent him from Damascus,
12 and had it ready against the king's return. When the king returned from Damascus, he saw the altar, approached it
13 and mounted the steps; there he burnt his whole-offering and his grain-offering and poured out his drink-offering, and he flung the blood of his shared-offerings against it.
14 The bronze altar that was before the LORD he removed from the front of the house, from between this altar and the house of the LORD, and put it on the north side of this
15 altar. Then King Ahaz gave these instructions to Uriah the priest: 'Burn on the great altar the morning whole-offering and the evening grain-offering, and the king's whole-offering and his grain-offering, and the whole-offering of all the people of the land, their grain-offering and their drink-offerings, and fling against it all the blood of the sacrifices. But the bronze altar shall be mine, to
16 offer morning sacrifice.' Uriah the priest did all that the
17 king told him. Then King Ahaz broke up the trolleys and removed the panels, and he took down the basin and the Sea of bronze from the oxen which supported it and put
18 it on a stone base. In the house of the LORD he turned round the structure*a* they had erected for use on the sabbath, and the outer gate for the king, to satisfy the king
19*b* of Assyria. The other acts and events of the reign of Ahaz
20 are recorded in the annals of the kings of Judah. So Ahaz rested with his forefathers and was buried with them in the city of David; and he was succeeded by his son Hezekiah.

[a] structure: *mng. uncertain.*
[b] *Verses 19, 20: cp. 2 Chr. 28: 26, 27.*

✻ Quite a large amount of space is devoted to the reign of Ahaz but only because he made changes in the arrangements of the Jerusalem temple. Some scholars have suggested that the descriptions of the changes he made there, verses 10–18, came originally from a different source than the rest of the chapter. The political events of his reign are dealt with briefly, though more details can be found in Isa. 7–8.

2. The editors condemn Ahaz for apostasy and disloyalty to the traditions of the covenant people. They may be over-simplifying an issue which was more complex than they were willing to admit. Ahaz was under threat of foreign invasion and wanted to rally the nation to support him. To do this he may have been more permissive to Canaanite religious customs than the strict deuteronomists approved. Hence their condemnation. But his tolerance may only have been for the sake of national unity. The editors, however, give no indication of the causes which lay behind Ahaz's actions. For them the actions were evil and the doer of the actions equally evil. They may have been right in this judgement but they take no account of motive or purpose and so hide from us the aspects of the issue on which we would lay great stress in coming to our own judgement of Ahaz. Ahaz may have been weak rather than wicked – the picture of him given in Isa. 7 lends some support for this view – but the deuteronomists made no distinction between the two. They were writing their history as religious teachers whose aim was to use Ahaz as a warning to their readers, and as such were more concerned with the force of the lesson than the niceties of theorizing about motive.

3. *he even passed his son through the fire*: this means that he offered his son as a sacrifice. Mesha king of Moab sacrificed his son in this way on his city wall as a desperate sacrifice when he thought that defeat by the Israelites was imminent, and Israel was so convinced of the efficacy of the sacrifice that 'they struck camp and returned to their own land' (3: 27). This action of Ahaz may have been like that: the desperate act

of a man facing complete defeat. If so, it indicates Ahaz's weakness as much as his wickedness. On the other hand there is evidence that such sacrifices were fairly common practice among the Canaanites. They are condemned in the law codes of Deuteronomy and Leviticus (Deut. 12: 31 and 18: 10–12; Lev. 18: 21) and references in Jeremiah seem to imply that such sacrifices took place regularly in his day in the valley of Ben-hinnom just outside Jerusalem (Jer. 19: 5 and 32: 35). Such sacrifices are in some places said to be 'to Molech', as though they were offered to a pagan god of that name. 'Molech' is a composite word. Its vowels are taken from the Hebrew word *bosheth* which means 'shame' to indicate to the reader that when he met this word he should read *bosheth*, i.e. shame. MLCH may be the name of a deity connected with kingship; *melech* is the Hebrew word for king. Alternatively it may mean *malch* which some scholars suggest was the name given to this type of sacrifice. If this is the case, then the sacrifice could well have been offered to Yahweh and is an indication of just how little difference there was between the worship that some Israelites considered appropriate, and the worship of the Canaanites.

4. It was a feature of the reform of King Josiah which the deuteronomists supported, to destroy all the *hill-shrines*, and so any approval of them was condemned by the editors. Much worship in Canaan took place in the open air particularly on hill-tops and among groves of trees. The charge of taking part in false worship *under every spreading tree* was a reference to this, often repeated by the prophets (cp. Jer. 2: 20).

5. *Rezin* (see note on 15: 37): this attack on Jerusalem, often called the Syro-Ephraimitic war, is thought to have taken place in 735 B.C. It seems to have been an attempt on the part of Rezin and Pekah to build up a coalition against Tiglath-pileser. Ahaz sought advice from the prophet Isaiah and an account of the war is given in Isa. 7. There it is said that a part of the plan was to remove Ahaz from the throne and replace him by a usurper 'the son of Tabeal'. They *could not bring him*

to battle because Jerusalem was too strong a fortress to be taken by them.

6. Elath was the port on the Red Sea which controlled the rich trade with Arabia. It lay in the territory of Edom. David and Solomon had controlled Edom, but some of their successors lost control from time to time. Amaziah had re-asserted his authority over Edom (14: 7) but now when Ahaz was threatened from the north, the Edomites once more rebelled. A scribe has mistakenly read 'Aram' (see N.E.B. footnote) for *Edom*. The two words can easily be confused in Hebrew. Once the mistake had been made 'Rezin king of' was added to harmonize with verse 5. *to this day*: i.e. in per-petuity. After the destruction of Jerusalem, the Edomites took the opportunity to take over some Judaean territory. This led to great bitterness on the part of Judaeans to Edom (cp. the prophet Obadiah) which influenced the relationship between the two countries up to New Testament times. One of the reasons why many of the Jews hated Herod the Great was that he was an Idumaean ('Idumaea' is the Greek form of Edom). Something of the same feeling underlies this reference to Edom here and in other places in Kings.

7. Ahaz sought help against his attackers by offering to become a vassal of the king of Assyria. He felt that he had no option but to take part in the diplomatic intrigues and threw in his lot on the side of the Assyrians whom he believed would win. In so doing he lost his freedom of action and freedom to order the political and religious life of Judah. Isaiah had counselled him to put his trust in God, which seems to have meant that he should defy Rezin and Pekah without appealing to Assyria, on the ground that they had not the strength to capture Jerusalem, in Isaiah's view. Ahaz's submission to Assyria brought him no gain that time itself would not have brought if he had been resolute. On the other hand it com-promised his allegiance to Yahweh and limited his capacity to rule his kingdom by reference to the demands of the covenant. So Isaiah stigmatized Ahaz's decision as faithlessness. Ahaz

lacked the will to obey Yahweh, and therefore was not willing to put the weapon that Yahweh had placed in his hands – the impregnable fortress of Jerusalem – to the test.

9. Damascus fell in 732 B.C. and with it the kingdom of Aram. The territory was annexed as a province of the Assyrian Empire. *deported its inhabitants*: see note on 15: 29. The site of Kir is unknown. *to Kir* is not found in the Septuagint and so the suggestion has been made that it was added here by a late Hebrew scribe to show that the prophecy of Amos at 1: 5 had been fulfilled. Amos believed that Kir was the original home of the Aramaeans (Amos 9: 7) and so his prophecy was that God would return them to the obscurity from which they had originally emerged. That also may have been in the mind of the writer here.

10. Much significance has been seen in the altar that took Ahaz's fancy at Damascus. It has been suggested that it was an Assyrian altar of which Ahaz had to have a replica in his own temple at Jerusalem to declare his vassalage. If this interpretation is correct, it would have been used for the worship of Assyrian gods, and Ahaz's appeal to Assyria would have involved flagrant disregard of the religious traditions of Israel. On the other hand, Ahaz may have seen an altar of a design which was new to him, probably an altar of a Syrian pattern, of which he wished to have a copy in his temple at Jerusalem. If this were the case, then there need have been no intention to worship Assyrian gods at it. It would have been intended for the normal worship of Yahweh. The temple of Jerusalem was designed on the same pattern as Syrian temples as we know through the excavation by archaeologists of other temples in Syria. Maybe Ahaz discovered at Damascus that new liturgical fashions had come into vogue there and he was simply concerned that his own temple should not appear to be old-fashioned.

12–13. Ahaz as king dedicated the new altar by himself offering the first sacrifices, just as Solomon had dedicated the temple itself. The *whole-offering* was a sacrifice which was completely burnt. Its Hebrew name *'olah* means 'that which goes up', i.e. its smoke went up as an offering to God. Together with the whole-offering it was the custom to offer a cake made from cultivated grain, *the grain-offering*, and an offering of wine, *the drink-offering*. These three offerings represented all the products of the land. The law on this matter is set out at Num. 15: 1–12. All these sacrifices were offered wholly to God. There was another kind of sacrifice in which only a part of the offering was burnt. The rest was eaten by the priest and the worshippers. These offerings were communion sacrifices, the *shared-offerings*. Blood was the symbol of life which belonged to God and was never on any account to be eaten. In the ritual of the shared-offering the blood of the animal to be sacrificed was drained off from the carcase. The priest then flung it against the altar as a sign of offering the life of the animal to God. Only after this had been done was the carcase distributed among the worshippers.

14–15. *The bronze altar* was the altar of sacrifice which stood in the court outside the temple probably on the eastern side. The new altar was meant to become the new altar of sacrifice and was placed in line with the bronze altar, a little to the east of it. Ahaz removed the bronze altar to the north to show that it had taken on a new liturgical function. The daily sacrifices offered by the priest for the nation and the king, previously made at it, were now to be offered at the new altar. To the bronze altar a new purpose was assigned. It was reserved for the king, who in his own person represented the people before God. What the king intended to do at the bronze altar is not clear because the meaning of the Hebrew verb is doubtful. The N.E.B. translates *to offer morning sacrifice*. The Hebrew verb does come from the same root as the word for morning, but if this is the correct meaning, it is strange that in all the regulations about the offering of sacrifice it is never elsewhere used. The Revised Standard Version interprets the verb in a different way translating, 'the bronze altar shall be for me to inquire by'. 'Inquire' here means to seek the will of God by interpreting omens. This was a very common feature of religious practice at this time. There were recognized methods of inquiring, such as looking into the eyes of a dying animal as it was about to be sacrificed, or inspecting certain of its organs, in particular the liver. Archaeologists have discovered clay models of animal livers which must have been used to instruct novice inquirers. All such evidence comes from pagan temples and we have no direct evidence that such interpretation of omens was practised by kings of Judah. Certainly the deuteronomic reformers set their faces against such practices as being alien to the true traditions of Israel and condemned the practitioners (cp. Deut. 18: 10–12). It would be surprising, therefore, if they had recorded here that Ahaz set aside an altar in the temple for such practices without derogatory comment. Yet if it were an Assyrian altar which expressed the king's vassalage and his obligation to acknowledge the gods of Assyria, then this further betrayal of the tradition might well have been recorded by the editors without comment.

17. Solomon had provided these things as a part of the furniture for the temple. Ahaz removed them presumably in order to provide some of the metal which he needed for the king of Assyria.

18. *the structure they had erected for use on the sabbath*: the meaning of the Hebrew translated by these words is not certain. They refer to some structure in the temple that Ahaz removed, but precisely what it was it is impossible to say. The Revised Standard Version following the tradition of classical Jewish exegetes has 'the covered way for the sabbath'. The Greek suggests a small platform upon which a throne could be set. The N.E.B.'s *structure* is neutral and could mean either of these, but it is more likely that the structure was removed as the vessels had been, rather than *turned round*. It is not easy to see how Ahaz could turn round *the outer gate for the king*. This gate seems to be the one referred to in Ezek. 46: 1. It may have been removed, in the sense of blocked up, to indicate that the Assyrian king was now chief ruler and not Ahaz. ✳

THE REIGN OF HOSHEA IN ISRAEL

In the twelfth year of Ahaz king of Judah, Hoshea son **17** of Elah became king over Israel in Samaria and reigned nine years. He did what was wrong in the eyes of the 2 LORD, but not as the previous kings of Israel had done. Shalmaneser king of Assyria made war upon him and 3 Hoshea became tributary to him. But when the king of 4 Assyria discovered that Hoshea was being disloyal to him, sending messengers to the king of Egypt at So,*[a]* and withholding the tribute which he had been paying year by year, the king of Assyria arrested him and put him in prison. Then he invaded the whole country and, reaching 5 Samaria, besieged it for three years. In the ninth year of 6 Hoshea he captured Samaria and deported its people to Assyria and settled them in Halah and on the Habor, the river of Gozan, and in the cities of Media.

✶ Hoshea must have been a stronger king than most of his immediate predecessors since he kept the throne for nine years.

1. *In the twelfth year of Ahaz*: the date conflicts with that given earlier (15: 30).

2. *but not as the previous kings of Israel had done*: we do not know what underlies this mitigation of the usual editorial condemnation of the kings of Israel.

3. Shalmaneser V ruled Assyria from 727 to 722 B.C.

4. The prophet Hosea who lived at this time refers to alliances with Assyria and Egypt (Hos. 7: 11). *the king of Egypt at So*: in the Hebrew *So* is the name of the king of Egypt. There was no Pharaoh of this name and So has generally been understood as a reference to Sibe the Egyptian commander-in-chief, who is mentioned as an opponent in Assyrian records.

[a] to the king of Egypt at So: *prob. rdg.; Heb.* to So king of Egypt.

The N.E.B. conjectures that So is the name of a place in Egypt, but this is a less likely conjecture than the equation of So with Sibe. *arrested him*: Hoshea was probably visiting Shalmaneser to try to make his peace with him.

5. *besieged it for three years*: this indicates the great strength of the city of Samaria as a fortress.

6. According to Assyrian records, Samaria was captured by Sargon II, the successor of Shalmaneser. Sargon recorded in his annals, 'I besieged and conquered Samaria, led away as booty 27,290 inhabitants of it.' (Translated in *Ancient Near Eastern Texts*, p. 284.) Samaria was captured and the northern kingdom brought to an end in 721 B.C. It was the Assyrian custom to deport the leaders of a captive city in order to prevent future rebellion. Some of the Israelites were settled in the north of Mesopotamia – Halah was near to Haran, and the Habor was a northern tributary of the Euphrates: others were settled in Media, the hill country east of Mesopotamia. Sargon conquered Media for Assyria, and the Israelites were probably settled there in garrison cities. The much later story of Tobit in the Apocrypha is given a setting in this region. ✳

THE EDITORIAL JUDGEMENT ON THE KINGDOM OF ISRAEL

7 All this happened to the Israelites because they had sinned against the LORD their God who brought them up from Egypt, from the rule of Pharaoh king of Egypt; 8 they paid homage to other gods and observed the laws and customs of the nations whom the LORD had dis- 9 possessed before them*ᵃ* and uttered blasphemies against the LORD their God; they built hill-shrines for themselves in all their settlements, from watch-tower to fortified 10 city, and set up sacred pillars and sacred poles on every

[a] *So Pesh.; Heb. adds* those of the kings of Egypt which they practised.

154

high hill and under every spreading tree, and burnt 11
sacrifices at all the hill-shrines there, as the nations did
whom the LORD had displaced before them. By this
wickedness of theirs they provoked the LORD's anger.
They worshipped idols, a thing which the LORD had 12
forbidden them to do. Still the LORD solemnly charged 13
Israel and Judah by every prophet and seer, saying, 'Give
up your evil ways; keep my commandments and statutes
given in the law which I enjoined on your forefathers and
delivered to you through my servants the prophets.' They 14
would not listen, however, but were as stubborn and
rebellious as their forefathers had been, who refused to
put their trust in the LORD their God; they rejected his 15
statutes and the covenant which he had made with their
forefathers and the solemn warnings which he had given
to them; they followed worthless idols and became worthless themselves; they imitated the nations round about
them, a thing which the LORD had forbidden them to do.
Forsaking every commandment of the LORD their God, 16
they made themselves images of cast metal, two calves,
and also a sacred pole; they prostrated themselves to all
the host of heaven and worshipped the Baal, and they 17
made their sons and daughters pass through the fire. They
practised augury and divination; they sold themselves to
do what was wrong in the eyes of the LORD and so provoked his anger.

Thus it was that the LORD was incensed against Israel 18
and banished them from his presence; only the tribe of
Judah was left. Even Judah did not keep the command- 19
ments of the LORD their God but followed the practices
adopted by Israel; so the LORD rejected the whole race of 20

Israel and punished them and gave them over to plun-
21 derers and finally flung them out of his sight. When he
tore Israel from the house of David, they made Jeroboam
son of Nebat king, who seduced Israel from their alle-
22 giance to the LORD and led them into grave sin. The
Israelites persisted in all the sins that Jeroboam had
23 committed and did not give them up, until finally the
LORD banished the Israelites from his presence, as he had
threatened through his servants the prophets, and they
were carried into exile from their own land to Assyria;
and there they are to this day.

* The deuteronomists were great writers of sermons and this
passage is typical of their work. In this sermon the main points
of the deuteronomic teaching about God and Israel are clearly
made. God allowed the kingdom of Israel to be destroyed
because the people had refused to honour their obligation to
the covenant that he had made with them. God loved Israel,
and his love was the basis of the covenant. He was long-
suffering with Israel's backsliding, giving them every opportunity to repent of their ways (verse 13), until Israel showed
that she was so hardened in her sin that national destruction
was the only way that the evil could be brought to an end;
'they followed worthless idols and became worthless themselves'.

The sermon has a dual purpose: it teaches the deuteronomic
doctrine that suffering is the consequence of sin. The northern
kingdom had come to an end because its people were hardened sinners. Its end, therefore, was just, and there could be
no complaint against the justice of God because of it. Indeed
the sermon stresses God's loving concern for his people and
his willingness to forgive, if only they would have repented.
This point leads to the second purpose of the sermon. As it
now stands, it was written for the exiles after 587 B.C. By then

the kingdom of Judah had also been destroyed and many of the exiles were in despair. The sermon, by stressing God's love and his willingness to forgive the penitent, is offering hope to the readers. The loving God who made the covenant, and for its sake had had to destroy those who had made themselves worthless, would also renew his covenant with those who were willing to turn again to him in obedient love.

The passage, as we have it, is the work of more than one editor. Probably verse 18 and verses 21–3 were the comment of the first editor. To this was added verses 19–20 after the fall of Jerusalem. Then another editor added verses 7–17. In these verses the teaching given briefly in verses 18–23 is expanded and clarified.

8. The N.E.B. footnote is not accurate. The Hebrew does not refer to 'kings of Egypt' but 'kings of Israel'. The phrase is rightly omitted as a scribal addition to the text. The point that the Hebrew is making is that Jeroboam and his successors were just as pagan in their practices as the nations whom God had dispossessed in their favour. The same point is made at greater length at verse 16.

9. *and uttered blasphemies*: the Hebrew verb here has traditionally been understood as meaning 'to conceal', and this meaning underlies other translations, e.g. the Revised Standard Version and the Jerusalem Bible. The N.E.B. translation is based upon knowledge of a similar verb in Akkadian, another Semitic language. *hill-shrines* (see note on 15: 4): the worship practised at such shrines was greatly influenced by Canaanite worship. King Josiah's attempt to abolish all such shrines and confine worship to the temple at Jerusalem was an attempt to get rid of all Canaanite influence. *from watch-tower to fortified city*: i.e. from the smallest settlement to the largest city.

10. *sacred pillars and sacred poles* were objects connected with Canaanite religious practices (see note on 10: 26). The deuteronomists probably disliked them so intensely because they were linked with fertility rites (cp. Deut. 16: 21–2).

12. This may be a reference to Israelite participation in

Canaanite worship, or to the bulls which Jeroboam set up in his sanctuaries at Bethel and Dan which the editors regarded as pagan idols (1 Kings 12: 28–30).

15. *they followed worthless idols and became worthless themselves*: the same phrase is used in Jer. 2: 5, though there the N.E.B. translates, 'pursuing empty phantoms and themselves becoming empty'. The vocabulary of much of Jeremiah's writing is closely linked with that of the deuteronomists. Either Jeremiah was closely associated with them, or his words were edited and elaborated in the same circles.

16. *two calves*: this refers to Jeroboam's bulls (see note on verse 12). The *commandment* is the second of the ten commandments: Deut. 5: 8. The bulls were probably not idols but a throne upon which the invisible Yahweh was believed to sit. However, the deuteronomists always treat these bulls as examples of the debased pagan worship of the northern kingdom. *the host of heaven* was the stars. They were objects of worship in Mesopotamia more than in Canaan. Their inclusion here points to the passage probably having been written in the exile, though such worship could have been introduced to Samaria and Jerusalem through the influence of the Assyrians. *Baal* means Lord or husband. It was the typical Canaanite name for god since the Canaanites looked upon their gods as being the masters and husbands of the land who ensured its fertility.

17. *they made their sons and daughters pass through the fire*: see note on 16: 3. *augury and divination* were various kinds of magic, the object of which was to control future events or to reveal their nature. They were condemned by the deuteronomists because they were linked with Canaanite religious practices (cp. Deut. 18: 9–13).

19–20. These verses were added after the destruction of Jerusalem.

20. *gave them over to plunderers*: the same phrase is used in Judg. 2: 14, which is also part of a sermon written by the deuteronomists.

23. *and there they are to this day*: i.e. in perpetuity. The writer was emphasizing the terrible consequences of the apostasy of the people of Samaria. ✳

THE ALIEN RELIGIONS OF THE NORTH

Then the king of Assyria brought people from Baby- 24
lon, Cuthah, Avva, Hamath, and Sepharvaim, and settled them in the cities of Samaria in place of the Israelites; so they occupied Samaria and lived in its cities. In the early years of their settlement they did not pay 25
homage to the LORD; and the LORD sent lions among them, and the lions preyed upon them. The king was 26
told that the deported peoples whom he had settled in the cities of Samaria did not know the established usage of the god of the country, and that he had sent lions among them which were preying upon them because they did not know this. The king of Assyria, therefore, gave orders 27
that one of the priests deported from Samaria should be sent back to live there and teach the people the usage of the god of the country. So one of the deported priests 28
came and lived at Bethel, and taught them how they should pay their homage to the LORD. But each of the 29
nations made its own god, and they set them up within[a] the hill-shrines which the Samaritans had made, each nation in its own settlements. Succoth-benoth was wor- 30
shipped by the men of Babylon, Nergal by the men of Cuth, Ashima by the men of Hamath, Nibhaz and 31
Tartak by the Avvites; and the Sepharvites burnt their children as offerings to Adrammelech and Anammelech, the gods of Sepharvaim. While still paying homage to the 32

[a] *Or* in niches at.

LORD, they appointed people from every class to act as priests of the hill-shrines and they resorted to them there.

33 They paid homage to the LORD while at the same time they served their own gods, according to the custom of the nations from which they had been carried into exile.

34 They keep up these old practices to this day; they do not pay homage to the LORD, for they do not keep his[a] statutes and his[a] judgements, the law and commandment, which he enjoined upon the descendants of Jacob whom

35 he named Israel. When the LORD made a covenant with them, he gave them this commandment: 'You shall not pay homage to other gods or bow down to them or serve

36 them or sacrifice to them, but you shall pay homage to the LORD who brought you up from Egypt with great power and with outstretched arm; to him you shall bow

37 down, to him you shall offer sacrifice. You shall faithfully keep the statutes, the judgements, the law, and the commandments which he wrote for you, and you shall

38 not pay homage to other gods. You shall not forget the covenant which I made with you; you shall not pay

39 homage to other gods. But to the LORD your God you shall pay homage, and he will preserve you from all your

40 enemies.' However, they would not listen but continued

41 their former practices. While these nations paid homage to the LORD they continued to serve their images, and their children and their children's children have maintained the practice of their forefathers to this day.

∗ Taken at its face value this narrative tells what happened in Samaria after the destruction of the northern kingdom. New

[a] *Prob. rdg.; Heb.* their.

settlers imported by the Assyrians added the worship of Yahweh to that of their own gods. The result was that a corrupt form of the worship of Yahweh persisted in Samaria. This account is however distorted. It may well be based in part on historical memory but its purpose is propaganda, and that purpose has determined, as we have found in other places in Kings, the manner of the presentation of the story. The narrator implies that the Assyrians deported the whole Israelite population and replaced them by new settlers. This was not the case: only the leaders of a defeated people and their best craftsmen – those who were either dangerous or useful to the Assyrians – were deported. The great mass of the peasantry were left in their villages. In some areas the population would have been decimated during the period of the Assyrian conquest, either in battle or by starvation. New settlers would have been brought in to farm the empty lands and the increase of wild beasts would be due to this temporary decline in the population and the villages being left empty. The worship of the people was carried on in much the same way after as before the Assyrian conquest, though some influence from the religious practices of the new settlers is likely to have happened. The editor, writing from a southern point of view, describes the old Yahwism of the northern kingdom as having come to an end. The new worship, when it began, he depicted as being a little Yahwism added to foreign pagan religion. This picture is certainly more propaganda than history. The northern kingdom and its worship were always regarded by the editors as an aberration; a rebellion against the true worship which had its centre in Jerusalem. God had tolerated it as long as there was any hope of its return to Jerusalem, but when its corrupt nature had become inflexible, then he had allowed it to be destroyed for ever.

This story of Samaria and its alien practices has often been regarded as an account of the origins of the Samaritan community. But as such it has no historical basis at all. The Samaritan religious community was associated with Shechem and Mount Gerizim, not with Samaria. Their whole later history and their religious beliefs and practices show them to have been a very strict and conservative group. It seems likely that they are the successors of a group of Jews who separated themselves from the rest of the Jewish religious community sometime during the period after the exile; not earlier than the fourth century B.C. and quite possibly even later. The hostility which developed between Jews and Samaritans (cp. Ecclus. 50: 26, 'the senseless folk that live at Shechem' and John 4: 9) led to this passage being interpreted as a description of the origin of the Samaritans.

24. Cuthah is thought to have been Tel Ibrahim, a city near to Babylon. Cuthim in later times came to be a term of abuse used by Jews to describe Samaritans. Avva is probably the same place as that referred to as 'Ivvah' at 18: 34. Its site is uncertain. It was probably a Syrian city near Hamath. Hamath was a Syrian city on the river Orontes (see map on p. xii). Sepharvaim may have been the Sibraim mentioned in Ezek. 47: 16. It would have been a neighbouring city to Hamath.

27. *one of the priests*: one would hardly have been sufficient for such a task.

28. *and lived at Bethel*: it is probable that Bethel was not destroyed as Samaria was, and some worship continued there. Later, Josiah is said to have destroyed an altar at Bethel during his reform of the temple at Jerusalem (23: 15).

29. *made its own god*: the editor has in mind idols set up at the shrines as the sacred pillars and poles had been. *the hill-shrines*: see comment on 15: 4. *Samaritans*: i.e. inhabitants of Samaria and not the religious community later called Samaritans. This community thought of themselves as 'keepers' (of the Law). The Hebrew for 'keepers' is *shomerim*. They seem to have been nicknamed *shomeronim*, i.e. Samaritans.

30. *Succoth-benoth*: the name is not found elsewhere. It has been suggested that Sarpanitu the goddess consort of Marduk, the god of Babylon, may be meant. The editors may have deliberately falsified the name to show their contempt. Nergal

was the god of the underworld, worshipped at Cuthah. Ashima is also referred to in Amos (8: 14). The name of the goddess may have been Asherah, for which the editors have substituted *Ashima*, a word meaning guilt.

31. Nibhaz and Tartak are not known elsewhere. Adrammelech and Anammelech were possibly a god and his consort. The original names may have been Hadad (this was the Syrian equivalent of Baal) and Anat. Both were linked with the royal house. *melech* means 'of the king'.

32. *they appointed people from every class to act as priests*: the editors made exactly the same accusation against Jeroboam I when he made Bethel a royal sanctuary after the rebellion of the northern tribes (1 Kings 12: 31). The point is that such men would have no means of learning the traditional priestly knowledge, and therefore, would not be able to pass on the true tradition of the covenant people.

34–40. This paragraph, from the words *they do not pay homage to the LORD*, is an addition made by a second editor who wished to add to the condemnation already expressed. It condemns the people of the north as being totally pagan, which goes far beyond what is written in verse 33.

41. Here the same view is expressed as in verse 33. ✶

THE INTRODUCTION TO THE REIGN OF
HEZEKIAH OF JUDAH

In the third year of Hoshea son of Elah king of Israel, **18** 1[a] Hezekiah son of Ahaz king of Judah became king. He 2 was twenty-five years old when he came to the throne, and he reigned in Jerusalem for twenty-nine years; his mother was Abi daughter of Zechariah. He did what was 3 right in the eyes of the LORD, as David his forefather had done. It was he who suppressed the hill-shrines, smashed 4

[a] Verses 1–3: cp. 2 Chr. 29: 1, 2.

the sacred pillars, cut down every sacred pole and broke
up the bronze serpent that Moses had made; for up to that
time the Israelites had been burning sacrifices to it; they
5 called it Nehushtan. He put his trust in the LORD the God
of Israel; there was nobody like him among all the kings
of Judah who succeeded him or among those who had
6 gone before him. He remained loyal to the LORD and did
not fail in his allegiance to him, and he kept the command-
7 ments which the LORD had given to Moses. So the LORD
was with him and he prospered in all that he undertook;
he rebelled against the king of Assyria and was no longer
8 subject to him. He conquered the Philistine country as far
as Gaza and its boundaries, alike the watch-tower and the
fortified city.

9   In the fourth year of Hezekiah's reign (that was the
seventh year of Hoshea son of Elah king of Israel)
Shalmaneser king of Assyria made an attack on Samaria,
10 invested it and captured it after a siege of three years; it
was in the sixth year of Hezekiah (the ninth year of
11 Hoshea king of Israel) that Samaria was captured. The
king of Assyria deported the Israelites to Assyria and
settled them in Halah and on the Habor, the river of
12 Gozan, and in the cities of Media, because they did not
obey the LORD their God but violated his covenant and
every commandment that Moses the servant of the LORD
had given them; they would not listen and they would not
obey.

* Hezekiah was clearly one of the heroes of the editors of
Kings. He is described here as a powerful king who had a long
and successful reign which included defiance of the Assyrian

emperor and the addition by conquest of new territory to his kingdom. The picture of him given in the Assyrian records is very different. There he is said to have rebelled against the emperor but to have been defeated and had part of his territory removed from his control (see *Ancient Near Eastern Texts*, p. 288). This latter account is the more likely of the two to be historically accurate. It may be that after the fall of Samaria and the destruction of the northern kingdom, Hezekiah felt that it now fell to him to reassert the authority of the Israelites over the remaining city states of Palestine. He seems to have tried to encourage the rulers of the city states to revolt and also to drive out such rulers as remained loyal to Assyria. His reform of the temple worship at Jerusalem would have been in part linked with his political aspirations, though it would also have had a genuinely religious basis. He would understand the destruction of Samaria as punishment for the apostasy of the people there, and his temple reform would be intended to make sure that such a fate did not overtake Jerusalem. He was a patriot but neither a strong nor successful king. In fact he left his kingdom far weaker than he found it.

All this the editors have chosen to ignore. Instead they have presented an idealized picture of Hezekiah, and devoted a large part of their book to describing certain incidents of his reign. (This idealization was carried still further by the Chronicler (cp. 2 Chron. 29–32) and by later rabbinic writers for whom Hezekiah became a messianic figure; that is, the future ideal ruler of the house of David.) These particular incidents have been recorded because Hezekiah successfully defended Jerusalem against the Assyrians. They confirm the Assyrian estimate of Hezekiah's reign in that they show that the whole kingdom other than Jerusalem was occupied by the Assyrians, but to the editors this point did not matter. What was important to them was the fact that Jerusalem was never taken by the Assyrians. The editors of the book of Isaiah were interested in the same point, and in the stories which are used both in Kings and Isaiah, the prophet Isaiah teaches that

Yahweh will never allow Jerusalem to be taken by any enemy because of his temple. This is the teaching often referred to as the doctrine of the inviolability of Jerusalem. It provides here one more indication that the main interest of the editors of Kings lay in the history of the temple rather than in the political history of the kingdom. It may seem strange that they should have included such lengthy stories to illustrate the inviolability of Jerusalem when, at the time that they were compiling their book, both Jerusalem and the temple lay in ruins. The reason is that they were writing to comfort and strengthen the exiles. The point that they were making was that Yahweh had promised to defend Jerusalem and the temple. Only the great wickedness of the people had deflected him from this purpose, and if the exiles were to renounce the evil ways of their fathers and return to Yahweh in obedient love, he would again protect Jerusalem and its temple. For them this hope was not of inviolability against destruction, but of the certainty of restoration.

3. *as David his forefather had done*: the comparison with David, who had been in the editors' eyes Israel's ideal king, is an indication of the great respect in which they held Hezekiah.

4. For the meaning of *hill-shrines*, *sacred pillars* and *sacred pole* see the notes on 17: 9 and 10: 26. According to tradition Moses had made the *bronze serpent* in the wilderness (Num. 21: 8–9). After the building of the temple it had been deposited there. The fact that Hezekiah is commended for destroying the serpent indicates that it was reckoned by the editors to be an idolatrous object. There is evidence of serpent images being used in Canaanite fertility cults. They were associated with Asherah, the mother goddess. This would account for the destruction of this serpent. Probably it had belonged to the pre-Israelite cult practised in Jerusalem by the Jebusites. Later it had come to be linked with Israel's early history, and may have been associated with Moses because the serpent was known to be a symbol of royalty in Egypt.

There appears to be here an implied criticism of Moses for

making an idolatrous object, but the criticism is intended not for Moses who made the serpent, but for those who treated it as an object of worship. Hezekiah's zeal was so great that he destroyed even an object associated with Moses since it had been debased by use and had become a stumbling block to true worship. *Nehushtan*: the name probably comes from one of two Hebrew words. One of them means 'serpent', the other 'bronze'.

5. This estimate of Hezekiah is contradicted at 23: 25 where similar claims to uniqueness are made for Josiah.

8. Hezekiah tried to remove all the vassal kings who were unwilling to revolt against the Assyrians. We know from Assyrian records that he imprisoned Padi, king of Ekron, in Jerusalem. Gaza was the most southern of the Philistine cities and therefore farthest from Jerusalem. The editor is implying that Hezekiah conquered all the Philistine cities. The extent of Hezekiah's victory was in his eyes equalled by its thoroughness. Every possible centre of resistance was taken by Hezekiah, from the watch-towers which guarded the smallest villages to the fortified cities.

9–12. These verses repeat the account of the fall of Samaria which has already been given at 17: 3–6. The only difference here is that the event is dated by Hezekiah's reign. ✲

SENNACHERIB ATTACKS JERUSALEM – THE
FIRST ACCOUNT

In the fourteenth[a] year of the reign of Hezekiah, 13[b] Sennacherib king of Assyria attacked and took all the fortified cities of Judah. Hezekiah king of Judah sent a 14 message to the king of Assyria at Lachish: 'I have done wrong; withdraw from my land, and I will pay any penalty you impose upon me.' So the king of Assyria

[a] *Possibly an error for* twenty-fourth.
[b] *Verses 13–37: cp. Isa. 36: 1–22; 2 Chr. 32: 1–19.*

laid on Hezekiah king of Judah a penalty of three hundred
15 talents of silver and thirty talents of gold; and Hezekiah
gave him all the silver found in the house of the LORD and
16 in the treasuries of the royal palace. At that time Hezekiah
broke up the doors of the temple of the LORD and the
door-frames which he himself had plated, and gave them
to the king of Assyria.

* Sennacherib succeeded his father, Sargon II, as ruler of
Assyria in 705 B.C. He reigned until 681 B.C. The chief event
of his reign was the destruction of Babylon. Merodach-
baladan, a former ruler of Babylon, who had been defeated
and exiled by Sargon II, returned to Babylon in 703 B.C. and
raised a rebellion against Sennacherib. He attempted to persuade the vassal kings of the western part of the Assyrian
Empire, including Hezekiah, to join in his rebellion. Sennacherib quickly defeated Merodach-baladan and undertook
some campaigns in the western part of his empire to put down
rebels there. We know from Assyrian archives that in 701 B.C.
Sennacherib mounted his third campaign against the west.
The record of this campaign has survived, and one copy of it
is now in the British Museum. It is known as the Taylor
Prism. A translation of this record can be found in *Documents
from Old Testament Times*, pp. 66–7, or *Ancient Near Eastern
Texts*, pp. 287–8, and an account of the Taylor Prism itself in
Old Testament Illustrations, p. 87. This Assyrian record is so
similar to the report of Sennacherib's attack given in these
verses that it is generally accepted that the two accounts must
refer to the same events. Sennacherib tells how he punished
Hezekiah for rebellion and devastated Judah. He released from
imprisonment in Jerusalem Padi, king of Ekron, who had not
taken part in the rebellion, and gave him extra territory from
Judah as a reward for his loyalty. His description of his siege
of Hezekiah in Jerusalem is very graphic. 'Himself I made a

prisoner in Jerusalem his royal residence, like a bird in a cage.' There are many chronological problems connected with the events described in Kings but here the Assyrian record for once allows us to attach a firm date to this particular event.

13. Samaria fell in 721 B.C., and if this was 'the fourth year of Hezekiah's reign' (verse 9) then 701 B.C. could not be *the fourteenth year*. It seems likely that *fourteenth* is a scribal error for 'twenty-fourth' (N.E.B. footnote). *all the fortified cities of Judah*: the Assyrian record states, 'I laid siege to 46 of his strong cities, walled forts and to the countless small villages in their vicinity and conquered them.'

14. The Assyrian headquarters were at Lachish, an important Judaean city some 30 miles (48 km) south-west of Jerusalem. Sennacherib commissioned for his palace in Nineveh a series of bas-relief wall pictures showing his capture of the city of Lachish. Those which have survived are now in the British Museum. Sennacherib is shown sitting on his throne in his camp receiving the homage of the citizens of Lachish. These pictures illustrate both the importance of Lachish and also the fact that Sennacherib never captured Jerusalem. (See *Old Testament Illustrations*, pp. 80–3.) *three hundred talents of silver and thirty talents of gold*: the Assyrian record gives the amount as 'thirty talents of gold and eight hundred talents of silver' and adds that Hezekiah also sent many other gifts including his own daughters and concubines. This illustrates the humiliation which Hezekiah suffered.

16. The destruction of the doors of the temple also illustrates to what straits Hezekiah was driven to satisfy the Assyrian demands. This picture of poverty and humiliation contrasts starkly with the editorial introduction to the reign; cp. verse 7. ✳

SENNACHERIB ATTACKS JERUSALEM – THE
SECOND ACCOUNT

✻ There now follows a lengthy section, 18: 17 – 19: 37, which also describes an Assyrian attack upon Jerusalem. The attack seems to be described twice, or rather, two originally separate descriptions of the attack have been joined together. The first account ends at 19: 8, and is immediately followed by the second so that it could be taken that the Assyrians attacked Jerusalem twice if the stories were not clearly duplicates. What is the relationship of these stories to the account of the Assyrian attack on Jerusalem already given (18: 13–16)? One suggestion is that these are longer accounts of the same attack; 18: 13–16 is a very brief account which has been taken from official archives. The editors considered this inadequate and supplemented it by other descriptions which were available to them. These descriptions were a part of the tradition about the prophet Isaiah which had been treasured and handed on by his disciples. They, therefore, look at the events from a point of view different from that of the official archives. They were also added to the book of Isaiah as an appendix to the teaching and tradition of the prophet Isaiah when these came to be written down (cp. Isa. 36: 1–22 and 37: 1–38).

However, many scholars think that these accounts differ so markedly from the two descriptions of the Assyrian attack of 701 B.C. (the Assyrian and Hebrew accounts) that they must be describing entirely different events. In verses 13–16 we have been told of Hezekiah's submission in humiliating circumstances to the Assyrians. In these accounts the whole emphasis is on his resistance and deliverance by the withdrawal of the Assyrian forces from Jerusalem. It has been suggested, therefore, that Sennacherib must have attacked Jerusalem twice; on the one occasion Hezekiah submitted but on the other occasion, stiffened by the support of the prophet Isaiah, he resisted and held out until the Assyrian forces were withdrawn from the city. Unfortunately there is no record of two attacks upon Jerusalem in Assyrian records. There is only the one description of the attack in 701 B.C. and this corresponds so well with the description in verses 13–16 that it has become generally accepted that these verses refer to the events of 701 B.C. If there was another attack, when did it take place? Two references in the stories have led those who support the hypothesis of a second Assyrian attack upon Jerusalem to assert that it must have taken place at the very end of the reign of Sennacherib. In 19: 36–7 we are told that Sennacherib was murdered in Nineveh by two of his sons, and this is told as though it happened shortly after Sennacherib's return from Jerusalem. Sennacherib was assassinated by his sons in 681 B.C. and so the reference to his death in Kings is based upon good historical knowledge. Hezekiah died in 686 B.C. and so a campaign in that year would be the latest possible date. Additional support for this date is given by the reference in 19: 9 to 'Tirhakah king of Cush' as an enemy of the Assyrians. Tirhakah reigned from 689 to 664 B.C. and so he could have planned a campaign against the Assyrians in 689 B.C. or later, but not earlier. A second Assyrian attack upon Jerusalem is likely to have taken place in 688 or 687 B.C. The suggestion is that the two long accounts in Kings are descriptions of a campaign which took place in one or other of those years and was not recorded in the Assyrian records because of its failure to subdue Jerusalem.

The question of the Assyrian campaign or campaigns against Jerusalem is an open one; 18: 17 – 19: 37 can be interpreted either as a second account of the campaign of 701 B.C., or as a description of an otherwise unrecorded Assyrian attack in 688 or 687 B.C. Here the former view is supported on the ground that the purpose of the narrative in 18: 17 – 19: 37 is to show that Yahweh did not allow his temple to fall into the hands of the Assyrians. It was to prevent this catastrophe that Isaiah encouraged Hezekiah to resist, and the fact that the resistance led the Assyrians to be content with imposing a heavy fine on Hezekiah rather than sacking the city is interpreted as a victory. The stories are concerned primarily to support theological doctrine, the doctrine of the inviolability of Jerusalem, and so are written from a different point of view and reflect a different outlook from descriptions based on archival material. An editor, to give extra force to the point being made, added the references to the death of Sennacherib and Tirhakah which are factual in themselves but here in the wrong context. The editors of Kings valued these stories so greatly because they fitted in with their own interest in the Jerusalem temple, and they added them to their book, placing them after their own account of Sennacherib's attack even though the length of the stories made Kings give much greater emphasis to Hezekiah than he deserved on strict historical grounds. *

SENNACHERIB ATTACKS JERUSALEM – THE SECOND ACCOUNT: PART I

17 From Lachish the king of Assyria sent the commander-in-chief, the chief eunuch, and the chief officer[a] with a strong force to King Hezekiah at Jerusalem, and they went up and came to Jerusalem[b] and halted by the conduit of the Upper Pool on the causeway which leads to
18 the Fuller's Field. When they called for the king, Eliakim son of Hilkiah, the comptroller of the household, came out to them, with Shebna the adjutant-general and Joah
19 son of Asaph, the secretary of state. The chief officer said to them, 'Tell Hezekiah that this is the message of the Great King, the king of Assyria: "What ground have you
20 for this confidence of yours? Do you think fine words can take the place of skill and numbers? On whom then do

[a] the commander-in-chief, the chief eunuch, and the chief officer: *or* Tartan, Rab-saris, and Rab-shakeh.
[b] *So Sept.; Heb. adds* and went up and came.

you rely for support in your rebellion against me? On 21
Egypt? Egypt is a splintered cane that will run into a
man's hand and pierce it if he leans on it. That is what
Pharaoh king of Egypt proves to all who rely on him.
And if you tell me that you are relying on the LORD your 22
God, is he not the god whose hill-shrines and altars
Hezekiah has suppressed, telling Judah and Jerusalem that
they must prostrate themselves before this altar in
Jerusalem?"

'Now, make a bargain with my master the king of 23
Assyria: I will give you two thousand horses if you can
find riders for them. Will you reject the authority of even 24
the least of my master's servants and rely on Egypt for
chariots and horsemen? Do you think that I have come to 25
attack this place and destroy it without the consent of the
LORD? No; the LORD himself said to me, "Attack this
land and destroy it."'

Eliakim son of Hilkiah, Shebna, and Joah said to the 26
chief officer, 'Please speak to us in Aramaic, for we
understand it; do not speak Hebrew to us within earshot
of the people on the city wall.' The chief officer answered, 27
'Is it to your master and to you that my master has sent
me to say this? Is it not to the people sitting on the wall
who, like you, will have to eat their own dung and drink
their own urine?' Then he stood and shouted in Hebrew, 28
'Hear the message of the Great King, the king of Assyria.
These are the king's words: "Do not be taken in by 29
Hezekiah. He cannot save you from me. Do not let him 30
persuade you to rely on the LORD, and tell you that the
LORD will save you and that this city will never be surrendered to the king of Assyria." Do not listen to Heze- 31

kiah; these are the words of the king of Assyria: "Make peace with me. Come out to me, and then you shall each eat the fruit of his own vine and his own fig-tree, and
32 drink the water of his own cistern, until I come and take you to a land like your own, a land of grain and new wine, of corn and vineyards, of olives, fine oil, and honey – life for you all, instead of death. Do not listen to Hezekiah; he will only mislead you by telling you that the
33 LORD will save you. Did the god of any of these nations
34 save his land from the king of Assyria? Where are the gods of Hamath and Arpad? Where are the gods of Sepharvaim, Hena, and Ivvah? Where are the gods of
35 Samaria?[a] Did they save Samaria from me? Among all the gods of the nations is there one who saved his land from me? And how is the LORD to save Jerusalem?'"

36 The people were silent and answered not a word, for the king had given orders that no one was to answer him.
37 Eliakim son of Hilkiah, comptroller of the household, Shebna the adjutant-general, and Joah son of Asaph, secretary of state, came to Hezekiah with their clothes rent and reported what the chief officer had said.

19 1[b] When King Hezekiah heard their report, he rent his clothes and wrapped himself in sackcloth, and went into
2 the house of the LORD. He sent Eliakim comptroller of the household, Shebna the adjutant-general, and the senior priests, all covered in sackcloth, to the prophet Isaiah son
3 of Amoz, to give him this message from the king: 'This day is a day of trouble for us, a day of reproof and contempt. We are like a woman who has no strength to bear

[a] Where are the gods of Samaria?: *so Luc. Sept.; Heb. om.*
[b] *Verses 1–37: cp. Isa. 37: 1–38; 2 Chr. 32: 20–2.*

the child that is coming to the birth. It may be that the 4
LORD your God heard all the words of the chief officer
whom his master the king of Assyria sent to taunt the
living God, and will confute what he, the LORD your God,
heard. Offer a prayer for those who still survive.' King 5
Hezekiah's servants came to Isaiah, and he told them to 6
say this to their master: 'This is the word of the LORD:
"Do not be alarmed at what you heard when the lackeys
of the king of Assyria blasphemed me. I will put a spirit 7
in him and he shall hear a rumour and withdraw to his own
country; and there I will make him fall by the sword."'

So the chief officer withdrew. He heard that the king 8
of Assyria had left Lachish, and he found him attacking
Libnah.

※ 17. *Lachish*: see note on verse 14 above. *the commander-in-
chief, the chief eunuch, and the chief officer*: the proper titles of the
Assyrian officers, of which these are the English equivalents,
are given in the N.E.B. footnote. *the chief eunuch* seems to be
out of place here, but the title, *Rab-saris*, is also used of a senior
military officer in Jer. 39: 3 (see the N.E.B. footnote). It may
have become, therefore, the title for a senior palace official and
lost its specific context. In the parallel account in Isaiah, only
one officer, 'the chief officer', is said to have been sent, and it is
he who made the speech to Hezekiah's officers. Some scholars,
therefore, have suggested that the words *the commander-in-
chief* and *the chief eunuch* should be omitted here. The site of
the conduit of the Upper Pool is not known. It may have been by
the spring of Gihon on the east side of the city, but this location would mean that the Assyrian officers were standing in a
valley much below Hezekiah's officers on the city wall. On
the other hand if the location were on the north or west of the
city then the Assyrians would have been standing at the same

height, or even higher than Hezekiah's officers, but we do not know of any water-supply on that side of the city. Isaiah had previously met King Ahaz at the same place during the attack on Jerusalem by Aram and Israel in 735 B.C. and there encouraged him to have faith (Isa. 7: 3).

18. The three officers who represented Hezekiah were among the most important officials in the kingdom, members of what could be called Hezekiah's cabinet.

19–25. The speech of *the chief officer* is clever and persuasive. It argues that all power is on the side of the Assyrians. The superiority of their army would have been obvious, but the argument that their very presence before Jerusalem indicated Yahweh's support for them must have been particularly telling. Isaiah also taught that Assyria was Yahweh's instrument, and that her might was being used to fulfil his purposes (Isa. 10: 5–19) but Assyria could do nothing that Yahweh did not permit. The issue then here was not one of judging which side had the superior power, but of discovering what was God's will. The speech has clearly been composed by an editor but its sentiments are appropriate to the occasion. The officer was obviously speaking to the people of Jerusalem to lower their morale.

21. Egypt was the great enemy of Assyria. The Egyptians were continually inciting the small states of Syria and Palestine to resist the Assyrians so that there should be some buffer states between the Assyrian Empire and Egypt, but the chief officer was correct when he maintained that Egyptian support was feeble and not to be relied upon. Isaiah also scoffed at those who trusted in help from Egypt (Isa. 31: 1–3), and Ezekiel used the same image of a staff which, when it was used for support, broke and injured the hand of the holder (Ezek. 29: 6–7).

22. The reference is to the reform which Hezekiah had begun; cp. verse 4 above.

23. Judah had never been able to maintain much of a cavalry force. The chief officer is telling the Judaeans that they cannot compete in military might with Assyria.

26. Hezekiah's officers were clearly afraid that the arguments of the Assyrian chief officer would impress the people of Jerusalem. To prevent this they asked that the exchange should be conducted in the language of diplomacy as an official exchange between two states. *Aramaic* was another Semitic language, used over a wide area and traceable from about the tenth century B.C. It had become the language of diplomacy for at least the western part of the Near East by this time and continued as such until the conquests of Alexander the Great. *do not speak Hebrew to us*: the chief officer may have been using the particular dialect of Hebrew spoken by the people of Jerusalem. The word translated *Hebrew* is not the usual one and may indicate a particular dialect. The Revised Standard Version translates, 'the language of Judah'.

27. This verse pictures the appalling conditions of a siege; cp. the cannibalism of 6: 26–9.

28–35. The chief officer now appeals directly to the people in their own language to abandon Hezekiah. His speech is typical propaganda, a combination of an appeal to fear and bribery. The Assyrian king is here made to claim the right and power to give land. The deuteronomists held that this was the prerogative of Yahweh alone, who had given Canaan to his people Israel as 'promised land' and in return looked for obedience to his law (cp. Deut. 6 and 30: 15–20). The editor has deliberately constructed the speech in this way to show that the Assyrian king by his arrogance had set himself against God, and must therefore eventually be destroyed (cp. 19: 22ff.).

32. Sennacherib recorded in his annals that in the campaign of 701 B.C. he took into exile 200,150 persons from Judaea. The people of Jerusalem would have known this and perhaps been encouraged to resist. The chief officer here claims that there is nothing for them to fear in exile.

34. Arpad is Tel Erfad to the north of Aleppo in Syria. Hamath, in the same area, has already been mentioned with Sepharvaim and Ivvah at 17: 24. The site of Hena has not been

identified, but probably it was in northern Syria. *Where are the gods of Samaria?*: this continues the polemic against the religion and people of the north (see comment on 17: 24–41).

37. *with their clothes rent*: the traditional sign of mourning and distress.

19: 3. *to give him this message from the king*: this action of Hezekiah seems to imply that Isaiah held an official position and was the right person to consult. The king was leading a day of prayer to discover what answer he should give to the Assyrians and looked to Isaiah as the voice through whom the message would be given. *the child that is coming to the birth*: a child was a symbol of hope and a sure sign of God's blessing on the parents. For a woman to carry a child to the moment of birth and then be unable to deliver it implied the most public humiliation possible for her, and since the Hebrews believed that suffering was a punishment for sin, it marked her off as a particularly wicked person. This was the nature of the humiliation to which Hezekiah and his people had been brought. The issue is whether Hezekiah or the Assyrians are going to be declared by events to be the true instrument of God at this time.

6. God's answer by the mouth of Isaiah was clear and un-equivocal. The Assyrian chief officer's interpretation of past victories as showing God's wholehearted approval of Assyria was wrong. To interpret past successes as indicating God's wholehearted and unconditional commitment to the cause of Assyria, when Assyria's national character was so clearly out of harmony with God's concern for holiness and righteous-ness, was blasphemy (cp. Isa. 10: 5–19). The real test for Hezekiah and his people was not the military might of the army of Assyria as such but the response which the sight of that army drew from them. If they relied for security on military considerations, then the sight of that great army would cause them to fear, but if their confidence was in God and in the conviction that, if they served him in loyal obedience, the issue of their security could be left in his hands, then they need

have no fear. Such an attitude of obedience and total reliance
on the character of God was what Isaiah meant by faith. It was
expressed by absolute obedience to the demands of God and
the conviction that once such obedience was offered, God
himself could be trusted to know how to use it best to fulfil
his purposes.

7. *I will put a spirit in him*: the deliverance of the city would
be brought about in such a way that all would know it was
God's doing. It had often seemed in the past that God had
caused the enemies of Israel to panic and lose their nerve (cp.
Judg. 7: 21) and it may be that something of that kind was
meant by *spirit* here. *a rumour*: the rumour would be of the
disaffection of Sennacherib's sons, and *I will make him fall by
the sword* would refer to his assassination. An account of the
fulfilment of the prophecy is given later at 19: 35–7.

8. Sennacherib recorded that he fought the Egyptians at
Eltekeh which is north of Libnah. The site of Libnah may be
Tel es-Safi in the lowlands of Judaea south-west of Jerusalem.
The temporal clause, 'when the king...war on him' (verse 9),
which the N.E.B. translates as dependent on the main clause
that follows, can also be translated as dependent on the clause
that precedes it. Then the sense is that Sennacherib attacked
Libnah when he heard that Tirhakah was about to attack
him. *

SENNACHERIB ATTACKS JERUSALEM – THE
SECOND ACCOUNT: PART II

But when the king learnt that Tirhakah king of Cush was 9
on the way to make war on him, he sent messengers
again to Hezekiah king of Judah, to say to him, 'How 10
can you be deluded by your god on whom you rely when
he promises that Jerusalem shall not fall into the hands of
the king of Assyria? Surely you have heard what the 11
kings of Assyria have done to all countries, exterminating

12 their people; can you then hope to escape? Did their gods
save the nations which my forefathers destroyed, Gozan,
Harran, Rezeph, and the people of Beth-eden living in
13 Telassar? Where are the kings of Hamath, of Arpad, and
of Lahir, Sepharvaim, Hena, and Ivvah?'

14 Hezekiah took the letter from the messengers and read
it; then he went up into the house of the LORD, spread it
15 out before the LORD and offered this prayer: 'O LORD
God of Israel, enthroned on the cherubim, thou alone art
God of all the kingdoms of the earth; thou hast made
16 heaven and earth. Turn thy ear to me, O LORD, and
listen; open thine eyes, O LORD, and see; hear the message
17 that Sennacherib has sent to taunt the living God. It is
true, O LORD, that the kings of Assyria have ravaged the
18 nations and their lands, that they have consigned their
gods to the fire and destroyed them; for they were no
gods but the work of men's hands, mere wood and stone.
19 But now, O LORD our God, save us from his power, so
that all the kingdoms of the earth may know that thou,
O LORD, alone art God.'

20 Isaiah son of Amoz sent to Hezekiah and said, 'This is
the word of the LORD the God of Israel: I have heard your
21 prayer to me concerning Sennacherib king of Assyria. This
is the word which the LORD has spoken concerning him:

> The virgin daughter of Zion disdains you,
>   she laughs you to scorn;
> the daughter of Jerusalem tosses her head
>   as you retreat.
> 22   Whom have you taunted and blasphemed?
>   Against whom have you clamoured,

casting haughty glances at the Holy One of Israel?
> You have sent your messengers to taunt the Lord,   23
>> and said:

I have mounted my chariot and done mighty deeds:*a*
I have gone high up in the mountains,
> into the recesses of Lebanon.

> I have cut down its tallest cedars,
>> the best of its pines,

> I have reached its farthest corners,
>> forest and meadow.*b*

>> I have dug wells   24
and drunk the waters of a foreign land,
and with the soles of my feet I have dried up
> all the streams of Egypt.

> Have you not heard long ago?   25
>> I did it all.

In days gone by I planned it
and now I have brought it about,
making fortified cities tumble down
> into heaps of rubble.*c*

Their citizens, shorn of strength,   26
> disheartened and ashamed,

> were but as plants in the field, as green herbs,

> as grass on the roof-tops blasted before the east wind.*d*

> I know your rising up*e* and your sitting down,   27
>> your going out and your coming in.

[a] and done mighty deeds: *so Luc. Sept.; Heb. om.*
[b] forest and meadow: *so Sept.; Heb.* forest of its meadow.
[c] heaps of rubble: *prob. rdg., cp. Isa. 37: 26; Heb. obscure.*
[d] the east wind: *prob. rdg., cp. Isa. 37: 27; Heb.* it is mature.
[e] your rising up: *prob. rdg., cp. Isa. 37: 28; Heb. om.*

28 The frenzy of your rage against me[a] and your arrogance
    have come to my ears.
  I will put a ring in your nose
    and a hook in your lips,
  and I will take you back by the road
    on which you have come.

29 This shall be the sign for you: this year you shall eat shed
    grain and in the second year what is self-sown; but in the
    third year sow and reap, plant vineyards and eat their
30 fruit. The survivors left in Judah shall strike fresh root
31 under ground and yield fruit above ground, for a remnant
    shall come out of Jerusalem and survivors from Mount
    Zion. The zeal of the LORD will perform this.

32   'Therefore, this is the word of the LORD concerning the
    king of Assyria:

  He shall not enter this city
    nor shoot an arrow there,
  he shall not advance against it with shield
    nor cast up a siege-ramp against it.
33 By the way on which he came[b] he shall go back;
    this city he shall not enter.
  This is the very word of the LORD.
34 I will shield this city to deliver it,
  for my own sake and for the sake of my servant David.'

36   That night the angel of the LORD went out and struck
    down a hundred and eighty-five thousand men in the
    Assyrian camp; when morning dawned, they all lay dead.
36 So Sennacherib king of Assyria broke camp, went back

[a] *Prob. rdg., cp. Isa. 37: 29; Heb. repeats* the frenzy of your rage against
me.   [b] *So some MSS.; others* comes.

to Nineveh and stayed there. One day, while he was 37 worshipping in the temple of his god Nisroch, Adram-melech and Sharezer his sons murdered him and escaped to the land of Ararat. He was succeeded by his son Esarhaddon.

* These verses offer a second version of the second fuller account of Sennacherib's attack on Jerusalem. Here there is much less factual detail. There is little new information other than the speeches of Hezekiah and the oracles of Isaiah. In fact several oracles of the prophet which are concerned with the theme of God's deliverance of Jerusalem have been collected here. It seems probable that the words of the prophet in verses 32–3 were the reply which was given to Hezekiah's prayer in verses 15–19. To this some editor or editors has added three more oracles (21–8, 29–31 and 34), all of which give a promise of the deliverance of Jerusalem, though they are not so closely related to Hezekiah's prayer as verses 32–3. Two other additions were also made: the story about the sudden destruction of the Assyrian army in verse 35, and the account of Senna-cherib's assassination in verses 36–7. If the two longer accounts of Sennacherib's attack on Jerusalem do refer to a second attack in the closing years of his reign, then verses 36–7 must be the end of the original narrative, and the reference to Tirhakah in verse 9 must also be historical.

9. *he sent messengers again*: these may be the opening words of a new sentence (see note on verse 8). Verses 8–9 link to-gether the two descriptions of the attack. Tirhakah was the last pharaoh of the XXV dynasty. He was an Ethiopian who reigned 689–664 B.C. *Cush* was the Hebrew name for Ethiopia. In the first part of his reign Tirhakah was co-regent with his brother. The reference to him here cannot be historical if the events being described took place during Sennacherib's attack in 701 B.C.

10–13. The message of the Assyrian king is here even more

183   7-2

derogatory of Yahweh than that delivered by 'the chief officer'. *How can you be deluded by your god* is blasphemy. It poses sharply, as does the whole message, the spiritual issue. Either, Yahweh was a worthless idol and trust in him would lead Hezekiah and his people to a similar disaster as had befallen other earlier opponents of Sennacherib, or Yahweh was fully in control of events. He was able to fulfil his promises and was allowing Sennacherib success in his campaign as an instrument of his purposes. The thought that Sennacherib could be an instrument of Yahweh proved as difficult, perhaps in a sense more difficult for Israel to accept, as that he was outside Yahweh's power and able to ignore him. Most Israelites seemed to find it easier to live with an idea of a weak Yahweh who never questioned his people's attitudes and actions, than a strong Yahweh who could use his strength as much against Israel as against any other nation if they contravened his will. This particularly became the theological problem of the exiles after 587 B.C., and is one of the prominent themes in Isa. 40–55. It may well be that the final editing of verses 9–37 took place in the exile and that the various oracles have been set out in the way they are because of the dominance of that theological question in the minds of the final editors.

11. *exterminating their people*: the Hebrew verb used here referred originally to a religious custom practised in early Israel. When a campaign of the tribes was regarded as a holy war, all the gains of the war, including cities and their inhabitants, were offered as a sacrifice to God. The custom has been translated as 'being put to the ban', or 'being devoted'. The word is probably not used here in its technical sense, but it does describe that total destruction which had up to this time been the lot of those who had opposed Assyria. It indicates the extent of Hezekiah's foolhardiness, or faith.

12. Gozan and Harran were in the north of Assyria (cp. note on 17: 6). The site of Rezeph is disputed. It may have been the Assyrian city of Rasappa, north-east of Palmyra. Beth-eden was the part of Assyria known as Bit-Adini, near

the Euphrates south of Harran (cp. Amos 1: 5). Telassar may be
a corruption of Til-Asskur or Til-Basheri, cities of Bit-Adini.

13. Most of the cities noted here have already been mentioned at 18: 34. *Lahir* may not be a proper name. It may be
Hebrew for 'to the city'. Some scholars would omit it as a
scribal error, or understand it as a collective noun referring to
the three cities whose names follow it.

14. *the letter*: the Hebrew has the plural 'letters' but this
may here be understood as a singular as in the English
'despatches'. Hezekiah here acts as leader of the nation. The
spreading of the letter in the temple was a symbolic way of
bringing the need of the people as represented by that letter to
their God.

15–19. Hezekiah in his prayer expresses his faith that Yahweh is no idol. It follows from this that every event happens
because he allows it; he is Lord of history and this is as it
should be, and always has been, because he is the Creator of all
that exists. The words of this prayer give the answer of faith
to the problem set by Israel's sufferings and the victory of her
enemies. As such they apply to many situations since the time
of Hezekiah, and the editors may well have used them so that
the exiles could draw comfort from the faith and the deliverance of Hezekiah. For men of faith the joy of deliverance lay
not so much in saving their own lives as in the vindication,
which the deliverance showed, of the ways of God to man.

20. The oracle in verses 32–3 seems to be the most direct
answer to the king's prayer. Perhaps it was the original
answer to which the other oracles have been added.

21–8. This poem set as the first answer that Yahweh gave
to the king through the prophet Isaiah is what is called a
'Taunt Song'. It mocks the enemy and ridicules his intentions
and aspirations. He believes that he is all-powerful and able to
defeat and destroy all who oppose him, but this belief is
ignorant delusion. He is in reality a tool in the hand of God
and he can only do what God allows him to do. Taunt songs
such as this are at lowest the kind of morale boosters which

have always been used by nations in wartime. The enemy, particularly a powerful one, is made to look ridiculous and, therefore, less terrifying. But such a psychological weapon can only have a limited temporary effectiveness unless it is based on truth, and such taunt songs as this rise far above the level of psychological warfare because they express the faith of the author in his God, and the truth upon which that faith is founded. It encourages God's people to stand against armed tyranny, no matter how powerful or frightening, in the faith that God who controls all men is on their side.

The poem was probably added to the story by an editor who believed that it strengthened the original answer. There is no need to doubt that Isaiah originally wrote it, but it may not have been written for this occasion. It is general enough to be used against many of the enemies of the kings of Judah and may have been so used on more than one occasion. The reference to Egypt in verse 24 may mean that it was written against Sennacherib's son Esarhaddon who was the first Assyrian king to invade Egypt, but this is not certain. Even if it was not composed against Sennacherib, its sentiments are certainly applicable to the occasion. If the poem was added to the story by a later editor in the final editing of the book, then that editor may have had in mind not so much the application to Sennacherib's attack on Jerusalem as the comfort it offered, and the call to faith it uttered to the readers in exile after the destruction of Jerusalem in 587 B.C. It was then most of all that the covenant people of God needed to be reminded and assured that even the strongest king was no more than a tool in the hand of God.

21. a *virgin daughter* was least able to defend herself and had most to lose in the defeat and plundering of the city in which she lived. She might be taken away as a concubine or sold into slavery, and even if she was left at home she would have been raped and thus lose her hope of marriage. Isaiah by the use of this image portrays Jerusalem as being both defenceless and also an attractive prize for the enemy. Yet far from being

afraid, she openly mocks her enemy. *tosses her head* in mockery and contempt (cp. Ps. 22: 7).

23–4. The words ascribed to the *messengers* are in the style of Assyrian and other court records: such use of familiar language heightens the irony.

23. *and done mighty deeds*: these words are not found in the Hebrew (see the N.E.B. footnote). They are probably original since they improve the sense and the rhythm of the poetry. *forest and meadow*: the Hebrew herc, which means literally 'forest of its meadow', is difficult to understand. It may be that the Hebrew is a poetic phrase. The word translated 'meadow' can also be translated 'garden' and may be used here as an adjective meaning 'the thickest, richest forest'. The best and richest growth of plants is in the garden. The Revised Standard Version translates 'its densest forest'. The N.E.B. follows the Septuagint; but were there likely to be meadows in the farthest corners of a forest? The Septuagint translation may be a correction made by translators who took the Hebrew words literally and could make no sense of them.

24. Esarhaddon, Sennacherib's successor, was the first Assyrian king to invade Egypt. The song may first have been written about him, but it is more likely that these words are meant to express the boasting and arrogance of Sennacherib. He was so confident of his power that he spoke of his future plans as though they were accomplished facts. The hearers would know that Sennacherib had never set foot in Egypt, and this made him seem all the more ridiculous.

25. Here God replies to the boasting of the Assyrian king. *heaps of rubble*: here, and in verses 26, 27, and 28, the N.E.B. offers a probable reading for a Hebrew word or words which are difficult to understand. In each of these cases it translates the Hebrew of the parallel passage in the book of Isaiah as it is found in the Isaiah manuscript of the Dead Sea Scrolls.

26. The point of the comparison is to stress the feebleness of the citizens. The point is made by comparing them with increasingly weak things in each of the three similes. *green*

herbs, or *grass*, is weaker than *plants*, and grass growing on the roof top is most vulnerable of all since it has no depth of soil from which it can draw strength. The *east wind* came across the desert and was hot and dry. It parched all vegetation and, if it came in the wrong season, could destroy crops.

27. *know* implies 'able to control'. Familiar phrases are here used ironically (cp. Deut. 6: 6f.).

28. Captives taken from defeated cities were often led away ignominiously with a ring in their nose or hook in their lips. Many are shown like this on Assyrian wall pictures.

29-31. This sign seems also to be an addition to the original story. It implies a long siege lasting into a third year; but the deliverance was immediate; cp. verse 35. The normal processes of agriculture are to be discontinued for two years and the city will exist on such grain as grows of itself. *shed grain* is that which grows from ears overlooked in the previous year's gleaning. *self-sown* is grain growing wild. The sign may be related to the rules for keeping the sabbatical year and the year of Jubilee in Lev. 25: 1-7 and 19-22. The sign is that Assyrian occupation of the land which has prevented sowing and harvest; it is not to be understood as a disaster but as a sabbatical year ordained by Yahweh. Therefore the people need not fear starvation or permanent alienation from their land. As a sign it is directed to the Judaeans whose lands had been occupied by the Assyrians rather than to the people of Jerusalem, though the restoration, when it came, would emanate from Jerusalem. The reference to *a remnant shall come out of Jerusalem* probably accounts for its inclusion in this chapter. In the period of the exile it was an oracle which, like the poem in verses 21-8, would sustain the exiles and encourage them to maintain faith and hope.

32-3. This oracle promises directly that the Assyrians would not enter Jerusalem. It seems to be the original response to King Hezekiah's prayer.

32. Sennacherib did in 701 B.C. *cast up a siege-ramp against it*. The Assyrian inscription reads, 'I surrounded him with

earthwork in order to molest those who were leaving his city's gate' (*Ancient Near Eastern Texts*, p. 288).

33. *came*: the parallel passage in Isaiah also has the past tense. *This is the very word of the LORD*: this phrase translates two Hebrew words which were a set formula added by the prophets to their oracles to declare they were authentic. They complete the original oracle and indicate that verse 34 was added later.

34. This is an independent oracle of the prophet which has been attached to the original answer to Hezekiah. It states the teaching associated with Isaiah of the inviolability of Jerusalem. Isaiah taught that God would not allow the city to fall into the hands of the Assyrians because it contained his temple. This was God's house built by Solomon the first of the house (i.e. descendants) of David. In the tradition of Jerusalem great use had been made of this link between the house of David and the temple (cp. 2 Sam. 7). Later the words were interpreted as being an absolute promise that as long as the temple stood in Jerusalem, God would not allow the city to fall. This teaching led to superstition and false security. It caused the prophet Jeremiah to make violent attacks on those who in his time propagated it (cp. Jer. 7: 1–15). Ezekiel modified the teaching. He taught that God withdrew his presence from the temple before its destruction in 587 B.C. because of the wickedness of the inhabitants of the city.

35–6. If this story refers to the campaign of 701 B.C. this sudden deliverance is unlikely to be based on historical fact. The Assyrian records state that Sennacherib withdrew when his very heavy demands had been met (cp. 18: 14–16). If the story relates to a later campaign, it may have an historical basis. There is no Assyrian record of such a disaster but this need not surprise us. The Assyrian kings did not record their reverses. Even if the story as set down here is not historical, it may be based upon some historical event. Herodotus in his history reports a story that Sennacherib was defeated by the Egyptians at Pelusium because field mice gnawed the bowstrings of the Assyrians. This may be based upon a legendary account of an Assyrian defeat caused by plague, since mice were associated in the ancient world with plague. In 2 Sam. 24: 15–16 an outbreak of plague is referred to as a visitation of the 'angel of the LORD', so it may be that behind this story there is a memory of a similar disaster for the Assyrians. The editor, however, was chiefly concerned to underline the point already made more than once in the narrative that Judah's true protection lay with God. If the Assyrian king blasphemed by taking to himself rights which belonged only to God, then he would be overthrown by a supernatural agency.

37. The Assyrian records confirm that Sennacherib was assassinated by a son in January 681 B.C. *Nisroch* is not known as the name of an Assyrian god. It may be a corruption of Nusku or Marduk. Ararat was Armenia, called Ururtu by the Assyrians. Esarhaddon reigned from 681 to 669 B.C. after defeating his brothers who had murdered their father. ✳

HEZEKIAH'S ILLNESS

20 1[a] At this time Hezekiah fell dangerously ill and the prophet Isaiah son of Amoz came to him and said, 'This is the word of the LORD: Give your last instructions to your household, for you are a dying man and will not
2 recover.' Hezekiah turned his face to the wall and offered
3 this prayer to the LORD: 'O LORD, remember how I have lived before thee, faithful and loyal in thy service, always doing what was good in thine eyes.' And he wept bitterly.
4 But before Isaiah had left the citadel, the word of the
5 LORD came to him: 'Go back and say to Hezekiah, the prince of my people: "This is the word of the LORD the God of your father David: I have heard your prayer and seen your tears; I will heal you and on the third day you

[a] Verses 1–11: cp. Isa. 38: 1–8, 21, 22.

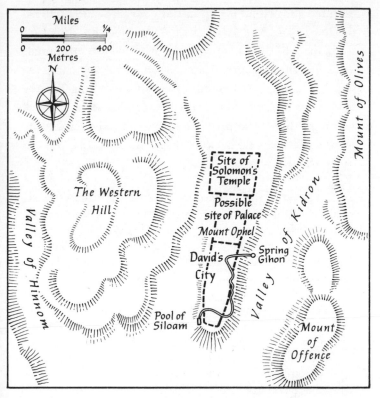

5. Plan of Jerusalem in the time of Hezekiah. His tunnel linked the Spring Gihon with the Pool of Siloam

shall go up to the house of the LORD. I will add fifteen 6 years to your life and deliver you and this city from the king of Assyria, and I will protect this city for my own sake and for my servant David's sake."' Then Isaiah told 7 them to apply a fig-plaster; so they made one and applied it to the boil, and he recovered. Then Hezekiah asked 8 Isaiah what sign the LORD would give him that he would

be cured and would go up into the house of the LORD on
9 the third day. And Isaiah said, 'This shall be your sign
from the LORD that he will do what he has promised;
shall the shadow go[a] forward ten steps or back ten
10 steps?' Hezekiah answered, 'It is an easy thing for the
shadow to move forward ten steps; rather let it go back
11 ten steps.' Isaiah the prophet called to the LORD, and he
made the shadow go back ten steps where it had advanced
down the stairway of Ahaz.

* At the end of their lengthy account of the reign of Hezekiah, the editors have added two stories which are meant to
portray their final verdict on him. This story of his illness
shows him as the recipient of God's special favour. The one
that follows indicates that even a king as blessed by God as
Hezekiah was could not change the doom that was coming
upon Judah.

This purpose of the editors has dictated the order of the
stories. They are not in chronological sequence. Hezekiah's
sickness may have happened before the Assyrian attack on
Jerusalem, though if we accept the fifteen years of verse 6, the
sickness must have happened in 701 B.C., the same year as
Sennacherib's attack. (If 18: 17 – 19: 37 describes a second
Assyrian attack towards the end of Hezekiah's reign, then the
sickness must have happened several years before that second
attack.) However, chronology is not of prime importance. The
editors have placed the story at the end of their account of the
reign of Hezekiah for a particular purpose. According to the
theological outlook of the deuteronomists there was a close
and rigid relationship between length of life and goodness.
One of the greatest blessings that God could bestow on any
man was a long life, and such a life was regarded as a particular
mark of God's blessing and approval. Equally one of the

[a] shall...go: *so Targ.; Heb.* has...gone.

surest marks of God's disfavour, and therefore a sign of particular sinfulness, was a short life. The description of Moses at the time of his death is an example of this (cp. Deut. 34: 7), and the problem which exercises the author of Ps. 37 is so acute for him because his thinking lies wholly within these terms of reference.

So the purpose of the editors in setting this story at the end of their account of Hezekiah's reign is to give their summary of him as a man who was specially blessed in life by God, and being specially blessed, was also extraordinarily good. This story has much the same function as the stories of miracles have in the mediaeval lives of the saints; it guarantees the evaluation of the character of the hero which the story has presented. In their introduction to the reign the editors gave their evaluation of Hezekiah (18: 5–6); now they round off their account by showing that God himself had given this evaluation to them.

The original story may have ended at verse 6. Verses 7–11 fit only awkwardly with the earlier verses. They are probably additional details added by another editor.

1. *Give your last instructions to your household*: this applies particularly to the nomination of a successor.

3. *loyal in thy service*: the Hebrew which these words translate refers literally to dedication of the heart (cp. the Revised Standard Version's 'with a whole heart'). The Hebrews linked parts of the body with particular emotional and psychological aspects of life. For them the heart was associated not with the emotions as with us, but with the intellect and the will. Hezekiah here means that all the intellectual force and volitional drive of his life had been consecrated to God so as to be pure and worthy to be offered as a sacrifice.

4. *he wept bitterly* because God's judgement implied that his own estimation of the value of his service could not be true. Death, especially premature death, implied punishment for sin. *the citadel*: the royal palace was a fortress within a fortress much in the same way as the keep was the inner fortress of a

Norman castle. The Hebrew here is literally 'middle city'. The Massoretes who added vowels to the original Hebrew consonantal text could not understand this and proposed to change it to 'middle court'. This is one of the places where the Massoretes added the vowels of a different word to the consonants they found in the text (see *The Making of the Old Testament*, p. 144).

5. *I have heard your prayer*: God acknowledges the justice of Hezekiah's claims about himself. The recovery was to be very rapid since Hezekiah would have had to be fully recovered by the third day to enter the temple.

7. The nature of Hezekiah's sickness is described here for the first time. *Isaiah told them*: this is a rare example of the work of a prophet as a healer. The verse may have been added to the original story. In the parallel passage in Isaiah it comes at the end of the narrative though the N.E.B. has rearranged the order (Isa. 38: 21-2). In an Ugaritic text discovered at Ras Shamra, there is a reference to a medical treatment consisting of a raisin-plaster. There it is used to heal a horse. *and he recovered*: the text as here translated makes it clear that the story ends at this point, and that verses 8-11 have been added as an extra detail. But the Lucianic Septuagint (cp. p. x) understood the words differently: 'let them take and lay it on the boil, that he may recover' (so the Revised Standard Version, and cp. Isa. 38: 21 which has this sense in the Hebrew). This links the two parts of the story together and represents a harmonizing of two originally quite separate themes.

8-11. This is a detail from a fuller version of the story which has been added to the story as given in verses 1-7. It is an integral part of the story in Isa. 38: 1-8 and may have been added here to make this version of the story fully parallel with that one. A 'sign' was a concrete, visible token asked for from God to authenticate the words of a prophet. It was often miraculous in character. Since the word of a prophet was usually declaring that some ordering of events, which was far from what seemed to be the probabilities or even possibilities of a situation, was in reality the will of God, the sign was the visible token that God was so in control of events that even the most improbable happenings would come to be if they were his will. The purpose of this sign is clear though its details are obscure. Isaiah has told Hezekiah that God will put back the moment of his death by fifteen years, and the sign authenticates this by the shadow, which marks the progress of the sun through the day, being reversed. In much the same way God was believed to have halted the sun when Joshua fought at Gibeon so that the Israelites should have sufficient time to exploit fully their victory (Josh. 10: 12-14). The story may be taken as a literal description of what happened and some who have so interpreted it, have suggested that the phenomenon was due to an eclipse of the sun. On the other hand the story may have developed out of some words of the prophet, much as the story of the sun's standing still at Gibeon seems to have grown out of an editorial attempt to show that the words of Joshua were literally fulfilled.

11. It used to be thought that Ahaz had introduced a sun-dial into the temple with his new altar (16: 10-11) and that the movement of the shadow was being noted on the degrees of the sundial. The word translated *steps* was understood in the sense of 'degrees', but it seems more likely that Ahaz added an upper room to one of the temple buildings, and the reference is not to the degrees of a sundial but to the steps leading to such an upper room. In the parallel passage in Isaiah, the Dead Sea Scroll Isaiah manuscript has 'upper room of Ahaz' in place of 'stairway of Ahaz'. The sun's shadow falling across the steps of such a stairway served as a primitive sundial. ✶

THE EMBASSY OF MERODACH-BALADAN

At this time Merodach*a*-baladan son of Baladan king 12*b* of Babylon sent envoys with a gift to Hezekiah; for he

[a] *So some MSS., cp. Isa. 39: 1; others* Berodach.
[b] *Verses 12-19: cp. Isa. 39: 1-8.*

13 had heard that he had been ill. Hezekiah welcomed[a] them and showed them all his treasury, silver and gold, spices and fragrant oil, his armoury and everything to be found among his treasures; there was nothing in his house and

14 in all his realm that Hezekiah did not show them. Then the prophet Isaiah came to King Hezekiah and asked him, 'What did these men say and where have they come from?' 'They have come from a far-off country,' Heze-

15 kiah answered, 'from Babylon.' Then Isaiah asked, 'What did they see in your house?' 'They saw everything,' Hezekiah replied; 'there was nothing among my

16 treasures that I did not show them.' Then Isaiah said to

17 Hezekiah, 'Hear the word of the LORD: The time is coming, says the LORD, when everything in your house, and all that your forefathers have amassed till the present day, will be carried away to Babylon; not a thing shall be

18 left. And some of the sons who will be born to you, sons of your own begetting, shall be taken and shall be made

19 eunuchs in the palace of the king of Babylon.' Hezekiah answered, 'The word of the LORD which you have spoken is good'; thinking to himself that peace and security would last out his lifetime.

* Merodach-baladan was a king of Babylon, referred to in Assyrian records as Marduk-apal-iddina. He rebelled successfully against Assyria for a time and reigned in Babylon from 721 to 710 B.C. He was driven out of Babylon by Sargon. After Sargon's death in 705 B.C. he again attempted to re-establish his position, but was defeated after enjoying a few months of independence in 703 B.C. His visit to Hezekiah was almost certainly more than a courtesy call. He was very likely attempting

[a] *So some MSS., cp. Isa. 39: 2; others* heard.

to stir up the subject states of Palestine and Syria to rebellion. It is impossible to date the visit with any certainty; it might have belonged to either period of his activity.

However, the main point of interest is the purpose of the editors in including the story at the end of their account of the reign of Hezekiah. For them its chief significance was as a sign. In the earlier part of the chapter they have shown Hezekiah being given a sign from God of outstanding blessing and this is consistent with their picture of Hezekiah as a king who was outstandingly loyal to God (cp. 18: 5). Yet even Hezekiah could not stand apart from the dynasty of which he was a member, and his reign could not be judged in isolation from the whole history of the covenant people under the kings. That history was one of consistent and flagrant disloyalty to God which could only lead, in the view of the editors, to national disaster. So at the end of their account of Hezekiah's reign they placed this story as a sign of the judgement that was to come. One of the lessons that the editors set before their readers consistently throughout Kings was that the guides to whom the people should turn were the true prophets. Their method was to give examples of such prophets making predictions about the future and then showing the predictions being fulfilled in future events. This is an example of such a prophecy.

12. *for he had heard that he had been ill*: this was an excuse. It may have been true, but the purpose in mentioning it here is to link the story with the incidents narrated in verses 1–11.

13. *welcomed*: the Hebrew verb for 'welcome' can be mistaken for the verb 'to hear' (N.E.B. footnote). The implication of the warmth of Hezekiah's welcome is that he was ready to fall in with Merodach-baladan's plans.

14. Isaiah was consistently opposed to intrigues and alliances with foreign powers.

16–17. Isaiah may have meant by his words to tell Hezekiah that such alliance or intrigue against the Assyrians could only end in disaster. For the editors the words *carried away to*

Babylon had a particular significance. This is what happened in 597 and 587 B.C., and for them Isaiah's words were a true prediction of the events of those years.

19. Hezekiah's answer was probably a conventional form of words which indicated that he accepted the wisdom of the prophet's words. As far as we know, he did not actively support Merodach-baladan. The final comment, *thinking to himself*, is the work of an editor who was concerned to reconcile the word of judgement with the description of Hezekiah as particularly blessed of God which has been given earlier. *

HEZEKIAH'S TUNNEL

20 The other events of Hezekiah's reign, his exploits, and how he made the pool and the conduit and brought water into the city, are recorded in the annals of the kings of 21 Judah. So Hezekiah rested with his forefathers and was succeeded by his son Manasseh.

* These verses give the final summary on Hezekiah, and incidentally record what has proved to be his most lasting work. In the ancient Near East, the weak point in the defences of most cities was the water-supply. Cities tended to be built on hills and the water supply was generally a spring which rose on the lower part of the hillside or in the valley. Thus the source of a city's water-supply was often outside the walls of the city and the difficulty lay in adequately protecting it. One solution was to drive a shaft from the spring horizontally into the hillside so that the water ran beneath the walls. A vertical shaft from the inside of the city was dug to reach the water, and that end of the horizontal shaft which was on the hillside outside the city walls was blocked up with great boulders. Access to the water down the vertical shaft was not easy, but at least it was reasonably secure.

Water shafts of this type have been found in several excavated cities in Palestine. At Jerusalem the water-supply, the spring Gihon, was outside the city wall on the eastern slope of Mount Ophel. It is now generally called the Virgin's Fountain. Horizontal and vertical shafts had been cut to bring the water within the city at some earlier date, probably even before David captured the city. The vertical shaft was rediscovered by Captain Charles Warren in 1867 and has since that date generally been referred to as 'Warren's shaft'. Hezekiah improved the water-supply into the city probably as a part of his preparation for his rebellion against the Assyrians. There seems to have been a canal running along the surface of the hill which led water around the southern part of Mount Ophel. This would have served to irrigate gardens. It may have been the 'conduit' referred to at 18: 17, but the *conduit* referred to here is the tunnel that Hezekiah had constructed to lead the water under Mount Ophel to the pool of Siloam on the western side of that hill. The tunnel still fulfils that function today. Captain Warren first explored it in modern times, but the most interesting discovery was made in 1880 when an inscription carved in the rock near the centre of the tunnel was discovered. This is known as the Siloam Inscription. It tells how the tunnel was cut from both ends of Mount Ophel and marks the place where the two sets of tunnellers met. The tunnel is 1700 feet (518 metres) long, and a considerable feat of engineering for the time in which it was made. The line of the western wall of the city of Hezekiah's time has not been found, and so it is not certain whether the pool of Siloam was inside or outside the city. This might not have been important if the pool was originally, as has been suggested, an underground reservoir. If this suggestion is correct, the roof of the reservoir at some time collapsed, probably as a result of one of the destructions of the city, leaving the pool visible and open to the air as it still is. (See *Old Testament Illustrations*, pp. 124–5.) *

The last kings of Judah

THE REIGN OF MANASSEH IN JUDAH

21 1[a] MANASSEH WAS twelve years old when he came to the throne, and he reigned in Jerusalem for fifty-
2 five years; his mother was Hephzi-bah. He did what was wrong in the eyes of the LORD, in following the abominable practices of the nations which the LORD had
3 dispossessed in favour of the Israelites. He rebuilt the hill-shrines which his father Hezekiah had destroyed, he erected altars to the Baal and made a sacred pole as Ahab king of Israel had done, and prostrated himself before all
4 the host of heaven and worshipped them. He built altars in the house of the LORD, that house of which the LORD
5 had said, 'Jerusalem shall receive my Name.' He built altars for all the host of heaven in the two courts of the
6 house of the LORD; he made his son pass through the fire, he practised soothsaying and divination, and dealt with ghosts and spirits. He did much wrong in the eyes of the
7 LORD and provoked his anger; and the image that he had made of the goddess Asherah he put in the house, the place of which the LORD had said to David and Solomon his son, 'This house and Jerusalem, which I chose out of all the tribes of Israel, shall receive my Name for all time.
8 I will not again make Israel outcasts from the land which I gave to their forefathers, if only they will be careful to observe all my commands and all the law that my servant

[a] *Verses 1–9: cp. 2 Chr. 33: 1–9.*

Moses gave them.' But they did not obey, and Manasseh 9
misled them into wickedness far worse than that of the
nations which the LORD had exterminated in favour of the
Israelites.

Then the LORD spoke through his servants the prophets: 10
'Because Manasseh king of Judah has done these abomin- 11
able things, outdoing the Amorites before him in
wickedness, and because he has led Judah into sin with
his idols, this is the word of the LORD the God of Israel: 12
I will bring disaster on Jerusalem and Judah, disaster
which will ring in the ears of all who hear of it. I will mark 13
down every stone of Jerusalem with the plumb-line of
Samaria and the plummet of the house of Ahab; I will
wipe away Jerusalem as when a man wipes his plate and
turns it upside down, and I will cast off what is left of my 14
people, my own possession, and hand them over to their
enemies. They shall be plundered and fall a prey to all
their enemies; for they have done what is wrong in my 15
eyes and have provoked my anger from the day their
forefathers left Egypt up to the present day. And this 16
Manasseh shed so much innocent blood that he filled
Jerusalem full to the brim, not to mention the sin into
which he led Judah by doing what is wrong in my eyes.'
The other events and acts of Manasseh's reign, and the sin 17
that he committed, are recorded in the annals of the kings
of Judah. So Manasseh rested with his forefathers and was 18
buried in the garden-tomb of his family, in the garden of
Uzza; he was succeeded by his son Amon.

∗ Manasseh reigned longer than any other king of Judah and
seems to have used his reign to undo all the reforms that his

father had introduced. The length of his reign shows that he was a loyal vassal of Assyria and as such, he would have followed a policy of appeasement, of which the reintroduction of the practices condemned by the editors would have been a part. In this he was doing no more than many of his predecessors had done and, even if he did it with extraordinary vigour, it may be doubted if he was as black as the editors have painted him. Certainly he deserved their condemnation. He was not loyal to the covenant tradition, but the vigour of their condemnation may owe as much to their doctrine as to his wickedness. They were writing their history to teach that God rewarded loyalty, obedience and faith, and punished disobedience and faithlessness. At this point in their story they were showing how Judah, in spite of the warning of the destruction of Samaria, was following the path of disobedience that Samaria had trodden, and heading for similar disaster. To do this they needed a king to follow Hezekiah who was as wicked as Hezekiah had been good, so that all the good of Hezekiah's reign was undone. They judged both Hezekiah and Manasseh simply on the basis of their attitude towards the worship of the temple. The result is a moral judgement on both kings which must appear to us as an oversimplification in view of the wider range of issues which we would wish to consider. So Manasseh may not have been so outrageously wicked as the editors believed him to be, but they were right in the judgement that his policies contributed to the coming destruction of the kingdom.

3. *hill-shrines*: see note on 15: 4. *he erected altars*: here and at verse 4 the Septuagint has the singular 'altar'. Ahab built a temple for Baal at Samaria but in it erected only one altar (cp. 1 Kings 16: 32). *a sacred pole*: see notes on 10: 26 and 17: 10. *the host of heaven*: see note on 17: 16.

4. *He built altars*: if the singular is read here and in verse 3, then both verses refer to the same altar which Manasseh placed in the temple at Jerusalem as a rival to the altar of Yahweh. If the plural is read, then the reference in verse 3 is to

altars erected at hill-shrines, and here to altars built in the Jerusalem temple for various Canaanite deities. *Jerusalem shall receive my Name*: the deuteronomists frequently used *Name* to mean the being of God. It particularly stressed the character of God. Names were believed to reveal character, and the significance of God revealing his name, Yahweh, to Moses at Sinai was that God thereby entered into a personal relationship with Israel. He became their God. Yahweh's character was such as to mark him off from all the gods of the neighbouring nations. Therefore he could not share his people with any other god. He demanded their exclusive worship and loyalty. It follows that any attempt to link the worship of Yahweh with the worship of any of the other gods of the surrounding nations could only mean that the character of the worship was being changed and the understanding of the character of Yahweh was being misrepresented. It was for this reason that the deuteronomists traced all the ills and shortcomings of their people to false worship.

5. *the two courts*: only one court is mentioned in the account of the building of the temple in 1 Kings 6. In Ezekiel's description of the temple there is a mention of an outer and an inner court. It has been suggested that the outer court was the court of the royal palace to which the temple was attached, though it might well be that there had been some modification of the temple buildings since their original erection by King Solomon.

6. *he made his son pass through the fire*: see note on 16: 3. *soothsaying, divination* and dealings with ghosts and spirits were condemned as practices used by the Canaanites, and also as implying powers which were believed to lie outside the control of Yahweh.

7. *Asherah* was the name of the Canaanite goddess of fertility; see note on 17: 10.

8. *the law that my servant Moses gave them*: this probably refers to the law code of Deuteronomy.

8–15. These verses are an editorial comment on the phrase

in verse 7, 'shall receive my Name for all time'. The people of Judah interpreted such promises as meaning that Yahweh was totally committed to them and would defend them against every enemy. The prophet Jeremiah, in particular, devoted much of his ministry to attacking this view as false. Yahweh would protect his faithful people, but equally would use the strength of Judah's enemies to punish them if they were disobedient, even to the extent of the destruction of the city and temple of Jerusalem (Jer. 7: 14–15). The same teaching is given here, though here it is probably directed to Israelites living in exile after the destruction of Jerusalem. They were inclined to believe that because Jerusalem and the temple had been destroyed, Yahweh was a feeble, discredited god who had been shown to be inferior to the gods of Babylon. The editors are concerned to counter that teaching by showing that the destruction of Jerusalem was Yahweh's act. It was his response to the depravity of his people. The editors were concerned to give hope to their readers. If Yahweh had sent them into exile, he could also rescue them from it.

9. If they were more wicked than those whom *the LORD had exterminated*, the logical consequence could only be their own extermination.

13. Samaria, the capital city of the dynasty of Ahab, had been destroyed by the Assyrians.

16. *innocent blood*: according to tradition the prophet Isaiah was one of the victims of Manasseh. He was said to have been sawn in two. This tradition is referred to in the New Testament in Heb. 11: 37.

18. Only Manasseh and Amon his son were buried *in the garden of Uzza*. It may be that the graveyard in which earlier kings had been buried was full, though it has been suggested that these two kings were buried in the garden of Uzza because it was associated with the false worship with which they were particularly identified.

The Chronicler (2 Chron. 33: 1–20) completely transforms the story of Manasseh by having him made a captive in

Babylon, and then a reformer when he had been restored to his throne after repentance. This story is the basis of the Prayer of Manasseh, a prayer of repentance, which is to be found in the Apocrypha. *

THE REIGN OF AMON IN JUDAH

Amon was twenty-two years old when he came to the 19[a] throne, and he reigned in Jerusalem for two years; his mother was Meshullemeth daughter of Haruz of Jotbah. He did what was wrong in the eyes of the LORD as his 20 father Manasseh had done. He followed in his father's 21 footsteps and served the idols that his father had served and prostrated himself before them. He forsook the LORD 22 the God of his fathers and did not conform to his ways. King Amon's courtiers conspired against him and mur- 23 dered him in his house; but the people of the land killed 24 all the conspirators and made his son Josiah king in his place. The other events of Amon's reign are recorded in 25 the annals of the kings of Judah. He was buried in his 26 grave in the garden of Uzza; he was succeeded by his son Josiah.

* 23. There seem to have been rival factions in the kingdom. This may have been the beginning of rival parties, one of which was loyal to Assyria while the other was bent on rebellion, relying for support on Egypt.

24. By *the people of the land* the free-born men of the country are probably meant (see note on 11: 17).

26. *the garden of Uzza*: see note on verse 18. *

[a] Verses 19–24: cp. 2 Chr. 33: 21–5.

THE REIGN OF JOSIAH IN JUDAH

22 1[a] Josiah was eight years old when he came to the throne, and he reigned in Jerusalem for thirty-one years; his 2 mother was Jedidah daughter of Adaiah of Bozkath. He did what was right in the eyes of the LORD; he followed closely in the footsteps of his forefather David, swerving neither right nor left.

✶ Like Hezekiah, Josiah was approved of by the editors, and for the same reason: both were said to have carried out a reform of the worship of the temple at Jerusalem. In fact Josiah was even more important to the editors than Hezekiah because the book which provided the basis for his reform, provided also the basis for their historical outlook and judgements. If Solomon is the hero of the earlier part of Kings, then Josiah is the hero of the latter part. Solomon was important in the history because he founded the most important institution in the kingdom, the temple at Jerusalem. Josiah was important because, after the temple had been corrupted by the influence of false worship over the course of several generations, and had largely lost its capacity to link the covenant people with their God, he carried out a radical reform in order to restore the temple to its original purpose. Solomon and Josiah, therefore, were the two kings who epitomized what the editors considered to be the most important lessons to be learned from the history of their people, namely that Israel had been created to be God's people; that the creation of the temple at Jerusalem was the sacramental expression of this relationship, and that the toleration of false worship in that temple was the outward sign of the people's rejection of their vocation.

In pointing to these lessons the editors were not greatly concerned that Josiah's reform was a failure, and that he died

[a] *Verses 1, 2: cp. 2 Chr. 34: 1, 2.*

defeated on the battlefield. They were writing after the destruction of Jerusalem and Judah. Their history and its lessons were meant for the exiles whose loyalty and faithfulness would provide in the future a new generation to rebuild the community. To those exiles Solomon and Josiah were presented as the great heroes of the past in that Solomon was the creator of the one institution which Israel needed for its very existence, and Josiah the 'upholder' of the law book which would keep that institution true in the future to its spiritual purpose. It was the lawbook and its continuing influence in later generations which made Josiah a greater king in the eyes of the editors than Hezekiah. Hezekiah's reform had no lasting influence. The policies of Manasseh destroyed it. Josiah's reform was also negatived by the policies of his successors, but in his case the lawbook remained and with it the hope of more permanent reform, even after the destruction of 587 B.C.

The editors, with Josiah as with other kings, made no attempt to relate their account of the reign with the history of the surrounding nations. Yet that history played a large part in determining the character of Josiah's reign. The Assyrians, who had been the dominant power in Mesopotamia for over two centuries, entered a period of rapid decline. The Babylonians rebelled against them and, after a struggle, destroyed the Assyrian Empire and replaced it with one of their own. So Josiah reigned through a period of Assyrian weakness and had a freedom of action which his immediate predecessors had not enjoyed. His reform of the temple might have been part of a policy of nationalist independence, and his actions in Bethel and Samaria part of a campaign to claim the old northern territories and to restore the united kingdom of David and Solomon. If so, this part of his policy was a failure. He was not strong enough to control Palestine as David had done. When Pharaoh Necho marched his army through Palestine to help the Assyrians against the Babylonians whose growing power he feared, Josiah tried to stop him. He was defeated and killed in battle at Megiddo, and with him died the last attempt, until the Maccabees 400 years later, to build an independent state in Palestine. Josiah's defeat and death was a problem to the editors. In their rigid theological system defeat and premature death were signs of God's displeasure and they had to seek reasons to explain these facts. Yet in spite of the circumstances of his death, Josiah was to them a hero because under him the deuteronomic reform had taken place and the lawbook in which they placed such trust had been restored to the people. *

THE FINDING OF THE BOOK OF THE LAW

3[a] In the eighteenth year of his reign Josiah sent Shaphan son of Azaliah, son of Meshullam, the adjutant-general, 4 to the house of the LORD. 'Go to the high priest Hilkiah,' he said, 'and tell him to melt down[b] the silver that has been brought into the house of the LORD, which those on 5 duty at the entrance have received from the people, and to hand it over to the foremen in the house of the LORD, to pay the workmen who are carrying out repairs in it, 6 the carpenters, builders, and masons, and to purchase 7 timber and hewn stones for its repair. They are not to be asked to account for the money that has been given them; 8 they are acting on trust.' The high priest Hilkiah told Shaphan the adjutant-general that he had discovered the book of the law in the house of the LORD, and he gave it 9 to him, and Shaphan read it. Then Shaphan came to report to the king and told him that his servants had melted down the silver in the house of the LORD and 10 handed it over to the foremen there. Then Shaphan the adjutant-general told the king that the high priest Hilkiah

[a] *Verses 3–20: cp. 2 Chr. 34: 8–28.*
[b] *So Targ.; Heb.* to count.

had given him a book, and he read it out in the king's
presence. When the king heard what was in the book of 11
the law, he rent his clothes, and ordered the priest 12
Hilkiah, Ahikam son of Shaphan, Akbor son of Micaiah,
Shaphan the adjutant-general, and Asaiah the king's
attendant, to go and seek guidance of the LORD for him- 13
self, for the people, and for all Judah, about what was
written in this book that had been discovered. 'Great is
the wrath of the LORD', he said, 'that has been kindled
against us, because our forefathers did not obey the
commands in this book and do all that is laid upon us.'

* 3. *In the eighteenth year*: this has usually been accepted as
621 B.C. The Assyrian Empire quickly declined after the death
of Ashurbanipal, and Josiah probably took advantage of that
decline to institute reforms which the Assyrians earlier would
have forbidden. The Chronicler's account places the beginning
of the reform earlier, in the eighth year of Josiah (2 Chron.
34: 3), but this is unlikely to have been historical. The Chronicler probably wished to defend Josiah against the charge of
being slow to begin his reform. *the adjutant-general* was one of
the most important officers of the royal household (cp.
1 Kings 4: 3).

4. *the high priest*: this is the first time that the title is used of
a priest in the temple at Jerusalem. In the temple that was
rebuilt after the exile, the chief priest was always known by
this title, and the priest who held the office was often the ruler
of Jerusalem. It has been suggested that *the high priest* is an
anachronism here, added by a scribe at a much later time to
make clear to the readers of his own day the function of
Hilkiah, but there is no reason to doubt that the temple in
Josiah's day had a chief priest and that he used the title. *to melt
down the silver*: see the note on 12: 10.

6. It seems that Josiah's first object was to repair the temple in much the same way as King Joash had earlier (12: 4–12).

8. It has generally been accepted that this *book of the law* was a part of our book of Deuteronomy. Most scholars agree that it must have included Deut. 12–26 and 28. These chapters contain the law code of Deuteronomy. Some scholars think that the earlier chapters of Deuteronomy, which are a summary of the traditional story of the Israelite wandering in the wilderness after their escape from Egypt, were also a part of the book of the law, but this is doubtful. The reason for the identification of the deuteronomic code with this book of the law is that the reforms undertaken by Josiah agree so closely with what is prescribed in Deuteronomy. In particular the law in Deuteronomy which orders the destruction of all the local sanctuaries and forbids the Israelites to offer their worship at any place other than 'the place which the LORD your God will choose out of all your tribes to receive his Name that it may dwell there' could well have provided the stimulus for Josiah's work (Deut. 12: 5).

But did Hilkiah actually discover the book? It has been suggested that the book was not so much discovered as planted; that Josiah as part of his general bid for independence wished to destroy all those religious influences which linked his people with their neighbours and, knowing that such a 'reform' would be unpopular, had a book written and then 'discovered' in the temple to give authority for what he wanted to do. His drive for independence caused him to turn for support to the prophets who were also, for their own reasons, opposed to Canaanite religious sanctuaries and customs. Some teacher or teachers among the prophetic groups rewrote the old laws in the spirit of the prophetic teachings and this book was then put in the temple to be discovered. Such a discovery has been called a 'pious fraud'.

However, there is little justification for the claim that Josiah manufactured his evidence. The book of the law may have been brought to Jerusalem from Samaria some time after

721 B.C. when the northern kingdom was destroyed. This would account for the clear links that Deuteronomy has with the north rather than with Judah; and the fact that, although the deuteronomic law insists on the legitimacy of only one Israelite sanctuary, it never names Jerusalem or any other particular place as that sanctuary, has suggested to some scholars that the book of the law goes back to the early days of Israel before the monarchy when the sanctuary was not identified with any one geographic place, but was moved from place to place according to the needs of the tribes. The essential thing for them was that there should only be one legitimate sanctuary to preserve their unity.

It is doubtful whether the deuteronomic code, as we now have it, can be traced back to those early days. The influence of the prophetic teaching on it, mentioned earlier, seems to discount that, but it may well incorporate elements from such an early law code. As it stands it seems to be a covenant document deposited in the Jerusalem temple and kept there to mark the bond which existed between Yahweh and Israel his covenant people. Emperors made treaties with their vassals and copies of such treaties were inscribed on temple walls and presumably recited from time to time. Deuteronomy shows some evidence of having been put together in the style of such treaties. The writer was probably using old Israelite material, but by the way in which he used it and constructed his book, he was declaring his faith that Israel as the covenant people of God was the vassal of Yahweh her God; looked to him for protection from all perils and evils; and owed him that total loyalty and obedience which was indicated in the character of the worship that she offered. This theology underlies the law that only worship in one sanctuary was legitimate. It also indicates the reason why the book had been laid up in the temple. It is impossible to give a date for this, but it was probably some time after the destruction of Samaria in 721 B.C. The book would have been ignored and forgotten during the period when the theology it taught was out of favour, and the long reign of Manasseh was certainly such a period. So there is no reason to doubt that the finding of the book of the law was genuine. It fitted in well with Josiah's political programme, and if up to that point, his aims had been more political than religious, it gave to them a theological justification which was to outlive all that Josiah achieved.

11. *he rent his clothes*: this was the sign of repentance and mourning. Josiah may have been expressing general contrition, or specifically setting out to avert the curses which Deuteronomy calls down on all who do not obey its laws (Deut. 28: 15–68).

13. *to go and seek guidance of the LORD* as to what atonement could be made that was acceptable to purge the sins of the past. The Israelites at the time believed that to break the law of God, even unintentionally, was sinful. They believed that there was no possibility of forgiveness for those who broke the law deliberately and wilfully. Unintentional breaches of the law by individuals could be atoned for by the offering of sacrifice, but special guidance was needed for this situation which the book of the law had now revealed; the whole nation was shown to be in breach of the law of Yahweh. *

THE WORD OF THE PROPHETESS

14 So Hilkiah the priest, Ahikam, Akbor, Shaphan, and Asaiah went to Huldah the prophetess, wife of Shallum son of Tikvah, son of Harhas, the keeper of the wardrobe, and consulted her at her home in the second quarter of
15 Jerusalem. 'This is the word of the LORD the God of Israel,' she answered: 'Say to the man who sent you to
16 me, "This is the word of the LORD: I am bringing disaster on this place and its inhabitants as foretold in the book
17 which the king of Judah has read, because they have forsaken me and burnt sacrifices to other gods, provoking

my anger with all the idols they have made with their own hands; therefore, my wrath is kindled against this place and will not be quenched." This is what you shall 18 say to the king of Judah who sent you to seek guidance of the LORD: "This is the word of the LORD the God of Israel: You have listened to my words and shown a 19 willing heart, you humbled yourself before the LORD when you heard me say that this place and its inhabitants would become objects of loathing and scorn, you rent your clothes and wept before me. Because of all this,[a] I for my part have heard you. This is the very word of the LORD. Therefore, I will gather you to your forefathers, 20 and you will be gathered to your grave in peace; you will not live to see all the disaster which I am bringing upon this place."' So they brought back word to the king.

* To the editors of Kings the true prophets were God's agents commissioned by him to ensure that the people did not turn away from the demands he had laid upon them. They possessed God's authority to declare his displeasure both to the whole nation and also to individuals when they turned away from God's will. A further aspect of their office was that in cases where there was doubt concerning exactly what was God's will, they would give an authoritative decision. In the account of the history of the two kingdoms given so far the editors have taken care to record the comment or judgement of prophets at decisive moments (cp. e.g. 1 Kings 11: 29–39). They regarded Josiah's reform as such a moment and so recorded this prophetic comment on it. The statement of Huldah may be based upon her actual words (cp. verse 20) but as set down here those words have been interpreted and probably expanded by the editors to make clear to the readers

[a] Because of all this: *prob. rdg., cp. Luc. Sept.; Heb. om.*

just how they were fulfilled in the events that overtook Judah after Josiah's death. The editors did not think that such interpretation was false or historically illegitimate. On the contrary they believed that by such interpretation they were doing their task of helping their readers to understand the true significance of the history of their people. Historians today take a different view of their task. They look upon it as being their duty to distinguish fact from comment so that the reader can make his own evaluation of the comment in the light of the facts. The editors of Kings did not give such choice to their readers because they were convinced that their interpretation was the true one.

14. *Huldah the prophetess*: she is otherwise unknown. The question has been asked why the king did not go to Jeremiah the prophet who was active in Jerusalem at this time. We do not know the answer to this question; it may be that Jeremiah in his lifetime did not have the kind of authority or prominence that we should now expect him to have had from our knowledge of his life and writings. Prophetesses had been active from time to time in Israel since at least the days of Deborah (Judg. 4: 4–5). *the second quarter of Jerusalem*: this would have been equivalent to the new town. Jerusalem had grown and expanded to the north, the only direction in which the city could expand.

15. *This is the word of the LORD*: i.e. the law as set down in the written code that had been found, ought to be obeyed.

16. *as foretold in the book which the king of Judah has read*: this refers to the curses which Deuteronomy calls down upon those who do not follow its teaching.

16–17. The destruction of Jerusalem and Judah in 587 B.C. was God's punishment on a disobedient people.

19–20. Josiah is to be rewarded for his reform in that the destruction will not take place until after his death.

20. *you will be gathered to your grave in peace*: Josiah died in battle at Megiddo. The words seem to have been spoken before Josiah's death and may be therefore the actual words of

214

Huldah. It is possible, however, that *in peace* refers to the fact
that Josiah died before the destruction of the kingdom. If this
interpretation is correct, then the words could have been
written by an editor after Josiah's death. This interpretation is
supported by the next clause.

The editor used the words of Huldah to convey to his
readers who were living in exile that the destruction of Jerusalem and the temple had happened because God had willed it.
It was a just punishment on the people not only because they
were frequently disobedient to God's will but also because
they had in the deuteronomic code clear directions as to what
God demanded from them. After the finding of the code, they
could no longer plead ignorance. There was a sense therefore
in which the finding of the book of the law itself contributed
to the destruction of the temple and Jerusalem. Since it did not
lead to things becoming better by a permanent reform, it had
to lead to things becoming worse. The purpose of the editors
in so stressing this to their readers was the deuteronomic
teaching that God punished the wicked and rewarded the
righteous. They wished their readers to understand that since
the evidence of God's punishment of evil was so clear, the
hope of his reward for the righteous would be just as sure. So
that if the readers were obedient, as their ancestors had not
been, some release from their misfortunes would be provided
by God. *

THE NATIONAL COVENANT

Then the king sent and called all the elders of Judah and **23** 1[a]
Jerusalem together, and went up to the house of the 2
Lord; he took with him the men of Judah and the inhabitants of Jerusalem, the priests and the prophets, the
whole population, high and low. There he read out to
them all the book of the covenant discovered in the house

[a] *Verses 1–3: cp. 2 Chr. 34: 29–32.*

3 of the LORD; and then, standing on the dais,[a] the king
made a covenant before the LORD to obey him and keep
his commandments, his testimonies, and his statutes, with
all his heart and soul, and so fulfil the terms of the
covenant written in this book. And all the people pledged
themselves to the covenant.

✶ By this solemn act Josiah committed the nation to accept
the obligation of being the covenant people of God. What
this meant in practical living was clearly set out in the words
that were read, and the people by their acceptance of the
obligations of the covenant would mark themselves off from
all their neighbours, most clearly by the demand laid upon
them for the exclusive worship of Yahweh in a distinctive
manner. Josiah was recalling his people to an allegiance from
which they had strayed. He probably knew the tradition that
Moses had bound the people to keep covenant with God in a
similar manner (cp. Exod. 24: 7–8), as had Joshua (Josh. 24:
25–7), but it is also likely that he believed that, as well as maintaining tradition, he was doing something new. With Moses
and Joshua it was the tribes who had been bound to the
covenant, but with the development of the kingdoms, the old
loyalty had broken down. Here Josiah was doing something
new in that he was committing the kingdom itself to the
covenant ideal. That very political development and all the
institutions, the growth of which had led the people away
from their covenant loyalties, were themselves to be committed to the covenant ideal.

Here is set out for the first time the ideal of a holy nation.
God has laid his covenant not on individual men, or families,
or local communities but on the nation itself and all that goes
to make up the national life. This is an idea which has had
great influence in the later history of both Judaism and
Christianity. Both these religions in different ways have

[a] *Or* by the pillar.

stressed the claim of God upon the nation and not just individuals or families.

2. *he read out to them*: Josiah may have read himself or given the task to one of his officials.

3. *on the dais*: see note on 11: 14. This would be a raised place in the forecourt of the temple which was the king's traditional place. Kings may have been crowned there. After the return from exile, Ezra, when he was binding the people to keep covenant with God, read the law from a similar platform (Neh. 8: 4) and from this has developed the custom of there being a platform in every synagogue from which the law is read at religious services. *and keep his commandments...with all his heart and soul*: these words are very reminiscent of Deuteronomy (cp. Deut. 6: 1–6). *all the people pledged themselves*: the Hebrew verb literally means 'stood'. The people who had been sitting may have stood up at this point to make their vow to God. ✵

THE REFORMATION IN JERUSALEM AND JUDAH

Next, the king ordered the high priest Hilkiah, the 4 deputy high priest,[a] and those on duty at the entrance, to remove from the house of the LORD all the objects made for Baal and Asherah and all the host of heaven; he burnt these outside Jerusalem, in the open country by the Kidron, and carried the ashes to Bethel. He suppressed the 5 heathen priests whom the kings of Judah had appointed to burn[b] sacrifices at the hill-shrines in the cities of Judah and in the neighbourhood of Jerusalem, as well as those who burnt sacrifices to Baal, to the sun and moon and planets and all the host of heaven. He took the symbol of 6 Asherah[c] from the house of the LORD to the gorge of the

[a] *Prob. rdg.; Heb.* priests.   [b] *So Luc. Sept.; Heb.* and he burnt.
[c] symbol of Asherah: *or* sacred pole.

Kidron outside Jerusalem, burnt it there and pounded it to dust, which was then scattered over the common
7 burial-ground. He also pulled down the houses of the male prostitutes attached to the house of the LORD, where the women wove vestments in honour of Asherah.

8 He brought in all the priests from the cities of Judah and desecrated the hill-shrines where they had burnt sacrifices, from Geba to Beersheba, and dismantled the hill-shrines of the demons*[a]* in front of the gate of Joshua,
9 the governor of the city, to the left of the city gate. These priests, however, never came up to the altar of the LORD in Jerusalem but used to eat unleavened bread with the
10 priests of their clan. He desecrated Topheth in the Valley of Ben-hinnom, so that no one might make his son or
11 daughter pass through the fire in honour of Molech.*[b]* He destroyed the horses that the kings of Judah had set up in honour of the sun at the entrance to the house of the LORD, beside the room of Nathan-melek the eunuch in
12 the colonnade, and he burnt the chariots of the sun. He pulled down the altars made by the kings of Judah on the roof by the upper chamber of Ahaz and the altars made by Manasseh in the two courts of the house of the LORD; he pounded them to dust and threw it into the gorge of the
13 Kidron. Also, on the east of Jerusalem, to the south of the Mount of Olives,*[c]* the king desecrated the hill-shrines which Solomon the king of Israel had built for Ashtoreth the loathsome goddess of the Sidonians, and for Kemosh the loathsome god of Moab, and for Milcom the abomin-

[a] *Or* satyrs.
[b] in honour of Molech: *or* for an offering.
[c] *So Targ.; Heb.* Mount of the Destroyer.

able god of the Ammonites; he broke down the sacred 14
pillars and cut down the sacred poles and filled the places
where they had stood with human bones.

* The measures that Josiah took to eradicate false worship
from Jerusalem and Judah are set out in detail. This was meant
to impress the first readers with the thoroughness of Josiah's
reform and doubtless did so, but it is difficult for us to understand all that Josiah did. Nevertheless his purpose, to reform
radically the worship offered to God in his kingdom, is
clear.

4. The same priestly officials are mentioned in 25: 18 and
Jer. 52: 24, and there *the deputy high priest* is referred to as a
particular individual. So here the singular has been substituted
for the plural (cp. the N.E.B. footnote). Baal was the Canaanite
fertility god, and Asherah was his consort. *the host of heaven*
were the stars and planets whose worship had been introduced
to Jerusalem (cp. 21: 3). *the Kidron* was the steep valley running north–south on the eastern side of the city. It divided the
temple from the Mount of Olives. There is very little *open
country* in such a valley. Possibly the place to the south of the
city where the valley of Hinnom joins the Kidron may be
meant. *and carried the ashes to Bethel*: this is an addition made by
a later scribe to link the reform in Jerusalem with the reform
later carried out at Bethel (cp. verses 15–20).

5. The Hebrew word translated *heathen priests* is not the
usual word for priests. It is the Hebrew equivalent of the word
used in neighbouring nations. The priests referred to here
were local village priests, the country clergy of the day, who
doubtless regarded themselves as faithful followers of Yahweh.
The writer is showing his estimate of them by his use of this
pejorative word. *to burn sacrifices*: the Hebrew reads the
singular of the verb instead of the plural (cp. the N.E.B. footnote). Some translations have 'to burn incense' here. The
Hebrew verb had this meaning in the period after the exile but

in earlier times had the more general meaning indicated by the
N.E.B.

6. *Asherah* is sometimes used as the name of a wooden pole
placed in the sanctuary as the symbol of the goddess (see note
on 10: 26). Here Josiah may have removed such a pole, or a
wooden image of the goddess which had been covered with
gold or silver. *scattered over the common burial-ground* in order
to show his contempt for the idol and maybe make it lose its
power in the eyes of the people.

7. *male prostitutes*: in Hebrew the masculine plural is used for
both sexes. The reference here is to prostitutes of both sexes.
The services of the prostitutes were employed by worshippers
taking part in the fertility cults which had been imported into
the temple along with other Canaanite customs. *vestments* for
use in worship.

8. *from Geba to Beersheba*: i.e. the kingdom of Judah. *the
hill-shrines*: i.e. the same kind of sanctuary as was used at the
hill-shrines. The word is being used as a technical term (see
comment on 15: 4). *the demons*: the Hebrew here has 'gates'.
The letters with other vowels mean 'satyrs' or demons. A
careless scribe may have added the vowels of the common
word 'gates' instead of those of the much rarer word *demons*,
but 'gates' may be correct and refer to 'gate-shrines' particularly aimed at protecting a city or a house. The site of the
gates referred to here is unknown.

9. Josiah's reform caused a great deal of redundancy among
the priests who had served the shrines which he destroyed.
They were brought to Jerusalem but the priests there refused
to accept them as equals and allow them to minister on equal
terms in the temple there. Nevertheless they were allowed a
share in the temple offerings. Their descendants may have
become the hereditary non-priestly officials of the temple such
as the singers (cp. Neh. 7: 44–59).

10. *Topheth* was the name of the sanctuary where human
sacrifices were practised. The word may mean 'fireplace'. *the
Valley of Ben-hinnom* is the valley running north–south on the

western side of the present-day old walled city of Jerusalem. It turns east and joins the Kidron valley thus marking the southern boundary of the city (see map on p. 191). It also marked originally the boundary between the territory of the tribes of Benjamin and Judah (Josh. 15: 8). Its use as a place where human sacrifice was offered made it notorious, and when in the first century B.C., the idea was accepted in Jewish thought of a place of fiery torment reserved for the wicked after the day of judgement, that place came to be called both in Greek and Latin Gehenna. This is a transliteration of the Hebrew words for Valley of Hinnom, *gai hinnom. make his son or daughter pass through the fire in honour of Molech*: see note on 16: 3.

11. This is the first reference to sun worship at Jerusalem. It is known to have been practised by the Assyrians and other nations. Sun worship was prominent in agricultural societies since the warmth of the rays of the sun was essential for the fertility of the land. Model horses and chariots were used as objects of worship. They seem to have represented the vehicle which the sun god used for his daily journey across the sky. These objects and their use were inconsistent with the faith that Yahweh controlled all the forces of nature (cp. Ps. 19: 1–6). In 1967 archaeologists discovered in a cave on the eastern slope of Mount Ophel a large number of pottery figurines, both human and animal. Many of the human figures were feminine and obviously associated with a fertility cult. Among the animals were figures of horses some of which had a disk on the forehead between the ears. The disk may represent the sun, and these figurines may have been used in the worship of the sun god.

12. *the upper chamber of Ahaz*: see note on 20: 11. *the altars made by Manasseh*: see 21: 5.

13. *Mount of Olives*: in Hebrew the words for 'destroyer' and 'oil' are very alike. The writer has used a pun to show his contempt for the shrines that Solomon built for his foreign wives by referring to 'Mount of the Destroyer' instead of

'Mount of Oil'. The southern part of the ridge east of Jerusalem, called the *Mount of Olives*, is still known as the Mount of Offence.

14. *filled...with human bones* so that they should be desecrated for ever. ✻

JOSIAH AT BETHEL

15 At Bethel he dismantled the altar by[a] the hill-shrine made by Jeroboam son of Nebat who led Israel into sin, together with the hill-shrine itself; he broke its stones in pieces,[b] crushed them to dust and burnt the sacred pole.
16 When Josiah set eyes on the graves which were there on the hill, he sent and took the bones from them and burnt them on the altar to desecrate it, thus fulfilling the word of the LORD announced by the man of God when Jeroboam stood by the altar at the feast. But when he caught sight of the grave of the man of God[c] who had
17 foretold these things, he asked, 'What is that monument I see there?' The people of the city answered, 'The grave of the man of God who came from Judah and foretold all
18 that you have done to the altar at Bethel.' 'Leave it alone,' he said; 'let no one disturb his bones.' So they spared his bones and also those of the prophet who came
19 from Samaria. Further, Josiah suppressed all the hill-shrines in the cities of Samaria, which the kings of Israel had set up and thereby provoked the LORD's[d] anger, and
20 he did to them what he had done at Bethel. He slaughtered on the altars all the priests of the hill-shrines who were

[a] *Prob. rdg.; Heb. om.*
[b] he broke...pieces: *so Sept.; Heb.* he burnt the hill-shrine.
[c] when Jeroboam...man of God: *so Sept.; Heb. om.*
[d] the LORD's: *so Sept.; Heb. om.*

there, and he burnt human bones upon them. Then he went back to Jerusalem.

✴ It has been doubted whether this story is historical. Bethel lay outside Josiah's kingdom in territory which the Assyrians had annexed after the destruction of Samaria, and since the story is clearly told to demonstrate how the prophecy of the man of God from Judah was fulfilled (cp. 1 Kings 13), it has been suggested that it was created by an editor for that purpose. However, we can acknowledge that purpose and still accept that the story has grown out of a reform that Josiah actually carried out at Bethel. Josiah saw himself as the successor of David and Solomon, and as such claimed authority over the territory of the northern tribes as much as over Judah. The growing weakness of Assyrian power meant that he was able to act upon his claims in a way that would have been impossible for his predecessors. So there is nothing historically improbable in Josiah exercising his authority at Bethel. Nevertheless the main purpose of the story is not simply to record what happened. The story has been told in such a way that its symbolic meaning is uppermost. By this act Josiah is shown to be claiming authority over the north as a true descendant of David and Solomon. He has been shown as restoring the worship of the temple at Jerusalem to that purity and loyalty to the covenant which the editors saw as the particular characteristic of David and Solomon. Now he is shown exercising authority over the north at Bethel, one of the two royal shrines which Jeroboam I had set up. (We know little of the other shrine at Dan, though a brief note in Judg. 18: 30f. indicates its overthrow at the time of the northern kingdom's decline. Bethel was a royal shrine in Amos' day (cp. Amos 7: 12f.).) So here Josiah is depicted as the true successor of David and Solomon who brought to an end the schism begun by Jeroboam. To this must be added a further piece of symbolism in that Josiah is shown as fulfilling the prophecy of the man of God from Judah. The editors of Kings took every opportunity open to them to demonstrate the fulfilment of prophecy and this is one example of that aspect of their work. The story of the man of God told in 1 Kings 13 is legendary and its fulfilment here is of the same character. The story was probably first attached to the grave of a holy man at Bethel to explain why that particular grave had escaped destruction. The editors seem to have believed it to be historical, and added it to their narrative as an example of the fulfilment of prophecy.

Here then is a story which has a historical basis. Legendary elements have become added to it and the editors use the story to present the picture of Josiah which they wished to portray, namely as the healer of Jeroboam's schism.

15. An altar was made of rough stones and would have been little affected by burning. Josiah broke down the altar and burned its ornaments such as *the sacred pole*. The Hebrew has confused these, and the N.E.B. rightly follows the clearer text of the Septuagint.

16. *the graves* were caves cut into the soft limestone of a nearby hillside. Since death together with sickness was regarded as the consequence of sin, all things associated with death had to be kept strictly separate from holy places. Thus a priest who had come into contact with a corpse had to undertake a purification ritual for some days before he could resume his work. Burning human bones on an altar made it unusable in the future and also showed the utmost contempt for the holiness of that sanctuary. *the word of the LORD announced by the man of God*: see 1 Kings 13: 1–2. The editors have included the story of the man of God to show that Jeroboam's altar at Bethel was never accepted by God as a true altar. Actually before Josiah's reform it never seems to have been claimed that sacrificial worship was invalid except when performed in the temple at Jerusalem. This restriction of sacrifice to Jerusalem was the teaching of Deuteronomy. In the light of that teaching, the editors used the story of the man of God to

justify their view that the sanctuary at Bethel was set up by Jeroboam in deliberate defiance of the law of the covenant. This is not so. Jeroboam simply wished to provide sanctuaries for his subjects within the borders of his own kingdom. The worship performed there was to be as thoroughly devoted to Yahweh as that at the temple at Jerusalem. However, the editors were so partisan in their support of Jerusalem and Judah, and so opposed to the evils of Canaanite religious influence which they believed had been brought into Israelite worship through the influence of the north, that they were willing to accept the most unfavourable view of the Bethel sanctuary, and used this story, which they probably accepted as historical, to support their point of view. *when Jeroboam... man of God*: in the Hebrew these words have been omitted because of the error of a scribe. In copying a manuscript in which the phrase *man of God* occurs twice in a brief space, he accidentally omitted the words between the two occurrences of the phrase. This is a mistake which is called haplography; reading once what ought to have been read twice. The N.E.B. has followed the original version, preserved in the Septuagint.

17–18. The story was first remembered to explain why *that monument* escaped destruction by Josiah. *the prophet who came from Samaria*: this must refer to the 'prophet living in Bethel' of the story (cp. 1 Kings 13: 11). At the time that Jeroboam made his altar, Samaria had not yet been founded.

19. This shows Josiah carrying out his reform throughout the old northern kingdom as he had already done throughout Judah. The editors want to show him carrying out his work throughout the territory occupied by the covenant people.

20. In Judah, Josiah brought *the priests of the hill-shrines* to Jerusalem, see notes on verses 8 and 9 above. He probably treated the priests at Bethel in the same way. However, it was a part of the prophecy of the man of God that Josiah would slaughter the Bethel priests (1 Kings 13: 2) and the editors have recorded it as happening. They always looked upon the

shrines of the northern kingdom as pagan shrines and did not regard their priests as being even in the same category as those of the hill-shrines of Judah. ✶

THE COMPLETION OF THE REFORM

21 The king ordered all the people to keep the Passover to the LORD their God, as this book of the covenant pre-
22 scribed; no such Passover had been kept either when the judges were ruling Israel or during the times of the kings
23 of Israel and Judah. But in the eighteenth year of Josiah's reign this Passover was kept to the LORD in Jerusalem.
24 Further, Josiah got rid of all who called up ghosts and spirits, of all household gods[a] and idols and all the loathsome objects seen in the land of Judah and in Jerusalem, so that he might fulfil the requirements of the law written in the book which the priest Hilkiah had discovered in the
25 house of the LORD. No king before him had turned to the LORD as he did, with all his heart and soul and strength, following the whole law of Moses; nor did any king like him appear again.

26 Yet the LORD did not abate his fierce anger; it still burned against Judah because of all the provocation which
27 Manasseh had given him. 'Judah also I will banish from my presence', he declared, 'as I banished Israel; and I will cast off this city of Jerusalem which once I chose, and the house where I promised that my Name should be.'

✶ The story now returns to Judah and tells of the further measures that Josiah took to complete his reform.

21-2. *the Passover* was a religious festival which went back

[a] *Heb.* teraphim.

to the earliest nomadic days of Israel. Each family sacrificed a lamb and then ate the carcase. The festival probably originated earlier than the exodus from Egypt but came to be particularly linked in Israelite tradition with the people's deliverance from Egypt and was believed to commemorate God's acts which had compelled Pharaoh to release the Israelites from slavery (cp. Exod. 12: 21–7). It was thus the particular feast which commemorated the creation of Israel by God as his covenant people, and the editors have made particular mention of it for this reason, and also because they viewed Josiah as the recreator of Israel.

21. *as this book of the covenant prescribed*: i.e. in accordance with the regulations laid down in Deut. 16: 1–8.

22. Josiah changed the character of the Passover festival. Previously it had been simply a family feast. Each family had gone to the local sanctuary to sacrifice its lamb, and had then kept the festival at home. The deuteronomic law insisted that the festival should be kept at Jerusalem and by so doing changed it from a family festival to a pilgrim festival. Every Israelite family was compelled to go to Jerusalem, offer its lamb in the temple there, and spend the days of the feast in the city. By this regulation the festival became as much, if not more, a national festival than a family one, and the element in it which commemorated the creation of Israel as the covenant people of God was strengthened.

In the description of the Passover taken from the code which was earlier than Deuteronomy, the J code (Exod. 12: 21–7) no mention is made of eating unleavened bread. It has been suggested that this custom originated as a separate feast, and that Deuteronomy linked them for the first time. This could also have been the sense in which *no such Passover had been kept* before, though these words seem to refer directly to Josiah's establishment of Passover as a pilgrim feast.

24. The practice of calling up *ghosts and spirits* had been introduced into the temple by Manasseh (see note on 21: 6). The practice is condemned in Deut. 18: 11. *household gods*

seem to have been small, easily portable statuettes. No objection had been made to them in earlier times. David possessed some (1 Sam. 19: 13) as did Jacob. In the story of Jacob the possession of household gods appears to be associated with the right to inherit property. In Josiah's reform many objects and practices which had previously been regarded as innocuous, were swept away probably because of their association with Canaanite life and culture.

25. *No king before him*: this contradicts the judgement made on Hezekiah at 18: 5. The editors have probably used two written sources which they greatly respected and would not alter in spite of the contradiction. *with all his heart and soul and strength*: this is clearly based on Deut. 6: 4–5. These verses are the opening words of the prayer, called the *Shema*, 'Hear', from its opening word in Hebrew, which the devout Jew repeats daily. Josiah is being described as the ideal king and ideal worshipper of Yahweh.

26–7. According to the rigid view of retributive justice which formed such a large part of the deuteronomic teaching, the life of a king such as Josiah should have led to great blessing and prosperity. In order to defend this teaching and to reconcile it with the disasters which were about to fall on Judah, the editors explain that even the perfection of Josiah could not atone for the evil of his predecessor Manasseh. *

JOSIAH'S DEATH

28 The other events and acts of Josiah's reign are recorded
29 in the annals of the kings of Judah. It was in his reign that Pharaoh Necho king of Egypt set out for the river Euphrates to help the king of Assyria. King Josiah went to meet him; and when they met at Megiddo, Pharaoh
30*a* Necho slew him. His attendants conveyed his body in a chariot from Megiddo to Jerusalem and buried him in his

[a] Verses 30–4: cp. 2 Chr. 36: 1–4.

own burial place. Then the people of the land took Josiah's son Jehoahaz and anointed him king in place of his father.

* The power of the Assyrians who had dominated Meso-potamia and Syria for generations was in Josiah's day broken by the Babylonians and Medes. In 612 B.C. Nineveh, the Assyrian capital, was captured and destroyed. The Assyrians tried to hold out against the Babylonians in the western part of Upper Mesopotamia, in the land called Harran. Pharaoh Necho was no friend of Assyria but he saw his primary interest as preventing the rise of a new strong Mesopotamian power, and also perhaps gaining himself control over Palestine and Syria. Consequently as soon as he had established himself – he reigned as Pharaoh from 609 to 593 B.C. – he marched north through Palestine to help to support what remained of Assyrian power against Babylon. Josiah judged that both Necho's aim and his ambition were hostile to Judah. He, Josiah, had been working throughout his reign to secure in-dependence from Assyria and to regain the old Israelite terri-tory that Assyria had annexed. He was content, therefore, to see the destruction of Assyrian power. At the same time Necho's ambitions to control Syria and Palestine were a threat to the independence he was working to secure. Therefore when Necho marched north through Palestine, Josiah tried to oppose the passage of his army at the pass through the Carmel range of mountains leading to the Esdraelon valley. This pass was controlled by the great fortress of Megiddo. His plan was unsuccessful and he died either on the battlefield or as a result of it (cp. 2 Chron. 35: 24). The editors record his death with-out comment. In view of their praise for his reform and their assurance that God favoured him, his death must have been to them a great mystery. They probably explained it as a further part of the price that had to be paid for Manasseh's sins.

29. *to help the king of Assyria*: this is historically correct and a possible idiomatic meaning of the Hebrew; but the text

could mean 'against the king of Assyria', and it has often been so understood. The later scribes may no longer have understood the situation correctly. *Megiddo*: see map at p. 80. The site of Megiddo has been extensively excavated (see *Old Testament Illustrations*, pp. 66–8).

30. *the people of the land* seem to have been those with power to choose a new king; see notes on 11: 14 and 21: 24. Jehoahaz was the younger son but preferred by the people presumably because he had inherited some of the character and ideals of his father. ✱

THE REIGN OF JEHOAHAZ IN JUDAH

31 Jehoahaz was twenty-three years old when he came to the throne, and he reigned in Jerusalem for three months; his mother was Hamutal daughter of Jeremiah of Libnah.
32 He did what was wrong in the eyes of the LORD, as his
33 forefathers had done. Pharaoh Necho removed him from the throne*a* in Jerusalem, and imposed on the land a fine of a hundred talents of silver and one talent of gold.
34 Pharaoh Necho made Josiah's son Eliakim king in place of his father and changed his name to Jehoiakim. He took Jehoahaz and brought him to Egypt, where he died.
35 Jehoiakim paid the silver and gold to Pharaoh, taxing the country to meet Pharaoh's demands; he exacted it from the people, from every man according to his assessment, so that he could pay Pharaoh Necho.

✱ With the death of Josiah the destruction of Judah and Jerusalem became inevitable. The independence and sense of national pride for which he had worked came to an end. Judah became virtually a vassal of Egypt. But if Josiah's plans

[a] removed...throne: *prob. rdg., cp. 2 Chr. 36: 3; Heb.* bound him at Riblah in the land of Hamath when he was king...

failed, so did Pharaoh Necho's. After defeating Josiah at
Megiddo he moved on to the north, but he was unable to
prevent the final defeat of Assyria, and was himself decisively
defeated by the Babylonians in battle at Carchemish in 605
B.C. (cp. Jer. 46: 1–12). Judah became entangled more and
more in the struggle between Babylonia and Egypt, and this
entanglement led in the end to her destruction. After the death
of Josiah then, Judah entered a period of decay. There was a
general loss of direction on the part of her leaders. Their concern was not the vocation that God had laid upon them but
their own security and well-being. Their nerve failed. Their
faith in God and in themselves was eroded, and they became
mere pawns in the power politics of Babylonia and Egypt.
The prophet Jeremiah who lived in Jerusalem throughout this
period was one of the few who saw clearly what was happening to the nation. He spoke out fearlessly but could make no
impact on the kings or their advisers. He lived in increasing
isolation and eventually persecution. Jeremiah thought well of
Josiah (Jer. 22: 15–16) but not of his successors.

31. Jehoahaz was called Shallum by Jeremiah (Jer. 22:
11–17). He may have assumed the name Jehoahaz at his
coronation. Jeremiah of Libnah was not, of course, the same
person as the prophet Jeremiah.

32. This is a stereotyped judgement of the editors. In three
months he would not have had time to do very much.

33. *removed...throne*: with this translation the N.E.B. has
set aside the Hebrew and in its place put a phrase which is
based upon the parallel passage in Chronicles. The translation
of the Hebrew is given in the N.E.B. footnote. The only
difficult phrase in the Hebrew is that translated, 'when he was
king in Jerusalem' and that has been accepted as a difficulty
from the earliest times. The original text is likely to have been,
'Pharaoh Necho bound him at Riblah in the land of Hamath,
and imposed on the land...' To this a scribe added two
words of further explanation after 'Hamath' which have been
translated 'when he was king in Jerusalem'. The first letter of

this phrase is 'b', and from the earliest times its accuracy was doubted by the Massoretes. (For an explanation of the Massoretes and their work see *The Making of the Old Testament* in this series, pp. 143–4.) They read 'm' in its place as did the translators of the Targum and the Septuagint. With this slight change the phrase then means 'to prevent him being king at Jerusalem'. There seems to be no justification for the N.E.B.'s conjecture. The meaning of the Hebrew is not in doubt. Hamath was in the far north of Syria. Riblah was in the southern part of that land (see map on p. xii). *one talent of gold*: a numeral may have been omitted. The Lucianic Septuagint and the Syriac version both have 'ten talents'. Metals were dealt in by weight. The standard measure was a shekel, from the Hebrew *shakal* which means 'to weigh'. The talent was the largest measurement. According to the Phoenician standard 3000 shekels made a talent, while by the Babylonian standard 3600 were needed. There was also at one time, one weight for a royal shekel and a smaller weight for an ordinary shekel. Because of such variations it is impossible to say what the value of these talents were in our money.

34. *changed his name* to indicate that Jehoiakim was his vassal. The particular name might have been chosen to please those who had supported Josiah's reform. In it 'el' the general name for god used by the Canaanites has been replaced by a form of Yahweh. ✳

THE REIGN OF JEHOIAKIM IN JUDAH

36 Jehoiakim was twenty-five years old when he came to the throne, and he reigned in Jerusalem for eleven years; his mother was Zebidah daughter of Pedaiah of Rumah.
37 He did what was wrong in the eyes of the LORD, as his
24 forefathers had done. During his reign Nebuchadnezzar king of Babylon took the field, and Jehoiakim became his vassal; but three years later he broke with him and

revolted. The LORD launched against him raiding-parties 2
of Chaldaeans, Aramaeans, Moabites, and Ammonites,
letting them range through Judah and ravage it, as the
LORD had foretold through his servants the prophets. All 3
this happened to Judah in fulfilment of the LORD's purpose to banish them from his presence, because of all the
sin that Manasseh had committed and because of the 4
innocent blood that he had shed; he had drenched Jerusalem with innocent blood, and the LORD would not
forgive him. The other events and acts of Jehoiakim's 5
reign are recorded in the annals of the kings of Judah. He 6
rested with his forefathers, and was succeeded by his son
Jehoiachin. The king of Egypt did not leave his own land 7
again, because the king of Babylon had stripped him of
all his possessions, from the Torrent of Egypt to the river
Euphrates.

* 36. Jehoiakim, though the elder brother of Jehoahaz, had
evidently been passed over by the people.

24: 1. *Nebuchadnezzar...took the field* when he defeated
Pharaoh Necho at Carchemish in 605 B.C. and that victory
may be what is referred to here. Jehoiakim may have submitted and become *his vassal* then. Nebuchadnezzar was also
campaigning against Egypt in 601 B.C. and was then defeated
by Necho. This may have caused Jehoiakim to revolt *three
years later.* It indicates how Judah was drawn into the struggle between Nebuchadnezzar and Necho to her own ultimate disaster.

2. *The LORD launched*: the Septuagint has 'he' referring to
Nebuchadnezzar, who clearly let it be known to Judah's
neighbours and his own garrisons in Syria that Judah could be
attacked with impunity.

3–4. This is the explanation of the editor to account for the
disaster.

4. *he had drenched Jerusalem with innocent blood*: cp. Jeremiah's comments on Jehoiakim and his 'cruel acts of tyranny' (Jer. 22: 13–17).

5. This is the last reference in Kings to *the annals of the kings of Judah*.

7. *the Torrent of Egypt* was the last settlement south of Gaza in the Sinai desert. Today it is called Wadi el-Arish (see map on p. xii). Nebuchadnezzar captured all the Egyptian strongholds in Syria and Palestine leaving Egypt very vulnerable to attack. This led Pharaoh Necho to do all that he could to stir up disaffection among Nebuchadnezzar's vassals. His success in doing this in Judah led to the final destruction of the state. ✳

Downfall of the southern kingdom

✳ The first edition of Kings may have ended at this point. Many in Judah were upheld through the troubles that followed the death of Josiah by a false optimism. They had interpreted the laws of Deuteronomy and the reform as meaning that God was totally committed to maintaining the temple at Jerusalem and the community that supported it. So they believed that, despite all appearances to the contrary, Jerusalem and Judah would come unscathed through the difficult times they were living in (cp. Jer. 7: 1–15). The editors of Kings presented a different interpretation of events, one which was much nearer to the point of view of the prophet Jeremiah. God had always desired and demanded from his people loyal acceptance of the covenant he had made with them. They had consistently refused to honour the covenant in such terms. They may have made professions of loyalty, but in practice, they had followed the customs and religious practices of the Canaanites because it was the values of Canaan which they really loved. For the editors the climax of this history had come in the reigns of the two kings Manasseh and Josiah. Manasseh gave his whole-hearted allegiance to Canaan and all that it stood for. Josiah brought about a reform, but the reform had to be not only an outward reform in the religious practices of Judah and the Jerusalem temple, but a genuine inner conversion of the hearts of the people to love of Yahweh. After the death of Josiah it became clear that such a conversion had not taken place. The prophet Jeremiah looked upon the reform as having been a failure. The sins of Manasseh remained and were the reason for the disasters that had come upon Judah.

The last section of Kings (24: 8 – 25: 30) seems to be an appendix added by an editor who worked on the book during the Babylonian exile. He added this section to bring the story up to date. He tells of the final destruction of Jerusalem and Judah, and ends with the release from prison in Babylon of Jehoiachin. This happened in 562 B.C. so the final ending of the book and the writing of this last section must have taken place shortly after that date. ✶

THE REIGN OF JEHOIACHIN

JEHOIACHIN WAS eighteen years old when he came to 8[a] the throne, and he reigned in Jerusalem for three months; his mother was Nehushta daughter of Elnathan of Jerusalem. He did what was wrong in the eyes of the 9 LORD, as his father had done. At that time the troops of 10 Nebuchadnezzar king of Babylon advanced on Jerusalem and besieged the city. Nebuchadnezzar arrived while his 11 troops were besieging it, and Jehoiachin king of Judah, 12 his mother, his courtiers, his officers, and his eunuchs, all surrendered to the king of Babylon. The king of Babylon, now in the eighth year of his reign, took him prisoner;

[a] *Verses 8–17: cp. 2 Chr. 36: 9, 10.*

13 and, as the LORD had foretold, he carried off all the treasures of the house of the LORD and of the royal palace and broke up all the vessels of gold which Solomon king of
14 Israel had made for the temple of the LORD. He carried the people of Jerusalem into exile, the officers and the fighting men, ten thousand in number, together with all the craftsmen and smiths; only the weakest class of people
15 were left. He deported Jehoiachin to Babylon; he also took into exile from Jerusalem to Babylon the king's mother and his wives, his eunuchs and the foremost men
16 of the land. He also deported to Babylon all the men of substance, seven thousand in number, and a thousand craftsmen and smiths, all of them able-bodied men and
17 skilled armourers. He made Mattaniah, uncle of Jehoiachin, king in his place and changed his name to Zedekiah.

* It was during this very brief reign that Jerusalem was captured by the Babylonians for the first time. A Babylonian record of the event has survived. It took place on the second day of the month of Adar (which has been reckoned as 16 March) 597 B.C.

8. Jehoiachin is called Jeconiah and Coniah by Jeremiah (Jer. 24: 1 and 22: 24). *Jehoiachin* may have been his throne name.

9. An editorial comment added to make the record conform with all the earlier records of the kings.

12. *now in the eighth year of his reign*: the event is dated by the reign of the Babylonian king and not, as previously in the book, by the reign of the king of Judah. This points to the account having been written in Babylon.

13–16. In these verses there are two parallel accounts of one event. The accounts differ in some details. Verse 15 probably originally followed verse 12. Then verses 13–14, a parallel account of verses 15–16, were inserted, perhaps because some of the details in that account differed from verses 15–16. The practice of Hebrew editors differed from our practice. They often inserted two accounts of one event side by side where there were differences of detail so that nothing should be omitted. We would regard this practice as illogical. Our practice is to construct from what is available to us a new account that contains what we consider to be the best evidence and irons out inconsistencies.

13. *as the LORD had foretold*: see 20: 17. This account records that Nebuchadnezzar melted down the gold vessels and turned them into bullion. If this is so, then there were no sacred vessels carried into exile to be returned, and later traditions about the desecration of the vessels (cp. Dan. 5: 2) and their return to Jerusalem (Ezra 1: 7–11) are legendary. No mention is made of the Ark of the Covenant of the Lord which had been placed in the 'inner shrine' of the temple by King Solomon (1 Kings 6: 19). This is surprising since the Ark was looked upon as the most sacred object kept in the temple. Perhaps no mention is made of its desecration out of motives of reverence. Alternatively, the priests may have hidden it before the temple was captured, but this is unlikely since it was never returned to the temple after the rebuilding by Zerubabbel. From this time the Ark disappears from history.

14. *the people of Jerusalem*: Nebuchadnezzar did not depopulate the city. He removed those who might assist in a future rebellion, *the officers and the fighting men* who would provide the army, and *the craftsmen and smiths* who would make weapons for them to use.

15. *He deported Jehoiachin to Babylon* where he was a prisoner for thirty-seven years until the death of Nebuchadnezzar (cp. on 25: 27–30). Records have been found in Babylon from the early part of this period which give the amounts of the oil that Jehoiachin was allowed (see *Ancient Near Eastern Texts*, p. 308, or *Documents from Old Testament Times*, p. 86). This would have been used in cooking, and indicates that Jehoiachin was

probably not kept in prison but under house arrest. It is also stated that he had five sons.

17. *Zedekiah*: the change of name was an indication of Zedekiah's vassal status (cp. 23: 34) though the actual name chosen was probably a concession to the religious feeling of the people of Judah. *Zedekiah* means 'Yahweh is righteous'. ✻

THE REIGN OF ZEDEKIAH

18[a] Zedekiah was twenty-one years old when he came to the throne, and he reigned in Jerusalem for eleven years; his mother was Hamutal daughter of Jeremiah of Libnah.
19 He did what was wrong in the eyes of the LORD, as
20 Jehoiakim had done. Jerusalem and Judah so angered the LORD that in the end he banished them from his sight; and Zedekiah rebelled against the king of Babylon.

✻ This is the briefest possible summary of the reign. All the interest of the story is concentrated on the description of the destruction of Jerusalem and its temple which follows. Nothing is said here of the nine years of Zedekiah's reign which preceded the Babylonian attack on Jerusalem. Some details of that period are available in the book of Jeremiah. Jeremiah lived in Jerusalem throughout that time and took an active part in its political affairs. Although Zedekiah was a vassal of the king of Babylon, there was an influential group of his nobles who were continually pressing him to be disloyal and to take part in the intrigues which the Egyptians never gave up trying to inspire. Jeremiah was an opponent of the pro-Egyptian party and one whose influence they evidently feared since they stopped him from speaking in public, and eventually had him arrested and almost murdered. In the end Zedekiah threw in his lot with the pro-Egyptian party, with disastrous

[a] 24: 18 – 25: 21: cp. Jer. 52: 1–27.

consequences. The pro-Egyptian party was influential because there seemed to be an improvement in the military fortunes of Egypt. Pharaoh Necho, who had been defeated by Nebuchadnezzar, died in 593 B.C. and was succeeded by Psammetichus II who did little against Babylon. He was followed in 588 B.C. by the Pharaoh called Apries in Greek sources and Hophra by Jeremiah (Jer. 44: 30). Apries attacked the Babylonians as quickly as he could, and it seems to have been this Egyptian offensive which led Zedekiah finally to rebel.

A copy of 24: 18 – 25: 21 has been added as an appendix to the book of Jeremiah, and a further account of the events of 25: 1–12 has been included in the book itself (Jer. 39: 1–10). Some of the details have been preserved more accurately in these accounts than in Kings, and the N.E.B. has incorporated some of the extra material (see footnotes). *

THE FINAL DESTRUCTION OF JERUSALEM

In the ninth year of his reign, in the tenth month, on **25** 1[a] the tenth day of the month, Nebuchadnezzar king of Babylon advanced with all his army against Jerusalem, invested it and erected watch-towers against it on every side; the siege lasted till the eleventh year of King 2 Zedekiah. In the fourth month of that year,[b] on the ninth 3 day of the month, when famine was severe in the city and there was no food for the common people, the city was 4 thrown open. When Zedekiah king of Judah saw this,[c] he and all his armed escort left the city and fled[d] by night through the gate called Between the Two Walls, near the king's garden. They escaped towards the Arabah, although

[a] *Verses 1–12: cp. Jer. 39: 1–10; verses 1–17: cp. 2 Chr. 36: 17–20.*
[b] In...year: *prob. rdg., cp. Jer. 52: 6; Heb. om.*
[c] When...this: *prob. rdg., cp. Jer. 39: 4; Heb. om.*
[d] left...fled: *so Pesh., cp. Jer. 52: 7; Heb. om.*

5 the Chaldeans were surrounding the city. But the Chaldaean army pursued the king and overtook him in the lowlands of Jericho; and all his company was dispersed.

6 The king was seized and brought before the king of Babylon at Riblah, where he[a] pleaded his case before him.

7 Zedekiah's sons were slain before his eyes; then his eyes were put out, and he was brought to Babylon in fetters of bronze.

8   In the fifth month, on the seventh day of the month, in the nineteenth year of Nebuchadnezzar king of Babylon, Nebuzaradan, captain of the king's bodyguard, came to

9 Jerusalem and set fire to the house of the LORD and the royal palace; all the houses in the city, including the

10 mansion of Gedaliah,[b] were burnt down. The Chaldaean forces with[c] the captain of the guard pulled down the

11 walls all round Jerusalem. Nebuzaradan captain of the guard deported the rest of the people left in the city, those who had deserted to the king of Babylon and any re-

12 maining artisans.[d] He left only the weakest class of people to be vine-dressers and labourers.

13   The Chaldaeans broke up the pillars of bronze in the house of the LORD, the trolleys, and the Sea of bronze,

14 and took the metal to Babylon. They took also the pots, shovels, snuffers, saucers, and all the vessels of bronze used

15 in the service of the temple. The captain of the guard took away the precious metal, whether gold or silver, of which

16 the firepans and the tossing-bowls were made. The

[a] *So some MSS.; others* they.

[b] Gedaliah: *prob. rdg.; Heb.* a great man.

[c] *So many MSS., cp. Jer.* 52: 14; *others om.*

[d] any remaining artisans: *prob. rdg., cp. Jer.* 52: 15; *Heb.* the remaining crowd.

bronze of the two pillars, the one Sea, and the trolleys, which Solomon had made for the house of the LORD, was beyond weighing. The one pillar was eighteen cubits 17 high and its capital was bronze; the capital was three cubits high, and a decoration of network and pome-granates ran all round it, wholly of bronze. The other pillar, with its network, was exactly like it.

The captain of the guard took Seraiah the chief priest 18 and Zephaniah the deputy chief priest and the three on duty at the entrance; he took also from the city a eunuch 19 who was in charge of the fighting men, five of those with right of access to the king who were still in the city, the adjutant-general[a] whose duty was to muster the people for war, and sixty men of the people who were still there. These Nebuzaradan captain of the guard brought to the 20 king of Babylon at Riblah. There, in the land of Hamath, 21 the king of Babylon had them flogged and put to death. So Judah went into exile from their own land.

* Most attention is paid to the destruction of the temple rather than the city. Kings began with the building of the temple by King Solomon and ends with its destruction. Throughout the book it has been the temple which has been the principal interest of the editors, not just for itself but as the symbol of the vocation which, they believed, God had placed upon Israel. This vocation, to be his covenant people, gave Israel its true status among all the other nations. It demanded that Israel should be different from all other nations, but Israel had proved itself unable and unwilling to live up to this demand. So first the northern kingdom and now Judah had been destroyed and the destruction of the temple at Jerusalem,

[a] *Prob. rdg.; Heb. adds* commander-in-chief.

the building which the editors had always portrayed as the outward sign of God's election and Israel's response, showed that the covenant people had come to an end, at least in the form in which they had existed during the period of the kings.

1. *In the ninth year of his reign*: Zedekiah's reign, 588 B.C. *Nebuchadnezzar...advanced*: this is not literally correct. Nebuchadnezzar was not present with his army at Jerusalem (cp. Jer. 38: 17). He was at Riblah (see verse 6 below) probably to protect the Lebanon against Egyptian attack. *erected watch-towers*: his object was to surround the city and to starve it into surrender much as the Romans succeeded in doing against Masada in A.D. 73.

2. *the eleventh year of King Zedekiah*: i.e. 586 B.C. This was a very long siege even against a city as strong as Jerusalem. Probably the Babylonians could not deploy their full forces against it because of the fear of attack from Egypt. Herodotus records that Apries attacked Tyre and Sidon from the sea. This attack may have taken place at this time. It would account for the length of the siege, Nebuchadnezzar's remaining at Riblah, and the fact that the Babylonians seem to have lifted the siege for a short time (Jer. 37: 5).

3. *In the fourth month of that year* has been added from the parallel account in Jeremiah.

4. *the city was thrown open*: i.e. the defenders surrendered. This interpretation is not certain. The Hebrew can be translated 'a breach was made in the city' (Revised Standard Version), i.e. the Babylonians broke through the walls and the defenders had become too weak to defend them properly. *he...left the city and fled*: Zedekiah may have intended to set up guerrilla warfare in the hill country between Jerusalem and the Jordan, which is ideal terrain for that purpose. *the gate called Between the Two Walls*: this was on the south-east side of the city. An additional wall may have been built there when Hezekiah improved the city's water-supply. *the Arabah* is that part of the great rift valley which lies to the south of the Dead Sea.

Several words have been omitted from the Hebrew of this verse. They have been added from the parallel account in Jeremiah.

6. Riblah was in Syria, south of Hamath (see note on 23: 33 and map on p. xii). *he pleaded his case*: Zedekiah was tried as a rebellious vassal.

7. *Zedekiah's sons were slain*: the Hebrews had no belief at this time in a personal immortality. A man's hope for the future lay in his family. By this action Nebuchadnezzar intended to wipe out the family and memory of a rebellious vassal.

8. *in the nineteenth year*: i.e. 586 B.C. Jeremiah seems to date the event a year earlier (Jer. 52: 29), but the difference is probably due to using different calendars.

9. *including the mansion of Gedaliah*: the Hebrew is 'every great house' (Revised Standard Version). The word for great, *gadol*, is very like Gedaliah. In fact Gedaliah means 'Yahweh is great'. The N.E.B. thinks that Gedaliah has been abbreviated and read as *gadol*, i.e. 'a great man'. Yet it is unlikely that this name Gedaliah could be mistaken, since he appears prominently a few verses later. The phrase may have been added by a scribe to make sure that his readers understood that *all the houses* included large as well as small.

13–14. *the pillars of bronze* were the two pillars which Solomon had made and stood on either side of the door of the temple (1 Kings 7: 15–22). The other objects were the furniture of the temple (cp. 1 Kings 7: 23–40).

18. The five priests mentioned must have been the most senior in the temple service.

19. *a eunuch*: he may have been a royal officer put in command of the troops. The title of one of the Assyrian officers who had led the attack upon Jerusalem in the time of Hezekiah, Rab-saris, means literally 'chief of the eunuchs'. *five of those...to the king*: members of the nobility who belonged to the council. *the adjutant-general*: the Hebrew has 'the secretary of the commander of the army'. *sixty men of the people*: they

seem to be noted because they were members of that rank in society called 'the people of the land' (see note on 11: 14 and 23: 30), probably provincial nobles. *

GEDALIAH, THE GOVERNOR OF JERUSALEM

22 Nebuchadnezzar king of Babylon appointed Gedaliah son of Ahikam, son of Shaphan, governor over the few
23 people whom he had left in Judah. When the captains of the armed bands and their men heard that the king of Babylon had appointed Gedaliah governor, they all came to him at Mizpah: Ishmael son of Nethaniah, Johanan son of Kareah, Seraiah son of Tanhumeth of Netophah,
24 and Jaazaniah of Beth-maacah. Then Gedaliah gave them and their men this assurance: 'Have no fear of the Chaldaean officers. Settle down in the land and serve the king
25 of Babylon; and then all will be well with you.' But in the seventh month Ishmael son of Nethaniah, son of Elishama, who was a member of the royal house, came with ten men and murdered Gedaliah and the Jews and
26 Chaldaeans who were with him at Mizpah. Thereupon all the people, high and low, and the captains of the armed bands, fled to Egypt for fear of the Chaldaeans.

* A much fuller account of Gedaliah's governorship can be found in Jer. 40: 7 – 41: 18. The author of this version of the story seems to have known far fewer details, which supports the view that he was writing in Babylonia during the exile. After the punishment of the rebellious vassal, Nebuchadnezzar wished the government of Judah to proceed as smoothly as possible. It was a generous gesture on his part to appoint a Judaean as governor, but some at least of the Judaeans could not accept this as being in their own best interest, and regarded

Gedaliah as a traitor. The result was that all hope of any continuance of control and government of Judah by Judaeans was lost. Nothing was saved from the wreck of the kingdom.

22. *Gedaliah*: some contemporary records have been discovered by archaeologists at Lachish. They are the remains of letters written on sherds of pottery and are known as the Lachish letters. According to one of them a Gedaliah had been 'comptroller of the household' for Zedekiah. This was probably the same Gedaliah. Nebuchadnezzar had thus chosen a senior member of Zedekiah's household as governor. Gedaliah had probably been sympathetic to the pro-Babylonian party. His father, Ahikam, had once helped to save the prophet Jeremiah from harm (Jer. 26: 24) and his grandfather, Shaphan, had been adjutant-general to King Josiah at the time of the reform (22: 12).

23. *the captains of the armed bands*: those who were still resisting the Babylonians as guerrillas in the wilderness of Judaea. Mizpah was 9 miles ($14\frac{1}{2}$ km) north of Jerusalem. It is now called Tel en-Nasbeh (see map on p. 80).

25. Ishmael because of his membership of the royal family may have felt that Gedaliah was usurping his position. We hear no more about Ishmael.

26. *fled to Egypt* to seek refuge with the enemies of the king of Babylon. The prophet Jeremiah was forced reluctantly to join this party (cp. Jer. 42–4). *

THE RELEASE OF JEHOIACHIN

In the thirty-seventh year of the exile of Jehoiachin 27[a] king of Judah, on the twenty-seventh day of the twelfth month, Evil-merodach[b] king of Babylon in the year of his accession showed favour to Jehoiachin king of Judah. He brought him[c] out of prison, treated him kindly and 28

[a] *Verses 27–30: cp. Jer. 52: 31–4.*   [b] *Or* Ewil-marduk.
[c] He brought him: *so Sept., cp. Jer. 52: 32; Heb. om.*

gave him a seat at table above the kings with him in
29 Babylon. So Jehoiachin discarded his prison clothes and
30 lived as a pensioner of the king for the rest of his life. For
his maintenance, a regular daily allowance was given him
by the king as long as he lived.

* The story of Gedaliah shows the hopelessness of the situation in Judaea. Everything had come to an end there. In
contrast is this brief note from Babylon. After the death of
Nebuchadnezzar, his son released Jehoiachin who had been a
prisoner for thirty-seven years. The editors seem to be pointing out that there is hope for the Jews who have been taken
into exile in Babylon, and that any future for the covenant
people must come from them. They have a king of Judah, a
descendant of Josiah, and if they will learn the lessons that the
history of the kings is meant to teach them, God will yet use
them to re-establish his covenant people. The prophets who
lived among the exiles preached such a message. Ezekiel, for
example, taught that though the nation was dead, God would
breathe new life into it and restore it (Ezek. 37: 1–14), and the
author of Isa. 40–55, the unknown prophet of the exile who is
usually called the Second Isaiah, preached much the same
message (Isa. 40: 1–6). *

THE MESSAGE OF THE BOOK

It will have been obvious to all readers that the story of the
kings of Israel and Judah has been told as a cautionary tale.
For the most part it has been told as a story of follies and mis-
spent opportunities. It had an obvious value for those Israelites
living in exile in Babylon who first read it. Its lessons were
directly relevant to their hopes, and it is likely that many of
them profited by their reading. Certainly when the exile was
ended, the community that was established again in Jerusalem
was determined that never again would it be tempted to com-

promise its religious loyalty by any association with the religious ideas or customs of neighbouring peoples. The restored community was determined to be holy, and the first step in holiness was rigid separation from any contact with the world around.

We, however, are not reading Kings from a Babylonian exile or even a restored Jerusalem. That is not our situation. What then is in Kings for us? The answer to that question depends very largely on our willingness and capacity to enter sympathetically and imaginatively into the life portrayed by the book. If we cannot do that, then Kings has probably nothing to offer us, but then neither will any other history or even biography, because sympathetic and imaginative understanding is necessary for any profitable reading of history. Such a reading of Kings will make us take seriously the standpoint from which the book is written. We shall not always agree with the judgements of the authors. We know that at times they put things into their history that we would have left out, and left out things that we feel ought to have been put in, but we shall face seriously the judgements that the editors of Kings make; that in the lives of the peoples with whom they were concerned God was at work. And as the story is unfolded a great deal is stated or implied about the nature of the God of Israel; his choice and use of Israel; his generous love for them which caused him to try time and again to bring them back from their faithless and corrupt life. So the story of Kings is about God's dealing with his people and it tells us much about the nature of God.

Again no-one can read Kings without understanding that what was at stake was the identity of the people who were the subject of the book. What does Israel make of itself? What does it see its purpose to be in the events in which it had a part to play? The editors were clear on this point. They saw Israel as having been called to be the covenant people of God, and they viewed the story that they had to tell as a tragedy simply because of Israel's unwillingness, and even at times her

247

inability, to accept that vocation. The vocation to be the people of God meant for the editors certain clear and definite things in the life of the people. It meant the acknowledgement of the priority of worship. That was what all the emphasis laid upon the temple meant. Israel could not be what God wanted her to be without accepting that. The priority of worship does not simply mean that worship should go on, but that worship of a kind which was acceptable to God should go on. That these two are very far from meaning the same thing is one of the great lessons of Kings. Worship is the offering of the worshippers to God, as community and as individuals. False worship is false because the community is false; its life and values are such that they are unacceptable to God. So worship is the instrument by which the spiritual health and well-being of a society can be measured. Worship cannot be isolated from the everyday life of the community. The two go together. This was the claim made by the code of Deuteronomy upon which King Josiah's reform was based. It was the claim made by the prophets to whom, as a class, the editors of Kings paid such respect.

This concern for worship is set within a particular context. We are shown the people of Israel at a particular point in their development. They had established themselves in Palestine as a kingdom in such a way that they could compete effectively with their neighbours. They were in close contact with a society and a way of life that possessed power and affluence far greater than any they had ever known. They wanted such power for themselves. They believed that they needed it if they were to continue to exist in the conditions of the time. They had to develop the organization and the institutions of a kingdom as their neighbours had done. Thus they faced the temptation of imitating their neighbours totally, copying their way of life and adopting their values, even though that meant abandoning the way of life, the values, and the God who had made them what they were. The kings were prepared to lead the people along this path. The prophets were not. The dilemma for the people was one which everyone who is committed to follow an ideal must face at some time or other; to be in the world but not of the world. The exploration of this problem must result from any sensitive reading of Kings. All the issues involved in that problem are at work in the pages of Kings. They are what the struggle between Yahweh and the Baals of Canaan were in the end about, and they are still live issues for today.

✳   ✳   ✳   ✳   ✳   ✳   ✳   ✳   ✳   ✳   ✳   ✳   ✳

A NOTE ON FURTHER READING

Fuller commentaries on 2 Kings are to be found in J. A. Montgomery, *The Book of Kings*, International Critical Commentary (T. & T. Clark, 1951), and John Gray, *I and II Kings*, S.C.M. Old Testament Library, 2nd ed. (S.C.M., 1970).

Readers will find background material in B. W. Anderson, *The Living World of the Old Testament* (Longmans, 1959), and in E. W. Heaton, *The Hebrew Kingdoms*, New Clarendon Bible (Oxford University Press, 1968). Translations of Assyrian and Babylonian texts are to be found in J. B. Pritchard, *Ancient Near Eastern Texts relating to the Old Testament*, 2nd ed. (Princeton University Press, 1955) and in D. Winton Thomas, *Documents from Old Testament Times* (Nelson, 1958).

Maps and illustrations will be found in C. M. Jones, *Old Testament Illustrations* in this series (1971) and in H. G. May, *The Oxford Bible Atlas* (Oxford University Press, 1962). Those who wish to learn more about the archaeology of Palestine should consult K. M. Kenyon, *Archaeology in the Holy Land* (Benn, 1969) and the same author's *Digging Up Jerusalem* (Benn, 1974), and those who are interested in the institutions of Israel will find a vast amount of information in R. de Vaux, *Ancient Israel: its Life and Institutions* (Darton, Longman and Todd, 1965). Fuller information about the struggle with Canaanite religion will be found in Th. C. Vriezen, *The Religion of Ancient Israel* (Lutterworth Press, 1967); Helmer Ringgren, *Israelite Religion* (S.P.C.K., 1966) and Georg Fohrer, *History of Israelite Religion* (S.P.C.K., 1973). Information on all these and many other subjects will be found in the articles of the Bible Dictionaries, such as *Peake's Commentary on the Bible*, rev. ed. (Nelson, 1962), and the four volumes of *The Interpreter's Dictionary of the Bible* (Abingdon, 1962).

A TIME CHART OF THE PERIOD

THE DIVIDED KINGDOM		OTHER POWERS			
Judah	*Israel*	*Damascus*	*Egypt*	*Assyria*	*Babylon*
Jehoram 849–842	Ahaziah 850–849	Ben-hadad II 860–843	Tirhakah 689–664	Shalmaneser IV 782–772	Merodach-baladan 721–710 and 703
Ahaziah 842	Joram 849–842	?860–843	Necho II 609–593	Tiglath-pileser III 745–727	Nabopolassar 626–605
Athaliah 842–837	Jehu 842–815	Hazael 843–796	Psammetichus II 593–588	Shalmaneser V 727–722	Battle of Carchemish 605
Joash 837–800	Jehoahaz 815–801	Ben-hadad III ?796–770	Apries (Hophra) 588–569	Sargon II 722–705	Nebuchadnezzar II 605–562
Amaziah 800–783	Jehoash 801–786	Rezin *about* 740–732		Sennacherib 705–681	Ewil-marduk 562–560
Azariah (Uzziah) 783–742	Jeroboam II 786–746	Fall of Damascus 732		Esarhaddon 681–669	
Jotham 742–735	Zechariah 746–745			Ashurbanipal 669–663?	
Ahaz 735–715	Shallum 745			Fall of Nineveh 612	
Hezekiah 715–687	Menahem 745–738				
Manasseh 687–642	Pekahiah 738–737				
Amon 642–640	Pekah 737–732				
Josiah 640–609	Hoshea 732–724				
Battle of Megiddo 609	Fall of Samaria 721				
Jehoahaz 609					
Jehoiakim 609–598					
Jehoiachin 598–597					
Zedekiah 597–587/6					
Fall of Jerusalem 587/6					

APPENDIX

MEASURES OF LENGTH AND EXTENT

	span	cubit	rod[a]
span	1	...	...
cubit	2	1	...
rod[a]	12	6	1

The 'short cubit' (Judg. 3: 16) was traditionally the measure from the elbow to the knuckles of the closed fist; and what seems to be intended as a 'long cubit' measured a 'cubit and a hand-breadth', i.e. 7 instead of 6 hand-breadths (Ezek. 40: 5). What is meant by cubits 'according to the old standard of measurement' (2 Chr. 3: 3) is presumably this pre-exilic cubit of 7 hand-breadths. Modern estimates of the Hebrew cubit range from 12 to 25.2 inches, without allowing for varying local standards.

Area was measured by the 'yoke' (Isa. 5: 10), i.e. that ploughed by a pair of oxen in one day, said to be half an acre now in Palestine, though varying in different places with the nature of the land.

MEASURES OF CAPACITY

liquid measures	equivalences	dry measures
'log'	1 'log'	...
...	4 'log'	'kab'
...	$7\frac{1}{5}$ 'log'	'omer'
'hin'	12 'log'	...
...	24 'log'	'seah'
'bath'	72 'log'	'ephah'
'kor'	720 'log'	'homer' or 'kor'

[a] Hebrew literally 'reed', the length of Ezekiel's measuring-rod.

According to ancient authorities the Hebrew 'log' was of the same capacity as the Roman *sextarius*; this according to the best available evidence was equivalent to 0.99 pint of the English standard.

WEIGHTS AND COINS

	heavy (Phoenician) standard			light (Babylonian) standard		
	shekel	mina	talent	shekel	mina	talent
shekel	1	...	...	1	...	...
mina	50	1	...	60	1	...
talent	3,000	60	1	3,600	60	1

The 'gerah' was $\frac{1}{20}$ of the sacred or heavy shekel and probably $\frac{1}{24}$ of the light shekel.

The 'sacred shekel' according to tradition was identical with the heavy shekel; while the 'shekel of the standard recognized by merchants' (Gen. 23: 16) was perhaps a weight stamped with its value as distinct from one not so stamped and requiring to be weighed on the spot.

Recent discoveries of hoards of objects stamped with their weights suggest that the shekel may have weighed approximately 11.5 grammes towards the end of the Hebrew monarchy, but nothing shows whether this is the light or the heavy shekel; and much variety, due partly to the worn or damaged state of the objects and partly to variations in local standards, increases the difficulty of giving a definite figure.

Coins are not mentioned before the exile. Only the 'daric' (1 Chr. 29: 7) and the 'drachma' (Ezra 2: 69; Neh. 7: 70–2), if this is a distinct coin, are found in the Old Testament; the former is said to have been a month's pay for a soldier in the Persian army, while the latter will have been the Greek silver drachma, estimated at approximately 4.4 grammes. The 'shekel' of this period (Neh. 5: 15) as a coin was probably the Graeco-Persian *siglos* weighing 5.6 grammes.

INDEX

Abana, river 54
Ahab 4, 15, 83; his family 98
Ahaz 147, 195; his new altar 150
Ahaziah, 17, 76, 78, 89; his family 96
Amaziah 129
Amon 205
Amos 133
Apries (Hophra) 239
Aram map p. xii; 36, 52, 60, 106, 133
Aramaic 177
Arpad 177
Assyria map p. xii; 4, 143, 149, 178, 229
Athaliah 109
Azariah (Uzziah) 136

Baal 31
Baal-shalisha map p. 80; 48
Baal-zebub 18
Babylon map p. xii
Babylonia map p. xii; 229, 231, 236
Ben-hadad 65, 72
Beth-haggan 88
Beth-shemesh map p. 30; 130
Bethel map p. 80; 24, 162, 223
Black Obelisk 105
Book of the Law 209, 210

calves, golden 103, 158
Carchemish map p. xii; 231, 233
Carmel map p. 30; 45
chariots of fire 25, 61, 67, 124
Chemosh 37
chronology 12
coronation rite 111
covenant 112, 216

Damascus map p. xii; 133, 134, 135, 150
Deuteronomic History 10
deuteronomic reform 6: 210, 211, 219, 220
deuteronomists 6: their teaching 9, 103, 144, 156, 202, 234

Dothan map p. 80; 60

Edom map p. xii; 35, 36, 75, 129 149
Egypt map p. xii; 176, 230, 238, 245, kings of Egypt 67
Ekron map p. 30; 18
Elath map p. xii; 131, 149
Elijah 4, 15, 17, 20; his ascension 23
Elisha 14, 61, 68, 70; his miracles 15, 27, 38, 40, 46, 48, 49, 56, 58; his commissioning 21; his illness and death 124
Esarhaddon 187
eunuch 70

Gath 119
Gedeliah 243, 244
Gilgal map p. 30; 24, 47

Hamath map p. xii; 162
Hazael 70, 72, 116, 122
Hezekiah 12, 143, 164, 170, 183; defends Jerusalem 168; his prayer 185; his illness 192, 196; his tunnel 198
high priest 118, 209
Hilkiah 209, 210
hill-shrines 136, 148, 157
Hittites, kings of 67
Hophra see Apries
Hosea 135

Isaiah 148, 178, 185, 189, 194, 197
Israel, kingdom of map p. 30; 2

Jehoahaz 121, 230
Jehoash 124
Jehoiachim 233
Jehoiachin 236, 237, 246
Jehoiada 110, 112
Jehonadab 99
Jehoram 29
Jehu 78, 82, 94, 103
Jeremiah 204, 231

Jericho map p. 30; 27
Jeroboam II 106, 121, 132
Jerusalem map p. xii; temple of
  Baal at 113; inviolability of 165,
  189; Assyrian attack on 168, 170;
  capture of 241
Jezebel 90, 96
Jezreel map p. 30; 77, 86
Joash 116
Jonah 134
Joram (Jehoram) 21, 75, 78, 86
Josiah 9, 206, 209, 210; his reform of
  the temple 219; at Bethel 223;
  celebrates Passover 226; his death
  229
Jotham 142
Judah, kingdom of map. p. 30; 3

Kir-hareseth map p. 30; 36

Lachish map p. 30; 169, 245
Lebo-hamath map p. 30; 126, 134
leprosy 53, 67, 137
LORD of Hosts 35

Manasseh 201
Megiddo map p. xii; 9, 229
Menahem 140
Merodach-baladan, 168, 196
Mesha 18, 31
Mizpah map p. 80; 245
Moab map p. 30; 17
Moabite stone 18, 34

Naaman 49
Naboth 87
Nebuchadnezzar 233, 237
Necho 229, 239
Nehushtan 67
Nineveh map p. xii; 229

Omri 4, 17

Passover 227
'peace' (shalom), meaning of 87
Pekah 141
Pekaliah 141
Pharpar, river 54

prophecy, fulfilment of 99, 213, 214
prophetic revolt 78

Ramoth-gilead map p. 30; 70, 81,
  86
Rechabites 99
remnant, doctrine of 188
Rezin 148
Riblah map p. xii; 243
Rimmon 55

sacred pillar 31, 101, 157
sacred pole 101, 157,
sacrifice: human 37, 147, 158, 203
  221; drink-offerings 151; grain-
  offerings 151; guilt-offerings 119;
  shared-offerings 151; sin-offerings
  119; whole-offerings 37, 55, 100,
  151
Samaria, city of map p. xii; 2, 8,
  61, 154, 169; temple of Baal at 98
Samaria, kingdom of (= Israel)
  map p. 80; 2, 160; deportation of
  inhabitants 141
Samaritans 161, 162
Sargon II 8, 154
Sennacherib 168, 177, 179, 188, 190
serpent, bronze 166
Shallum 140
Shalmaneser III 105
Shalmaneser IV 133
Shalmaneser V 153
Shunem map p. 80; 42
Solomon 3

Taylor Prism 168
temple at Jerusalem 5; repair of 117;
  practice of sun worship at 221;
  destruction of 241
Tiglath-pileser III 135, 140
Tirhakah 171, 179, 183
Torrent of Egypt map p. xii; 234

Uzziah see Azariah

Zared, river map p. 30; 34, 36
Zechariah 139
Zedekiah 238